SLIDE RULES and SUBMARINES

The illustration on the title page is a bearing rate computer, a circular slide rule used by submariners to calculate attack and self-protection data. The slide rule photo is used through the courtesy of CAPT John Byron, USN.

Slide Rules
and
Submarines

American Scientists and Subsurface Warfare in World War II

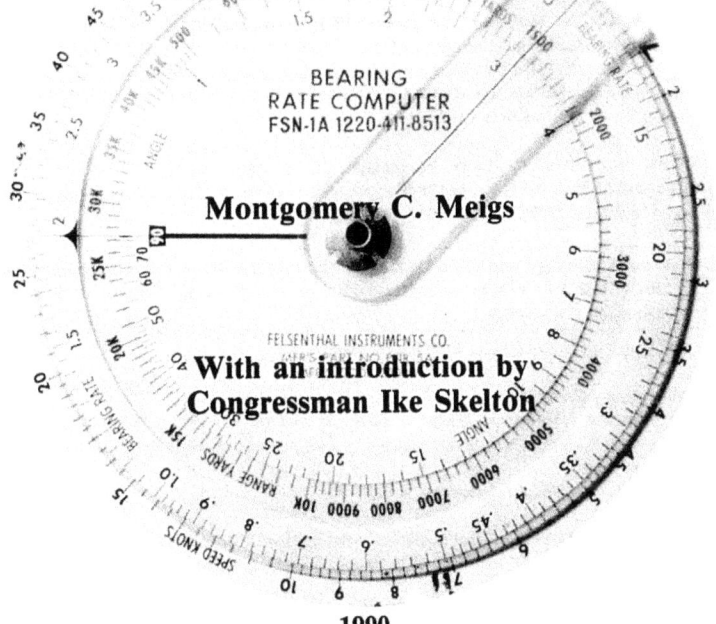

Montgomery C. Meigs

With an introduction by Congressman Ike Skelton

1990

National Defense University Press
Fort Lesley J. McNair
Washington, DC

To Mary Ann,
William, and Matthew,
on whose time
this book was written

SLIDE RULES AND SUBMARINES:

American Scientists and Subsurface
Warfare in World War II

Text and display lines in Times Roman

Advisory readers:
Stanley L. Falk; Capt. Edward L. Beach, USN-Ret.

Original water color for the cover painted by Laszlo L. Bodrogi;
artwork for cover, half-title pages, and endpiece by Laszlo L. Bodrogi.

Contents

Photographs   xi
Foreword   xv
Preface   xvii
Introduction by Congressman Ike Skelton   xxi

1. **Forgotten Naval Lessons of World War I**
   War at Sea and the Prize Ordinance   5
   Allied Failures, German Successes   8
   Wolves and Shepherds   19
   Role of American Scientists   24

2. **Lack of Preparation is Costly**
   German Advantage   39
   Confusion in Washington and Slow Progress at Sea   43
   R&D and Operational Analysis   54
   War Department Role   63

3. **Convincing Admiral King**
   German Success and Innovation   73
   Small Losses . . . Big Impact   83
   Turning Point   86
   Role of Tenth Fleet   97
   Payoff for Scientific Work   99

4. **Campaign Against the U-Boat**
   Tenth Fleet Brings Unity   112
   New Weapons Mean New Tactics   122
   Defeat of the U-Boat   126
   Tenth Fleet and Scientists Consolidate Advantages   134
   The Germans Respond   140

5. **American Submarine Campaign in the Pacific**
   Legacy of Prewar Years   154
   Caught Off Guard   157
   Strategic Offensive   163
   Results of Prosubmarine Program   174

6. **Victory in Subsurface Warfare**
   U-Boats Struggle to Survive   181
   BdU's Moves are Watched   190
   Scientific Effort Changes Emphasis   196
   Scientists Aid Submarine Warfare   200
   An Irony: Too Late, Too Much To Do   209

In Retrospect   211
Notes   221

Selected Bibliography   247
Abbreviations   255
Index   259
The Author   269

Photographs

Vice Admirals Low (COMSUBLANT) and Lockwood (COMSUBPAC) xviii
Convoy at anchor in Iceland xix

Depth charge explosion 4
German Admiral Doenitz inspects U-boat crew early in war 8
Admiral King, COMINCH 11
Convoy in North Atlantic early in war 18
British subchaser in 1942 22
Dr. Vannevar Bush, Chairman, National Defense Research Committee (and president of Carnegie Institute) 25
Secretary of the Navy Frank Knox 27
Ships in North Atlantic convoy 32
Mousetrap bomb projectors 35

Lookout scans sky, sea from sub's conning tower 38
Merchantman sinks in convoy 40
ROPER officer directs unloading of U-boat casualties 42
Atlantic convoy at dusk 45
Tanker burns off Cape Hatteras, March 1942 47
Legendary Cutter *SPENCER* in convoy, June 1943 50
Radio sonobuoys 56
Torpedo is loaded aboard submarine 59
General Arnold, Army Air Forces Chief, confers with Marine Major General Woods, June 1945 66
PB4Y (B-24 *Liberator*) on patrol, December 1943 68

Secretary of War Henry L. Stimson 72
Atlantic convoy, from stern of escort vessel 74
PB4Y on patrol over North Atlantic 76

Atlantic convoy in rough seas   79
Torpedoed merchantman in North Atlantic   82
Admiral Ingersoll, CINCLANT, watches *Operation Torch* task force stand out from Hampton Roads   84
Escort carrier USS *BOGUE* (CVE-9)   90
"Jeep" carrier *BOGUE*   102
Radar equipment in *BOGUE*   104
Radar on ships, the war's silent weapon   108

Dawn flight from USS *SANTEE*, November 1942   113
U-118 sunk by planes from *BOGUE*   117
U-boat under attack, July 1943   119
Bombing of submarine by aircraft   121
US Navy blimp over Atlantic convoy   124
HMS *BITER*, British escort carrier, 1942   128
Effects of fire from USCGC *SPENCER* on U-boat   130
Ingersoll honors *SANTEE* flyer with Navy Cross, April 1943   132
HMS *ARCHER*, British "jeep" carrier, 1942   133
Convoy in North Atlantic   135
Depth charge hunts U-boat from *SPENCER*'s stern   137
U-664 sunk in August 1943   139
Admiral Doenitz congratulates U-boat crews late in war   141
Snorkel of U-3008, Mark XXI U-boat   144
CIC team in "jeep" carrier *SANTEE* vectors a plot   148

GATO-class submarine on Pacific war patrol, May 1945   154
Admirals Nimitz, Lockwood greet submariners, June 1945   157
Admiral Nimitz, CINCPAC   160
Sampan seen through periscope near Luzon, January 1945   162
WAHOO skipper, officer on watch in conning tower   166
Pacific subs moored at Pearl Harbor, September 1945   167
Submarine *SPIKEFISH* surfaces at sea, September 1944   170
Sailor displays echo-ranging device   172
SEA DRAGON approaches torpedoed ship, June 1945   174
Japanese carrier through *HADDOCK* periscope, April 1943   176

SPENCER K-gun fires depth charge   180
Troop transport, escort vessels in Atlantic, 1942   181
Anti-radar *Alberich* coating shown on U-boat   184
German submarine nest   187
Survivor of *U-175* is rescued   191
German soldiers use *Enigma* encoding machine   194
US sailors ready *Hedgehog* bomb projector   198

Silhouette of HMS *ARCHER*, 1943   201
U-118 under attack from *BOGUE*'s planes, June 1943   203
U-boat sunk by planes from *BOGUE*, June 1943   205
GREENLING on patrol, January 1942   207
Quintet of subs returns to Pearl Harbor, September 1945   208
Destroyer through *WAHOO* periscope, January 1943   210

US Navy PBY drops bomb during hunt for U-boat   212
President Roosevelt confers with Admiral King, General Marshall during Yalta conference, February 1945   213
Captain of U-858, May 1945   216
Silhouette of HMS *BITER*, April 1943   218
SENNETT on patrol, September 1944   220

Foreword

The classic problem of when to depend on lessons learned from previous conflicts and when to employ new tactics and technology always confronts military leaders. At the beginning of World War II, for example, Allied naval strategists were prepared to do battle using traditional tactics against surface vessels, but—this study contends—not against submarines, because the strategists failed to appreciate either the damage done by submarines in World War I or the tactics that had worked successfully against them. Consequently, from the beginning of World War II to mid-1943, German U-boats were able to mount a devastating campaign against Allied shipping.

In *Slide Rules and Submarines*, Montgomery Meigs describes how the Allies learned to counter the U-boat threat. Using new technology—and new tactics derived from scientific methods—they devised countermeasures to defeat the German submarine menace. Then, continuing to apply those successful measures, they went on to negate the Japanese submarine threat in the Pacific. The author cites the crucial role of civilian scientists—the "outsiders"—who worked with military staffs and operational commanders of the campaign at sea. Their open minds and objective methods were essential for the application of such technical advances as sonar and radar, acoustic torpedoes, depth finders, and code breaking to the battle.

As this study illustrates, the importance of such timely and innovative cooperation among scientists, the research and development community, and military commanders in bringing technological knowledge to bear for operational and strategic advantage cannot be overstated. Meigs' study of how such cooperation succeeded in the crucible of wartime crisis is itself an example of how the lessons of the past can serve us well today.

J.A. Baldwin
Vice Admiral, US Navy
President, National Defense University

Preface

This study of the relationship between operational art and technological innovation attempts to gain insights about how scientific developments became military capabilities in the campaign of subsurface warfare in World War II. My interest in the general topic of science and strategy began with a fascination, kindled by the work of C. P. Snow, with how scientific developments influence decisions about strategy and operational art. Over a number of years as a serving officer, two years as a graduate student, and later as a member of the faculty at the United States Military Academy, I kept stumbling over the problem of how technological innovation makes an impact on decisions about national strategic policy and operational capability. A year as an Army Research Associate at the National War College afforded an opportunity to investigate the problem.

This effort began as a more ambitious attempt to look at a wide range of technologies and types of warfare in World War II and to draw conclusions about the strategic implications of a number of technologies taken together. But the realization that time was quickly slipping away and the advice of an editor wiser than I about what was achievable in a project done on a part-time basis made me decide to concentrate on subsurface warfare. This decision had two beneficial effects. It focused the study more directly on the operational level of command and the conduct of campaigns within a theater. And it allowed more detailed research into the relationships between the activities of scientists, fighting leaders at sea, and senior naval figures in Washington. The reader may not be surprised to find that the efforts of these three groups, while all directed at winning the war on and under the sea, often cut across one another.

Throughout the research and writing of the study, three questions kept reemerging and imposing themselves. They crop up again and again in the actions and reactions of the main figures encountered:

- How were scientists best able to contribute to the development of new military capabilities that proved significant at the operational level of command?

Vice Admirals Francis S. "Frog" Low (left) and Charles A. Lockwood, who commanded in the US Navy at the same level as German Admiral Karl Doenitz, experienced similar pressures and patterns of effects. As Commander, Submarines, US Pacific Fleet (COMSUBPAC), Lockwood rejuvenated the US submarine campaign in the Pacific. Low was Commander, US Submarine Forces, Atlantic Fleet (COMSUBLANT).

- What institutional factors aided or abetted this process?
- Once technological innovations became operational capabilities, how did they influence the campaign in terms of their psychological, operational, and tactical effect on the battle?

One caution to the reader: The term "operational level of war" is not used here. Operational is intended here in terms of a level of command, that is, command of a theater or of a type of warfare in a theater, one echelon removed from national authority. In this context, German Admiral Karl Doenitz and US Vice Admirals Francis S. Low and Charles A. Lockwood all commanded at the same level and experienced similar pressures and patterns of effects. These effects are peculiar to technologically intensive warfare in campaigns that have a fundamental import for the respective national command authorities. They are far different from the pressures and effects felt at lower levels of command.

A particularly frustrating aspect of research on this project stems from the amount of archival evidence available. One must go

National Archives

Convoy at anchor in Iceland. Only convoying, and mining egress routes into shipping lanes, promised solutions to concentrated attacks by U-boats against merchant shipping toward the end of the First World War. Iceland's location in the North Atlantic midway between North America and Europe made it an ideal stopping-off place for Allied convoys.

through literally thousands of boxes to exhaust the possibilities of the records of even one of the maritime theaters. And often, the most important records are effectively lost in the mounds of poorly catalogued material that remains a monument to the stinginess of a nation proud of its history but too shortsighted to invest the relatively tiny amount of national treasure needed to ensure protection of the historical record. One hopes at a minimum that the issues raised here and the notes that hopefully give clear paths to a variety of sources will encourage other scholars to follow and find new materials and insights I did not have the time and energy or the wit to turn up.

To the extent that this study breaks new ground, I am indebted to several extremely professional archivists: Bernard Cavalcante of the Operational Archives at the Naval Historical Center provided invaluable assistance, as did Marjorie Ciarlante, Tim Nenninger, and

George Chalou at the National Archives. A number of scholars read and commented on the text: I am especially indebted to the advice of William W. Kaufmann and Martin van Creveld. I am also very grateful to Captain Edward L. Beach, US Navy Retired, who spent a good deal of time with me working over the manuscript and providing his advice and encouragement. I appreciate the comments of Captain Paul Callahan, US Navy, and Captain J. B. Griggs, US Navy, Retired, and a bit of translation done by Lieutenant Commander Dennis Hopkins, US Navy. Dr. Fred Kiley, Director of the NDU Press, gave invaluable advice throughout the project, and Ed Seneff, my editor, worked long and hard to help to protect the reader from arcane terms and definitions known only to a vanishing generation of seamen.

Finally, I owe a debt of thanks to my classmates in the National War College class of 1987. As the project wore on, more and more of the fruits of my research into World War II materials crept into discussions in seminars on aspects of the operational art. The forebearance and support of my classmates is greatly appreciated. But in the final analysis, the author is left alone with the reader. Any errors in the work, and, in spite of the helpful efforts of a number of good people, any failures to convince are my responsibility, and mine alone.

Introduction

By Congressman Ike Skelton

The role of the submarine — by the Germans in the Atlantic and the Americans in the Pacific — figures prominently in this book, *Slide Rules and Submarines,* written by Colonel Montgomery C. Meigs, US Army. His study details scientific efforts brought to bear in responding to the serious challenge posed by German U-boats during the first half of the Second World War, in what came to be known as the Battle of the Atlantic. Equally interesting is Colonel Meigs' description of the various measures taken to bolster the deadly work of US submarines in the Pacific campaign. His work, in a unique manner, shows how antisubmarine warfare lessons learned in the Atlantic were exploited to help American submariners in the Pacific develop new equipment and tactics to counter Japanese antisubmarine efforts.

The reader may wonder about an Army officer writing on naval matters. And some naval officers may be quite surprised at the thorough treatment of the subject by a non-sailor. They shouldn't be, in this era of "jointness." Colonel Meigs has done a masterful job of chronicling the various policy and technological obstacles that the Allies, and more especially the Americans, had to overcome in meeting these two distinct submarine challenges on opposite sides of the world. He also provides a thorough description of steps taken by German Admiral Karl Doenitz to build up the German submarine force before the war, and how Doenitz tried to maintain his force's advantage once the war began. Equally important are the wide lessons that can be applied by officers who must coordinate the work of civilian outsiders, military staffers, and fighting leaders toward the use of technological advances to provide new military capabilities.

A particularly prominent theme of the book is the familiar one of military men preparing to fight the last war. At the same time, Colonel Meigs tells the more interesting story of how the biases of military men can be overcome. He highlights a corollary principle:

"That the needs of success for the next war lie in the experience of the last, if only the generals and admirals would look for them in an unbiased way, or listen to their subordinates who immerse themselves in warfighting disciplines." And it is those subordinates at operational levels who ultimately helped overcome these biases.

Possibly the most difficult task confronting generals and admirals is to overcome traditional and institutional thinking. Human nature in general tends to resist change, to want to stay with the familiar. In the military, this proclivity is further reinforced by other factors: One service tends to look to its own for the answers, for example, while within each service, institutional boundaries between occupational or warfare specialties exacerbate this tendency. Mental blinders can at times be fastened so tightly that opportunities to deal with serious problems are dangerously delayed, if not lost.

Such was the case with the threat U-boats posed to Allied merchant shipping at the beginning of World War II. Admiral Ernest J. King, who occupied the dual positions of Commander in Chief, US Fleet, and Chief of Naval Operations, developed his ideas about operational strategy as a study at the Naval War College in 1932-33. While creative in his notions about the use of aircraft carriers, King's thinking did not display the same openness about the possible role of submarines.

This weakness in thinking came about despite his unique background as both submariner and aviator. Submarines and aircraft had no independent function in his strategic outlook. He gave primacy to the role of the surface fleet. The object of naval power was to defeat the forces of the enemy fleet. Admiral King simply failed to appreciate the strategic implications of unrestricted submarine warfare to defeat a nation by attacking its maritime lines of communication. Yet, such thinking on King's part proved to be woefully inadequate, as first British and then American shipping losses mounted in the first half of the war. Not until 1943 was an American strategy developed for defeating the German submarine threat.

Crucial in promoting that strategy was a variety of "outsiders"—such as American scientists and officers of the Royal Navy, and especially Secretary of War Henry L. Stimson. But American scientists played key parts in bringing the Navy around in their thinking about the role of the submarine—how best to counter the German U-boat threat, and how best to improve the capability of American submarines in the Pacific. Scientists, in and out of government, brought to the task at hand open minds, research skills, scientific methods, and a willingness to continue their work, despite the institutional resistance of Navy leadership.

The Navy initially resisted, and then later came to accept, the use of airplanes as submarine killers and the development of acoustic torpedoes. Scientists not only contributed new weapons, but, more importantly, influenced changes in training, tactics, and strategy. From a defensive strategy based on convoys and escorts, scientists promoted an offensive strategy of seizing the initiative by seeking out the U-boats.

Slide Rules and Submarines may be more topical than some imagine. The House Armed Services Subcommittees on Research and Development and Seapower published the *Report of the Advisory Panel on Submarine and Antisubmarine Warfare* on 21 March 1989. The panel, made up of 10 distinguished scientists and retired Navy admirals, expressed great concern about current ASW developments:

> Our current antisubmarine warfare (ASW) capability rests almost entirely on listening for the sounds generated by Soviet submarines. But the future of that approach is very much in doubt. . . . We must build what will amount to an entire new ASW capability. But the Navy establishment . . . is burdened with internal vested and sometimes conflicting interests that encumber innovation and execution on the scale required here. Dramatic new initiatives are essential. . . .

Readers of Colonel Meigs's account of difficulties faced by an earlier generation of naval leaders will have a keener appreciation of the various institutional forces at play today. Military officers and civilians actually involved in efforts to correct current ASW problems may have the most to gain by reading *Slide Rules and Submarines*. They will have before them an interesting account about the sometimes torturous path that scientific innovations must overcome before becoming accepted military capabilities.

Rep. Ike Skelton (D-Mo.) of Lexington, Mo., was a rural state legislator when he was elected to represent Missouri's Fourth District in 1976. A lawyer, Skelton has spent much of his career on the House Armed Services Committee. He has been a leading advocate of Pentagon reform, working to revamp the Defense Department hierarchy and arguing that US military strength is being hindered by interservice rivalry. Rep. Skelton is a graduate of Wentworth Military Academy, the University of Edinburgh, and the University of Missouri.

SLIDE RULES and SUBMARINES

1
Forgotten Naval Lessons of World War I

The Great War of 1914-18 represented a watershed in the evolution of warfare. After the war, the lessons of the land campaigns made more of an impression than those learned at sea. World War I brought together forces of modernization and industrialization that swept away conventional ideas of fighting on land. The machine gun, modern artillery, the airplane, the tank, and the telephone made possible the unprecedented massing of destructive power.

The naval battles of World War I had a somewhat different result. The indecisive Battle of Jutland Bay did not provide insights for the evolution of capital ships and their role in naval warfare. In the negotiations of the Washington Naval Treaty and the development of fleets after the war, battleships remained the decisive weapon of choice. A postwar development, the aircraft carrier, emerged only slowly; its total dominance of naval warfare began only to suggest itself late in the postwar period. The submarine, however, had proved its worth as a new weapon for the classical *guerre de corse*. The development of tactics and techniques in submarine warfare in 1917 anticipated the dominant factors in the seesaw contest in subsurface warfare in World War II.

4 Slide Rules and Submarines/Meigs

National Archives

Depth charge explosion. The development of tactics in warfare by submarines, which proved their worth as new weapons for the classical waging of war during WWI, anticipated dominant factors in subsurface warfare in WWII.

I
War at Sea and the Prize Ordinance

The Germans began their submarine campaign in 1914 with a tactical doctrine dominated by the rules of war at sea. Bound by orders to follow the Prize Ordinance, U-boats operated much like normal surface raiders of commercial shipping. They intercepted merchant vessels, warned them, and after the crews had a chance to abandon ship, sank the vessel with fire from their deck gun and saved torpedoes for the *coup de grace*.

The British developed "submarine traps" or Q-ships, heavily armed merchant vessels that looked harmless but which broke out concealed weapons to engage an attacking U-boat once it came to close range to carry out the Prize Ordinance Rules. Coincidentally, the Germans toyed with unrestricted submarine warfare, though they remained sensitive to American public opinion. Until 1917, combat between U-boats and surface ships consisted of fighting on and beneath the surface. Armed merchant ships and naval escorts used gunfire and ramming to attack U-boats on the surface, obeying the Ordinance. In response, the German submarines began to stray from the rules of maritime warfare and increasingly to conduct submerged attacks. After the German High Command decided in 1917 to initiate unrestricted submarine warfare, U-boats preferred submerged attacks and almost exclusively attacked without warning. In April 1917, the British Merchant Marine lost 900,000 tons, or one-twentieth of its capacity. This loss forced the Admiralty to implement convoying and to discover its utility as a defense against the U-boat.[1]

By the end of the war, a variety of weapons had taken a toll of U-boats. (See the table on page 6 for a listing of U-boat losses in World War I.) With the exception of convoying, and mining the U-boats' egress routes into shipping lanes, no particular weapon or tactic promised a definitive solution to the problem of concerted attacks by submarines against merchant shipping. No one technology seemed dominant. Well trained, aggressive escorts generally kept submarines away from convoys and occasionally picked off the lone raiders that attempted to infiltrate the escort screen. Aircraft showed potential but time ran out before conclusive evidence became

---

U-boat losses in World War I

30%	mines in the North Sea
10%	sunk on surface by Allied submarines
25%	ramming or gunfire by surface ships
20%	sunk while submerged
15%	not due to Allied action

Source: National Archives and Research Agency, Record Group 227, The Records of Division 6 of the National Defense Research Committee, John Tate et al., *The Summary Technical Report of Division 6*, Vol. 1, pp. 7-10.

---

available. Only convoying and mining had demonstrated decisive results. Accordingly, as budgets grew tighter in the twenties, the potential of other tactics for antisubmarine warfare lost most of their impact. Arms conferences limited construction of new ships, and the victorious navies reoriented their attention to the traditional concern of admirals, the clash of surface fleets.

Some postwar analysts of the experience of World War I, however, did reveal lessons with great significance for any subsequent war at sea. Rear Admiral William S. Sims commanded the American naval forces operating from England in World War I. In 1920, he published *The Victory at Sea*, in which he discussed the operations of American naval units and the operational experience of the Allies' navies. In addition to noting the success of convoying, he discussed the potential of the airplane and acknowledged the success of the blimp in locating submarines.

The commander of the German submarine fleet corroborated American successes in developing the airplane as an antisubmarine weapon.[2] Sims also detailed the susceptibility of the talkative U-boat captains to high-frequency direction-finding and described the development of a command center in Britain, which successfully monitored and tracked German submarines. Operators became intimately familiar with the operational habits of certain German captains and the individual distinctive rhythm their radio operators exhibited on their keying devices. Plotting rooms also learned how to predict the movements of U-boats and how to route convoys away from areas where contact seemed most likely. Allied convoy commanders understood that along with destroying U-boats attempting to penetrate their defenses, they also accomplished their mission if they detected submarines at long range and forced them to submerge. Even unsuccessful attacks occupied the submarine while the convoy escaped at a speed that, though slow for surface ships, proved three or four times that of a submerged U-boat.[3] These patterns appeared again and again in WWII.

The German Navy had its innovators as well. At the end of the war, a young U-boat captain, Karl Doenitz, the father of the U-boat navy of World War II, successfully employed surfaced attacks at night. On his last cruise, he planned and attempted to execute a two-boat patrol. He believed strongly that U-boats operating in packs could wreak havoc with convoys and their escorts. Doenitz knew from experience the liabilities of early U-boats, the inadequacy of early radios, and the tactical advantage afforded by surprise. He understood that the merchant marine of a seapower like Great Britain presented her vital weakness.[4]

Improvements in equipment in World War I accompanied developments in tactics. Along with radio receivers for direction finding, the Allies developed underwater sound-ranging gear, called ASDIC by the British. In the United States, laboratories of the General Electric Company and the Submarine Signal Company began work on hydrophones for capturing underwater sound. The Allies tested these in the English Channel in 1917. Both the American and Royal Navies placed orders with their respective industrial establishments. By the war's end, crude second-generation equipment saw combat. In addition, Allied naval engineers worked on a variety

8   Slide Rules and Submarines/Meigs

National Archives

German Admiral Karl Doenitz inspects the crew of one of his U-boats in early days of World War II during campaign against convoys in the Atlantic. Doenitz (1891-1980) was creator of Germany's World War II U-boat fleet; he was named commander in chief of the German Navy in January 1943, replacing Admiral Erich Raeder.

of other gear, ranging from depth charges to improved submarines and subchasers.[5] But much of the momentum begun in the last year of the First World War played out in the years leading to the second.

II

Allied Failures, German Successes

The failure to capitalize on the lessons of World War I meant that Britain and the United States began the Second World War unprepared for antisubmarine warfare. With the exception of work done on specific pieces of equipment, little took place to prepare for the scope of campaigning that could have been expected in another war. The Versailles Treaty took the Germans out of naval competition. Until a bilateral agreement with Great Britain in 1935, their submarine building program remained a dead letter. In other quarters, the Washington Naval Treaty limited the size of the navies of the United States, Great Britain, and Japan. Depressed economies, a traditional fascination with big ships and big fleets, and institutional compartmentalization all preempted innovation.

The American and British navies failed to develop an operational concept for an antisubmarine campaign. Their weapons for sinking submarines carried over from the campaigns of 1917, with little improvement in capability. In spite of the development of the airplane as a naval weapon, admirals on both sides of the Atlantic overlooked its potential as an antisubmarine weapon, and concentrated on capital ships and the operation of big fleets.[6] British and American naval leaders failed to develop a doctrine for antisubmarine warfare that took an integrated approach to applying a broad range of capabilities to finding and killing submarines.

In the United States, this failure stemmed in part from an institutional problem. Between the wars, the US Navy did not conduct an organized program for development of weapons and doctrine for antisubmarine warfare. No agency survived World War I with "both the power and the interest necessary to carry on effective antisubmarine developments."[7] As a result, techniques languished. Laboratories worked on incremental improvements in equipment in isolation from operational needs. Without an institutional proponent, no process existed by which the interaction between operational needs and nascent capabilities made possible by new scientific development could generate requirements for new weapons. Lacking a cohesive group of young and ambitious antisubmarine officers to experiment with techniques and ideas and to push for improvements, doctrine atrophied and institutional compartmentalization stymied technological innovation. The Naval Research Laboratory persevered and perfected underwater sound-ranging gear. But no agency worked to integrate this improved capability for finding submarines with better weapons for killing them tied to a training program to make it all work. Antisubmarine weapons improved only marginally over those weapons available in 1918. The standard depth charge had a flight trajectory of a "falling leaf." It sank slowly through the water, giving a turning, diving U-boat a chance to put more space between it and its last known position.[8] Without an appreciation of the value of the airplane as a submarine killer, the Navy made no effort to adapt depth charges to aircraft.

Returning to traditional naval thinking, senior naval officers directed their attention to combat between surface fleets. In the late thirties, fleet exercises of the US Navy concerned maneuvers between similarly configured battlegroups of carriers and battleships, which attacked each other or in which one unit attacked and one defended a strategic objective like the Panama Canal. Seaplanes served only as scouts for the battle groups. Submarines saw employment only as a means of reconnoitering for surface ships and as a secondary weapon for attacking them. The exclusion of subsurface warfare from naval operations took place in the Royal Navy as well. Though in 1925 the British improved the design of their depth charges and placed them into service without trials in 1931, they never adapted the weapon to aircraft. In addition, the Air Ministry made an affirmative decision not to develop an antisubmarine bomb. British naval strategists confined themselves to combat between the big ships. Their appreciation of the threat to commerce concerned only the danger posed by surface task groups.[9]

One officer in particular personified the blindness in the US Navy toward subsurface warfare. After the disaster of Pearl Harbor, President Franklin D. Roosevelt selected Admiral Ernest J. King as Commander in Chief United States Fleet. In King, Roosevelt selected a man with an unusually rich background of operational experience. An outstanding seaman, King had trained as a submariner, commanded a division of submarines, and while in command of the navy's submarine base at New London had established his reputation in difficult

Admiral Ernest J. King (1878-1956), Commander in Chief, US Fleet (COM-INCH). President Roosevelt appointed him Commander in Chief, Atlantic Fleet (CINCLANT) in February 1941 and COMINCH in December 1941. In May 1943, King headed Tenth Fleet, the newly created command that monitored antisubmarine activities.

and politically very sensitive salvage operations of sunken submarines. One of a number of senior officers who in the thirties qualified as naval aviators, King served as head of the Bureau of Aeronautics, as commander of the Pacific Fleet's seaplane force, and later as commander of the carrier USS *LEXINGTON*. During his tour at the Bureau of Aeronautics, he worked on the design of aircraft and developed some of the doctrine for the operations of carrier task forces. Somewhat of an innovator, he advocated the separation of battleships and carriers and the formation of fast battle groups consisting of cruisers and carriers long before the concept proved itself in combat.[10]

King's ideas about operational strategy appear in work done during his tour as a student at the Senior Course of the

Naval War College in 1932-33. As part of his course of instruction, he submitted various appreciations and orders for operations of fleets against hypothetical Japanese enemies in the Pacific and British opponents in the Atlantic. King's staff work presented simply stated and precisely analyzed strategic estimates and courses of action that deserve the respect of contemporary scholars for their clarity and precision. However, they uniformly portray the location and activity of the enemy surface fleet as the threat to naval lines of communication. Decisive victory came only from a classic clash of capital ships. Either by direct confrontation or by placing one's own fleet across the enemy's maritime lines of communications, the goal was to force the enemy to battle at a time and place of your choosing. Submarines and aircraft operated solely to assist the battle line in its decisive role.[11]

King's work to improve the tactics of aircraft carriers and his experience with fleet submarines in the years following the Senior Course at Newport did not open his mind to the possibilities of unrestricted submarine warfare. His ideas about the primacy of the capital ship and the role of the surface fleet in naval warfare changed only slightly by 1940. In 1935, he wrote that aircraft and submarines served to extend the observation and fires of the capital ships, "to assist the battle line to the maximum in defeating the enemy."[12]

Five years later, his thinking about naval strategy reflected the same basic principle. In terms of rate and weight of fire, the guns of the heavy ships provided the primary destructive power of the fleet. Naval strategy had as its object bringing the fleet of the enemy within the range of destruction of those guns. Other means of naval warfare existed to "compel the enemy fleet to battle."[13] While King acknowledged the near success of the unrestricted operations of the German U-boats in 1917, he noted that their eventual failure provided a good example of the rule that "a serious menace impels the creation and development of countermeasures."[14] The power of the surface fleet possessed sufficient reserves to combat the submarine menace with gunfire, ramming, and depth charges. Given a resurgence of antisubmarine warfare the fleet would adapt to meet the challenge. In the mind of Admiral King, control of the sea depended solely on offensive action of battleships and the fast carrier groups against the enemy's fleet. Submarines and aircraft had no independent function. Because of these ideas, and because of his innate stubbornness, when in a position to assist the development of new solutions to the U-boat problem during the Battle of the Atlantic, King inhibited tactical and technical innovation.

The Germans had a completely different perspective toward naval strategy. The Versailles Treaty and the economic ruin of the interwar period prevented the buildup of a large fleet. As the losers of the 1914-18 War, they knew the value of a powerful surface navy. However, they also remembered that in 1917, the U-boat had almost delivered victory on Great Britain's maritime lines of communications. The submarine obviated the need for a great fleet. In 1935, the Anglo-German Naval Treaty allowed a German Navy of all types of ships. Germany could build ships with a total tonnage by type equal to 35 percent of Britain's total. Submarines fell into a special category; the treaty allowed Germany 45 percent of the Royal Navy's tonnage in submarines. This worked out to 24,000 tons. The door for naval modernization and expansion of the German Navy stood open.

In July of that year, the German High Command appointed as Officer Commanding Submarines a World War I veteran of submarine warfare and believer in the potential of the U-boat, Karl Doenitz. In the years leading to 1935, Doenitz had worked his way through positions in command of German surface ships. Between 1918 and assumption of his new duties, he added a thorough exposure to surface operations to his combat experience in submarines. Once given the nod, he immediately began building his undersea service with what turned out to be a vengeance.[15]

Doenitz brought to submarine warfare insights gleaned from his experiences both on and under the sea. Operations on the surface allowed the U-boat better observation and a greater chance of sighting the enemy. Surface speeds of over 15 knots allowed the U-boat making a sighting and its fellows the operational mobility to bound ahead to intercept their quarry. Individual submarines gained the tactical mobility to move about the convoy to select an approach to get into torpedo range, as well as the ability to sidestep out of harm's way. From his own experience, Doenitz knew the effectiveness of night attacks. Like any good military man, a believer in the principle of massing combat power at the decisive point, he felt certain that this concept applied to U-boats attacking convoys.[16]

The Germans immediately faced the problem of developing a submarine arm. They set aside the design of the old cruiser submarine, one optimized for surface attacks using deck guns. For operations in the North Atlantic, the German submariners wanted a handy, nimble, quick-diving boat with a low profile. Doenitz settled on a 517-ton submarine with redesigned fuel bunkers that gave the range to allow prolonged deep-water operations. To maximize the number of submarines permitted under limits of the Anglo-German treaty, the German Navy planned for a fleet consisting of three-quarters Mark VII, 500-ton boats and one-quarter Mark IX, 750-ton U-boats. Doenitz wanted the Mark IX, the redesigned cruiser (itself much smaller than Germany's 2,000-ton WWI cruiser submarine), for operations in distant waters.

Next, Doenitz set about developing tactics. Beginning with the doctrine that existed for torpedo boats, he and a small group of officers spent a great deal of time training with their units in the most realistic scenarios they could conceive. In 1935 and 1936, by trial and error, they derived a doctrine from operational experience. In peacetime, Doenitz sought to put his submariners through the stresses they could expect in wartime. He wanted the high morale that comes from confidence. He drove his crews through surface tactics, diving drills, and simulated attacks. Each submarine had to complete over 60 successful practice attacks before it could attempt a live torpedo run. By 1937, Doenitz had his submariners ready for the German Navy's Fleet Maneuvers.

The following year, he ran a wargame in the Atlantic to perfect tactics of the submarine groups. The tactics proved a success. Doenitz continued to refine his ideas about surfaced attacks, centralized command and control, and concentration against one target by submarines that operated independently. He experimented with a new tactic of guiding U-boats onto convoys from a distant headquarters and began to perfect what later became *Rudeltaktik*, wolfpack tactics, in which U-boats in a reconnaissance screen followed directions from a distant operational headquarters to swarm onto a convoy. After his successes in 1938, Doenitz believed that with a fleet of 300 U-boats, a figure that meant he could keep 100 submarines on patrol, he had a chance of strangling Britain by destroying its merchant marine.[17]

While the US and British navies focused their energies on strategies for fighting on the surface and neglected antisubmarine warfare, the German Navy developed equipment, doctrine, and training optimized for a new kind of combat. Doenitz made no bones about his ideas and in 1939 published *Die U-Bootswaffe*, in which he discussed the potential of the U-boat. His American and British contemporaries simply overlooked the challenge the U-boat presented to naval lines of communication, and they failed to develop capabilities to meet it. In his *Memoirs*, Doenitz gives an insight into the peculiar myopia of the military man that stems from his tendency to prepare for the future by revisiting lessons of his past:

> How difficult it is for a naval officer who has been educated and trained for surface warfare clearly to appreciate and assimilate the importance of any other type of fighting, such as submarine warfare. From the human point of view, this is readily understandable, for he lives in the atmosphere of his own type of war, and if he is energetic and keen on his job, he concentrates all his thoughts on those means which will enable him to win the surface engagement he seeks, and he pins his hope on them and believes in them.[18]

Doenitz might better have said that the soldier and sailor eat, sleep, and breathe the atmosphere of their own type of warfare. Successful operations at sea or in the field require intense concentration and effort and unremitting discipline to overcome horrible weather and great fatigue and to obtain results in exercises in spite of confusion and muddle. The shared experience of success makes for susceptibility to tradition and a collegial loyalty to the ideas and techniques that have worked in the past.

Institutional boundaries of branches, corps, and departments provide an organizational focus for shared experience and parochial consensus. Even an officer as broadly experienced as Admiral King overlooked the potential of new weapons for which he was the proponent. His professional schooling and the large fleet exercises in which he gained his operational insights in the late thirties only recreated strategic problems posed in geographical terms. Only when the iconoclasts design the big exercises and the large fleet maneuvers can unconventional thinkers obtain results that support challenges to institutionally sanctioned policies about force structure, capabilities, and doctrine.

Not that the US Navy completely ignored the threat posed by the German submarine. Just before war broke out, King and the then Chief of Naval Operations, Admiral Harold R. Stark, tried to initiate a building program for escorts. Short of time and despairing of consensus, the Navy's General Board settled on the design of the Hamilton Class Coast Guard Cutter as a satisfactory prototype. Relatively large at 327 feet in length, seaworthy, and fast, these ocean-going cutters carried heavy armament and provided a stable platform that could accept new weapons. They proved to be the outstanding American escort vessels of the war. Unfortunately, the General Board's recommendation went awry in the navy staff over the issue of proper armament. When Stark finally got to President Roosevelt with his recommendations, the President objected to the size and cost of the program and backed away. Roosevelt favored using smaller craft like submarine chasers.[19]

In 1939 and 1940, the US Navy struggled to prepare for war. Problems and liabilities seemed larger than those long-term programs that eventually contributed to defeating the U-boat. Congress provided funds for new ships, though naval planners underestimated the numbers of destroyers and destroyer escorts they would require. Franklin D. Roosevelt's keen interest in the Navy brought mixed blessings. While he badgered the Navy into moving ahead with construction of escort carriers, his sponsorship of small craft for antisubmarine work preempted the construction of escort craft capable of continuous operations in the heavy seas of the North Atlantic. His reticence and the bumbling of the navy staff cost the US Merchant Marine dearly in 1942.[20]

In spite of advances Doenitz had made by 1939, the war came before his fleet of U-boats was anywhere near ready for a contest with the Royal Navy. Instead of 300 ocean-going U-boats, he had less than 60 submarines, 30 of which could conduct prolonged operations at sea. Of these, only 10 were of the newest 500-ton class. In September 1939, the six German U-boats then on patrol began their attacks on British shipping. Along with the very capable Mark VII submarine, the Germans had developed an electric, wakeless torpedo that was superior to its US counterpart. However, the Germans had not applied the potential of their scientific community to protecting the ability of their submarines to remain hidden. They ignored the possibilities of the combined effect of radar, sonar, and airplane.[21] Doenitz's emphasis on training and tactical doctrine yielded a small force, but one with extremely high combat readiness and a potential for growth. However, he had not surveyed the whole range of possible countermeasures of relatively low technological risk available to combat his U-boats.

Doenitz, however, did have a well-defined strategic concept. The Royal Navy existed to assure Britain control of the sea. For centuries, English seadogs protected their country from invasion, patrolled the sea-lanes that tied Britain to the remote outposts of her Empire, and provided foodstuffs and raw materials to her workers and factories. The German Navy planned to avoid the power of Britain's surface fleets and destroy her trade:

> The strategic task of the German Navy was to wage war on trade; its objective was therefore to sink as many enemy ships as it could. The sinking of ships was the only thing that counted.[22]

Doenitz called his theory integral tonnage. Sinking of ships without regard to geographical reference gave him an ad-

Convoy in the North Atlantic early in World War II. The war erupted before Admiral Doenitz's U-boats were ready for the contest with the Royal Navy.

vantage over American and British naval strategists. While the Allies worked to move surface units to strategic locations and to protect sea lanes, the U-boats could always use the waters they neglected to maneuver to attack merchantmen where they were most weakly defended. The German Navy could win so long as, at a cost in U-boats that did not threaten the integrity of his command, it could sink more ships than the Allies could replace.

III
Wolves and Shepherds

In the first year of the war, U-boats and the Royal Navy picked up the pace they had achieved in 1917-18. Very early, both sides adopted a pattern of tactic and countermeasure that continued throughout the war. U-boats began their attacks in the northeastern waters of the Atlantic close to the United Kingdom. From September 1939 to June 1940, they usually attacked in daylight from periscope depth. Concentrating on the large amount of independent shipping that sailed early in the war, and capitalizing on the inability of the Royal Navy to provide heavy escorts to convoys, they lay in wait of shipping, acquired a target, used their relatively fast surface speed to sprint ahead to gain a good firing position, and closed in for the kill once their prey came into range.

This work was not easy for the German submariners. The proximity of their patrol areas to the coast of Britain allowed the British to maintain an air umbrella over their coastal waters. While at this point in the war aircraft possessed neither radar nor weapons designed specifically to attack submarines, their presence forced the U-boat to submerge and thus surrender its advantage of surface speed. This tactic cut the area a U-boat could search and geometrically reduced its probability of acquiring a target. A submarine on the surface could outmaneuver a slow merchant vessel making 10 knots. Submerged, it could not keep up the chase.

Doenitz also had his problems. His submarines caused a great ruckus in British coastal waters, but he could not keep enough U-boats on station to support initiating *Rudeltaktik*. The High Command also diverted U-boats from their primary operational objective. Through the winter of 1939-40, submarines on patrol never exceeded 10 and at one time dropped to 2. Hitler also diverted submarines from the main strategic objective by insisting that a number remain in the Arctic off Norway as a reconaissance screen against the Royal Navy. Later, he ordered submarines into the Mediterranean. Once in, they could not get out. Doenitz also had problems with torpedoes that lowered the confidence of his commanders and took months to correct.[23]

Though short of escorts in the first phase of the war, from September 1939 to the summer of 1941, the Royal Navy aggressively defended its merchant ships and acquired experience in tough months of fighting. Of the six submarines the German Navy could keep on station, the Royal Air Force and Royal Navy claimed between two and three a month. The average U-boat during this phase of the war survived for three months in combat. But monthly, the U-boats in their turn sent an average of 26 merchant ships to the bottom, approximately 11 for each of their own casualties.[24] Since the British lost 280,000 gross tons of shipping to all causes monthly and built on the average 90,000 gross tons to replace them, the future looked grim.

In the summer of 1940, the Germans altered their operational strategy, always a sign in the campaign that they felt countermeasures had placed their units at a disadvantage. Convoy procedures instituted by the British and costs of operating near the enemy's coast made a strong argument for change. In addition, production of U-boats had increased, and the defeat of France made French coastal ports available as operating bases. A growing fleet and shorter lines of communication and deployment made it possible to position more raiders farther into the Atlantic away from the nuisance of Coastal Command's airborne patrols. Doenitz began ordering his captains to take up patrol zones farther west along the

Atlantic approaches to Great Britain. Because of increases in production, he could now plan to keep an average of 10 boats on station.[25]

The Germans also changed their tactics. They used the same techniques for patrolling and positioning themselves for attack as in the previous period; however, they abandoned daytime attacks and began primarily penetrating the increasingly heavy convoy escorts on the surface at night or in fog. They slipped by the escorts, fired their first spread of torpedos, and raced away. If undetected in the confusion that ensued, they reloaded and attacked again, submerging only to escape a surface escort in hot pursuit. Doenitz adapted his tactics to maximize sinkings and minimize the exchange ratio of U-boats for enemy ships. Enough submarines now remained on patrol to support reconnaissance sweeps and concentrations that the U-boats had practiced before the war. The summer of 1940 and the months leading to March 1941 saw the introduction and perfection of *Rudeltaktik*.[26]

The British had not been idle. They fought through a debate over merits of a strategy based on defense of convoys as opposed to an offensive concept that envisioned the formation of "hunter groups" of escorts positioned to intercept U-boats on their way to convoy routes. The Royal Navy experimented with the offensive concept until the losses of early 1940 forced a return to tactics of defense of convoys that had proven effective in 1917. In addition to instituting convoy rules for shipping, the British also began to develop new weapons and tactics. Ships in convoys increased dispersion, making it harder for U-boats to score hits with unaimed torpedos fired in a fan pattern into the convoy. The Admiralty developed rules for attack by surface ships and organized escort groups that trained and then fought together for as long as possible. They developed a training program for escort vessels. New ships received initial training at an escort training school, HMS *WESTERN ISLES*, and then continued their instruction under the captain in command of escort groups before they joined a particular escort group. The Admiralty recognized the importance of habitual association as a factor in top performance.

British subchaser in 1942. When the Germans changed their U-boat tactics early in the war, the British instituted new convoy rules for shipping and began to develop new weapons and tactics.

Once they organized a group, they made every effort to keep it together for the duration of the war.[27]

In October 1940, the loss of 38 ships from 3 convoys pushed the Admiralty to look for additional technological improvements. The Royal Navy had an advantage in the idiosyncratic system of committees that supported the parliamentary Cabinet. The Admiralty's weekly Trade Protection Meeting discussed operational problems and immediately forwarded recommendations to the Prime Minister for expeditious approval. As a number of programs began and received support at the highest level, scientists adapted meter-wave radar to aircraft and then to ships. They also began developing a network of direction-finding stations to locate U-boats on patrol and make possible evasive routing of convoys.[28]

In the second phase of the Battle of the Atlantic, from the summer of 1940 to the summer of 1941, German submariners increased their take. The average of 10 U-boats kept on patrol sank just over 40 merchant ships, double the monthly tonnage of the previous phase. Escorts had less success in the more open expanses of the mid-Atlantic. They sank only 2 U-boats a month, giving the Germans a ratio of 22 merchant ships for every submarine lost, the best exchange rate they achieved throughout the war. However, the antisubmarine operations of the Royal Navy kept improving. In March 1941, as Doenitz added the final touches to his wolfpack tactics, they bagged Germany's three top-scoring submariners. By June, the Royal Navy had enough operational escort ships to provide end-to-end coverage of Atlantic sea-lanes from Halifax to ports in Britain. Aircraft kept submarines out of Britain's coastal waters and away from Newfoundland, but proved a disappointment as submarine killers. To make aircraft into effective submarine killers, weapons and training had yet to be mastered. In addition, improvements in command and control made a contribution, direction-finding nets began to track U-boats, and evasive routing began to pay off.

By January 1942, the campaign for Atlantic sea-lanes had assumed the general pattern that continued until the end of the war. Doenitz maintained the strictest central control over his boats, constantly moving them about the Atlantic, advising them on a daily basis on tactics and procedures, and demanding frequent situation reports and status on fuel and torpedoes. When a given operational strategy began to result in too many losses, he shifted the geographical focus of attack and changed tactics. To improvements in Allied capabilities, the Germans responded with a shift of U-boats to more lightly defended sectors. So long as they could find independent shipping or convoys with ineffective escort screens, the Germans met their strategic objective of integral tonnage and found no incentive for a review of operational and tactical capabilities. Following his functional objective of sinking merchantmen, and able to exploit geographical weaknesses, Doenitz failed to assess changes in countermeasures made available by technological innovation. He did not look to scientists and engineers for ways to improve capabilities of submarines until the summer of 1943, when the slide toward defeat had become obvious.

The British and, subsequently, the Americans adapted their ideas about the role of submarines as an independent element in naval warfare. They had to control critical parts of the ocean by checkmating the U-boats' unique capabilities. Killing submarines was important, but it was achieved by attacking the problem systemically, that is, by analyzing U-boats and their supporting logistical network as a system. This system had two types of exploitable weaknesses. The capabilities of equipment created tactical limitations, like the requirement to recharge batteries, or operational ones, like limits on range imposed by the submarine's fuel capacity. In addition, each part of the system operated in the environment provided by the sea, the atmosphere, and the electromagnetic spectrum. Scientists, by training, possessed the special aptitude of measuring and analyzing environmental factors, like the manner submarine noise carried in sea water, or the possibility of bouncing a radio wave off a submarine's hull. The need to surface for high-speed operations and to recharge, and the U-boat's radar cross section created exploitable weaknesses in the U-boat system. Radar cross section, underwater noise, radio-electronic signatures, and susceptibility to acoustic torpedoes when submerged to attack all became exploitable to scientists who investigated and measured the interaction between the submarine and its environment.

IV

Role of American Scientists

As the war raged in Europe, American scientists began to mobilize themselves for the inevitable. This activity included their unprecedented participation in developing weapons. Vannevar Bush, President of the Carnegie Institute, a former proimage not included owing to copyright restrictions

National Archives/The Bettmann Archive

Dr. Vannevar Bush, president of the Carnegie Institute, helped scientists mobilize for the development of weapons needed for the war that was raging in Europe. He formed the National Defense Research Committee (NDRC) in June 1940 and turned his position in NDRC over to Dr. James B. Conant when the Office of Scientific Research and Development (OSRD) was formed. Bush then ran OSRD, to which NDRC was subordinate.

fessor and vice president of MIT, formed the National Defense Research Committee (NDRC) in June 1940. This organization grew out of the concern of Bush and other similarly minded leaders of the scientific community, like chemist James B. Conant, president of Harvard, that American scientists must prepare to make their skills available for winning the war that would surely come. As part of his overall program, Bush sold his ideas to President Roosevelt and received a charter in the form of an Executive order, and funds from the President's own budget.

Bush and his colleagues arranged for a committee sponsored by the National Academy of Science to study subsurface warfare. The Colpitts Report, named after the committee's chairman, scientist Edwin H. Colpitts, roundly criticized the scientific background of the Navy's antisubmarine effort, noting, "We feel an altogether inadequate research effort on fundamentals has been put forth since the last war." Colpitts noted as well that the scientific contribution to antisubmarine warfare was, "also a question of tactics and tactical doctrine, of personnel and training and of operational records."[29] The Navy responded by challenging the report and competence of its authors to comment on operational matters.

Bush and his colleague Frank B. Jewett, head of Bell Labs, tactfully stood by their guns, emphasizing their desire to support the Navy's program. Initially, the authorities in the navy staff resisted this interference. Bush cajoled and pushed and eventually reached Secretary of the Navy Frank Knox. By March, he and Jewett met with the Navy's General Board. The Bureau of Ships subsequently requested that NDRC conduct a study of antisubmarine devices.[30]

Bush and Jewett actually had used the device of committees and studies to get their foot in the door to the Navy's research effort. Jewett already had formed a group of scientists who, parallel with Colpitts' group, by January 1941 surveyed technologies relevant to antisubmarine warfare and had let contracts for work on acoustic torpedoes and magnetic detection of submarines (Magnetic Anomaly Detection or MAD).* The official request of the Bureau of Ships

---

* The process of finding a submarine by locating the disturbance in the earth's magnetic field caused by the magnetic field of the submarine.

Forgotten Naval Lessons of World War I   27

National Archives

Frank Knox, Secretary of the Navy during the Roosevelt administration (1940-44). Knox (1874-1944), emphasized the need for naval supremacy. An American journalist and newspaper publisher (Sault Sainte Marie, Mich., Manchester, N.H., and Chicago, and the Hearst organization), Knox was Republican vice presidential nominee in 1936.

(BUSHIPS) allowed Jewett officially to organize a new section of his division of NDRC to consolidate an informal program of work already in progress. Jewett picked scientist John T. Tate of the University of Minnesota to run Section C-4. By 18 April, in response to the request by BUSHIPS, Tate and his colleagues published their "Plan for Handling of a Comprehensive Investigation of Submarine Detection."

Tate and his colleagues refused to confine themselves narrowly to what they disdained as "gadgetry." They insisted on applying scientific method to the whole problem of the detection and destruction of submarines and to the environment in which the submarine operated, in their words,

> the most complete investigation possible of all factors and phenomena involved in the accurate detection of submerged or partially submerged submarines and in antisubmarine devices.[31]

In their comprehensive analysis of the operational problem of the U-boat, its atmospheric and oceanic environment, and all possible technologies available for detection and destruction of submarines, Tate and his colleagues opened the possibility of an unprecedented application of technological innovation to antisubmarine warfare, an application unfettered by military tradition, institutional boundaries, or vested points of view.

Tate and his fellow researchers did not fail to acknowledge the contribution of the Naval Research Laboratory in perfecting underwater sound-ranging gear. They recognized the scarcity of funds that had preempted research on other means of detection. Critical of the Navy's overall program of antisubmarine warfare, they also pointed out the discontinuity between the Navy's improving capabilities for detection and its lagging capabilities for destroying U-boats:

> The rest of the antisubmarine gear had not been correspondingly improved. The ordnance, depth charges, had hardly changed at all; and equipment designed to help the aircraft make submarine attacks was practically nonexistent.[32]

No body of theory and empirical data existed on which to base tactical doctrine and a training program. No data was available on sound propagation underwater, a crucial element in predicting how sonar could be expected to perform in different ambient conditions at sea. Nor were attack aids or displays available to help operators locate submarines and ships' captains solve the three-dimensional problem of calculating an aiming point for depth charges given a moving, diving target and a moving firing platform. The capability of sound-ranging equipment had outstripped the ability of the Navy to train sailors who could operate it at top efficiency.[33]

Tate traveled to England in June 1941 to learn from the British scientific community and naval staffs anything that might help the efforts of his scientists. He found the officials of the Royal Navy more cooperative than those at home. In England, he immersed himself in all aspects of Britain's experience with antisubmarine warfare. From officials anxious for help in winning the war, he received tutorials on tactics of escorts and convoy formations and capabilities of U-boats. Scientists and naval officers alike discussed with him the idiosyncracies of sound gear and depth charges, as well as possibilities for future research. They stressed "the tendency of researchmen (sic) to continually improve and delay production" and the corresponding requirement for one man who could and would "say stop! and go!"[34]

Displeased with the US Navy's antisubmarine effort, Tate lost no time organizing his program. By June, fresh from his liaison trip to England, he obtained the Navy's support for laboratories on the East and West coasts. On 12 June 1941, NDRC authorized $90,000 for contracts to be let that month. In July, NDRC authorized an additional $1,569,500 for contracts for work on antisubmarine warfare. On 5 September, the Bureau of Ships sanctioned the work of Tate's Section by incorporating it into the Navy's program for research and development. Rear Admiral A. H. Van Keuran, head of BUSHIPS, accepted the significance of Section C-4's research on propagation of sound underwater, the problem of locating a submerged submarine, and oceanic surveys. He declared that "depth determination and speeding of descent of depth charges" were then the most critical elements of "the whole problem of antisubmarine warfare."[35] Two weeks later, Tate outlined to his subordinates some of the challenges as he saw them:

> The types of problems facing the section may be classified in the following way:
> (1) Determination of maximum range of present echo-ranging equipment in terms of oceanographic conditions and practice.
> (2) Extension of the range. . . .
> (3) Improvements in present equipment as far as range and bearing are concerned and the development of a new device or addition to present equipment to determine the depth of the submarine.
> (4) The transmission of the measurements of range, bearing, and depth to the conning officer of the ship.
> (5) Probability studies of the relative advantages of various attack procedures utilizing the data obtained.[36]

Tate's description of the problem highlights the unique perspective scientists brought to development of antisubmarine warfare. They looked at the problem systemically, divided it into stages of location, tracking, and attack, and isolated causal links at each stage. This view allowed them to isolate and string together the series of tasks required for a surface escort to find and kill a submerged U-boat. It also brought to light the need for data on such things as the propagation of sound waves in salt water at different depths and temperatures, the better to understand the problem of locating a submarine. Once this data became available in the form of charts, they led to a system for surveying the ocean immediately around a convoy, to allow operators to understand more clearly the sound picture their sonar gave to them. The data further allowed an unbiased assessment of results.

As they began to study the problem, the scientists came up with some astounding findings. From a study of the problem of attack on a submerged U-boat by a surface vessel, they discovered that the theoretical possibilty of success was less than 1 in 20. Agreeing that the operational experience of the Navy must validate parameters of their theory, they requested information on the performance of ships, sonar gear, and depth charges. They soon discovered that naval authorities

> did not know in any quantitative manner the *operational* characteristics of their antisubmarine craft and gear when used by the average crew in actual wartime conditions.[37]

During Tate's absence in England, Frank Jewett consulted his colleagues about the organization of work on subsurface warfare. They decided on a five-part structure, consisting of a central control group, an oceanographic laboratory, laboratories for fundamental studies in underwater propagation of sound and for prototype development, and a group of agencies under contract to develop individual pieces of equipment. Tate used the central control group as a coordinating agency for liaison with the Navy and for access to research being done in other divisions of NDRC. He also drew on Jewett and Bush for scientific personnel to fill his ranks and established a program analysis group to collect and analyze operational data and develop the theory of attack. But the important first step toward new technological innovations depended on fundamental studies to quantify the characteristics of the ocean as a medium.

To bring together fundamental studies and to continue work done there in 1940, NDRC awarded contracts to the Oceanographic Institute at Woods Hole, Mass. This work included development of the bathythermograph, a device for measuring the temperature profile of the ocean. Personnel at Woods Hole also began surveying and charting the ocean floor and evaluating the effect of depth on reflectivity and propagation of sound waves. Woods Hole eventually developed sound propagation charts for the whole Atlantic. Because of its proximity to Washington, DC, the war zone, and the most likely manufacturers of equipment, the East Coast laboratory contracted to Columbia University received the charter for testing

Ships in North Atlantic convoy. Early work by scientists helped improve range and receptivity of sound gear, making shipping by Allied convoys relatively safer.

and refining equipment to bring it from prototype to the point where it could be manufactured in quantity in a configuration ready for issue to the field. The University of California received contracts for a laboratory in San Diego to develop the physics of underwater acoustics and quantify the effect of salinity, temperature, density, and depth on the propagation of waves of different frequency through seawater. In addition, Harvard University began work on the ambient sound profile of the ocean, the sounds of various ships, and the reflectivity and sound of submarines underwater.[38]

Work on the basic physics of the propagation of sound underwater suggested improvements to existing gear, as well as possibilities for new equipment. The constant feedback between the labs and the central group and its analysis section played a unique role in guiding the work of engineers and physicists trying to improve the range and receptivity of sound gear. Stemming from work commissioned at Harvard in 1940 by the US Navy's Bureau of Ordnance, scientists developed the idea of an acoustically guided torpedo. The Navy resisted the idea until December 1941, arguing that the weapon would be too big and too slow. But the scientists went ahead on their own. They had control of the contracting process. Results gained from their studies of the fundamental science of acoustics and their access to operational data gave Tate and his colleagues a unique insight both to what was needed in the field and to what was technologically achievable. As a result, the acoustic torpedo, MAD, which in October demonstrated a range of 300 feet, the echoscope (a short-range sonar using frequency modulation, FM), radio sonobuoys, and other promising equipment received attention with or without the blessing of the Bureaus of the Navy.[39]

In November, the leaders of Tate's Section C-4 had their first joint meeting with representatives of all agencies in the Navy with an interest in antisubmarine warfare. These agencies included the Office of the Coordinator of Research and the Bureau of Ships, Bureau of Ordnance (BUORD), and Bureau of Aeronautics (BUAER). As in April 1941, each Bureau wanted NDRC to work on narrow applications relevant to its particular functional responsibility. BUORD, for instance, asked for research on "weapons of attack, detection of ground mines, and acoustic radiation of ships." Because of the independence of the Bureaus, a long-standing source of controversy between naval officers, who wanted unified control over operations and research and development, and civilians, determined to avoid the consolidation of too much power under the Chief of Naval Operations (CNO), the Navy had no one person who could say "stop!" and "go!"

The Bureaus wanted work that satisfied their parochial requirements. A staff officer with no executive authority, the Coordinator of Research, lacked the clout to force consensus between them. Nor could the CNO do so, until after Pearl Harbor and King's elevation to both positions of CNO and Commander of the US Fleet. A reluctance to have civilian scientists interfere in navy matters also acted to keep requests to NDRC along narrow lines. But Tate and his colleagues were not about to limit the scope of their work to narrow categories defined by the institutional interests of the Bureaus.

After the initial meeting adjourned and the uniformed representatives departed, Tate reconvened the meeting. As they had in April, in their first meeting with BUSHIPS, the scientists again resisted restriction to work on specific applications:

> It was apparent to all of us that the vital need was for overall intelligent planning to ensure that our resources were directed into well-conceived programs of development and research and not into a welter of gadgetry.[40]

Accordingly, they agreed to continue their broad inquiry into the whole field of subsurface warfare with a view to matching technology to operational possibilities suggested by their scientific analysis of the U-boat system and the oceanic and atmospheric environment in which it operated. For another 18 months, until May 1943 and the formation of Tenth Fleet, the US Navy had no senior official charged with effective day-to-day authority over technological developments for antisubmarine warfare. Authority over research and development fell by default into the hands of three men: John T. Tate; his deputy, Dr. William Shockley of Bell Labs; and Dr. Philip M. Morse of MIT, whose interest in operational research eventually led to a position on King's staff.

By December 1941, Section C-4 was pushing hard on a variety of projects suggested by the theoretical work of the scientists, their analysis and measurement of the process of search and attack on a submarine, and their understanding of what current technology of low risk might be put to use. These technologies included faster-sinking conventional depth charges armed with magnetic proximity fuses; *Mousetrap*, a forward-firing launcher that fired a number of new, smaller, fast-sinking depth charges filled with a better explosive; acoustic torpedos; MAD; and attack aids (information displays) for skippers and their sonar operators. They also added to

National Archives

US sailors work on *Mousetrap* bomb projectors. This forward-firing launcher, one of the projects suggested early in the war by the theoretical work of scientists, fired several fast-sinking depth charges filled with a better explosive.

Section C-4 a branch devoted to development of training for sound operators and for conning teams of ships.[41]

In spite of initial resistance to their ideas, the scientists already had begun to affect the thinking of the Navy's operational staff. Admiral Richmond K. Turner, then in charge of planning, felt that the breadth of the program was formidable.[42] However, the Navy's planning staff felt comfortable, in the sense that its members believed everything was being done that needed to be done without extraneous organizational additions. Operational data collected by scientists and their work on a variety of antisubmarine weapons, in the words of one of Turner's subordinates, only "showed what things had the most effect on the probability of hitting."[43] The encouraging thing was that planners began to accept the scientists' assessments of the antisubmarine problem and their conclusions on how to improve chances of success. This change took place in spite of a general resistance to outsiders and an effort by the Navy Bureaus to restrict the latitude of civilian scientists.

The year 1941 had seen extended preparation by NDRC scientists for an effort to defeat the U-boat. They had opened channels to England to allow them access to operational experience from the Royal Navy. They organized a complete review of the field of antisubmarine warfare and because of NDRC's contracting authority could conduct work they believed essential, in spite of apathy or opposition by bureaucratic agencies of the US Navy. They reoriented the perspective of antisubmarine strategy from one based on geographical position of fleet units to one that focused on the U-boat's environment and functional requirements of finding, tracking, and killing it. This reorientation proved an excellent base for the work done in the crisis-ridden year that followed, as well as the foundation for the work done by the scientists in 1943 and 1944 to assist American submarines.

2
Lack of Preparation is Costly

BY THE END OF 1941, THE PATTERN OF FIGHTING IN THE Atlantic centered on convoys. The number of U-boats on patrol tripled to 30. On the other hand, as the Royal Navy improved its capabilities for antisubmarine warfare and gradually instituted end-to-end coverage of shipping lanes from Halifax to England, convoys with weak though aggressive complements of escorts proved much harder to crack open. From April to December 1941, U-boats sank 34 merchant vessels monthly, at a cost of between 2 and 3 of their own. In December 1941, in heavy weather, escorts of convoy HG 76 soundly defeated the attacking submarines.

As the year closed, U-boat commanders in general became less aggressive. In late 1941, each U-boat on patrol sank an average of four merchant ships monthly. As the Japanese attacked Pearl Harbor and opened the door to attacks on American shipping, the success rate for U-boats in the North Atlantic dropped to one merchant ship per month per submarine on patrol in that area. Independent, unescorted shipping then presented U-boats with their most lucrative opportunity. Centralized control continued. German Admiral Karl Doenitz's strategic objective remained constant: Sink as many merchant ships as possible at the smallest cost in U-boats.[1]

Lookout scans sky and sea from US submarine conning tower. Enemy attacks came from above and below as World War II progressed.

As 1942 began, Doenitz consolidated his own operations and shifted the focus of attack to the unprotected American East Coast, with terrible effect. The Americans stumbled badly. A defensive campaign strategy against the U-boat surrendered the initiative to the German submariners.

American scientists were already working inside and outside the Navy to improve equipment and tactical doctrine, pushing for the offensive campaign designed to seize the initiative from the U-boat. Their efforts began to lay the foundations of a change of momentum.[2] Countermeasures still unknown to *Befehlshaber der Unterseebooten* (BdU) (Commander in Chief, submarines) were under development but had not asserted themselves. Doenitz believed he held the stronger hand, based on advantages of the U-boat's tactical invisibility and its resulting capacity for surprise attack, and BdU's ability to move the wolfpacks to the most weakly defended parts of the sealanes.

I

German Advantage

Early in the war, aircraft posed more of a nuisance than a threat. Escort ships did not yet carry the 10-centimeter wave radar (*ra*dio *de*tection *a*nd *r*anging) and high-frequency direction-finding gear that in late 1942 began to make nighttime attacks on the surface increasingly hazardous for the U-boats. In Doenitz's words,

> The U-boat attack in 1942 was superior to the defense. The finding of convoys was facilitated by the large number of boats. The U-boat's greatest possession, the element of surprise, was still effective. The U-boats, when on the surface, were not spotted soon enough for the enemy to be able to avoid them; and, when attacking, they could not be detected early enough by surface or underwater means of detection.[3]

In addition, Doenitz had new cards he would soon play: New 1,600-ton supply submarines approached commissioning. These supply submarines, combined with the increasing monthly production of Mark VII and Mark IX U-boats, promised to give BdU greater numbers of submarines in the patrolling areas. In early 1942, the Germans added another weapon to their inventory: They broke British Naval Cipher Number 3, the code used by Allied convoys. By July 1942, the Germans read 80 percent of all messages sent in this cipher.[4] In fact, the Japanese attache in Berlin was so impressed with German successes with British naval codes that he recommended to Tokyo cooperation in attacking American ciphers.[5]

Overshadowed by successes of Allied codebreakers, the German *Beobachtungsdienst,* or *B-dienst* (cryptological unit), had some notable successes in the war, not the least of which gave Admiral Doenitz a cloudy picture of convoy sailings and locations from early 1942 until the Allies recognized the problem and changed their codes in June 1943.

German cryptologists, however, lived in a far different environment than those in Britain and the United States.

National Archives

Sinking merchantman in Convoy PQ-17, seen from gun tub of escort ship in 1942. The German cryptological unit, *B-dienst,* **helped orient U-boats on convoy locations, until the Allies changed their codes in June 1943.**

For example, in the fall of 1941, as Soviet reinforcements gathered to counterattack to save Moscow, the head of the Intercept Control Station of *B-dienst,* a Colonel Kettler, forwarded to General Alfred Jodl, Chief of the *Wehrmacht* (German armed forces) Operations Staff, a complete order of battle of the building Soviet threat. Jodl noted to Hitler that the good colonel was "soiling his britches" and should be relieved. In his marginal note, Hitler concurred. Word of Kettler's demise more than likely made a long-lasting impression on his colleagues. Doenitz seems to have used communications intelligence effectively, though Colonel Kettler's experience may explain why the German High Command failed to sponsor a more comprehensive cryptological effort and why analysts might have been reluctant to forward controversial findings up the chain of command.[6]

In general, proven tactics, extensive and realistic training, good equipment, and highly centralized command and control contributed to the early successes of the U-boats. After the Japanese attack on Pearl Harbor and Hitler's long-awaited authorization to sink American ships, Doenitz anticipated even greater successes. He suspected that the Americans, like the British in 1940, would take some time to consolidate the defense of coastal waters. Giving his operation the Wagnerian title of *Paukenschlag* (roll of the kettle drums), he ordered six Type-IX U-boats into American waters. On 12 January 1942 they attacked with a vengeance and began what the U-boat crews called their second "happy time." (The first was during the free-for-all on the undefended convoy routes in 1941.)[7]

The U-boats looped down the great circle route "with the regularity of commuter trains" into the coastal shipping lanes of New York, Hatteras, and Florida. U-boats also individually ambushed convoys encountered en route. Once in American waters, they slaughtered Allied shipping. In February, the Allies lost 85 ships totalling more than 570,000 gross tons; more than 90 percent of them went down off North America.

Doenitz had much to be pleased with. His new form of naval warfare promised a decisive victory. He believed that by inflicting 700,000 tons of losses on the Allies monthly, his

An officer of USS *ROPER* (APD 20) directs unloading of dead German U-boat crew members at Naval Operating Base, Norfolk, Va., on 12 April 1942. They were buried at the National Cemetery, Hampton, Va., on 14 April 1942. The submarine was sunk off the North Carolina coast.

U-boats would impose a naval victory in short order. However, though his submariners seemed well on their way to achieving the necessary sinking rates, problems did exist. At this point in the war, Doenitz could not obtain priority for the U-boat construction program that came after his elevation to command of the German Navy in 1943 and the opportunity to work directly with Minister of Armaments Albert Speer. Nor could Doenitz get the *Luftwaffe* (German air force) to give him the aircraft to contest the airspace over the Bay of Biscay.[8] The German High Command required BdU to keep patrols of submarines off Gibraltar and Norway, effectively halving the number of U-boats available for the attacks on Allied shipping on the American East Coast. Nonetheless, despite the minuses, the U-boats were succeeding and promised potentially decisive results. Perhaps Doenitz felt too comfortable in the successes of his U-boats to dig deeply into the application of technological innovation to subsurface warfare. For a year later, as the U-boats approached the critical point in the Atlantic campaign, it would be too late to start the process of fielding the weapons and tactics needed to counter the work done by American scientists in 1942.

II

Confusion in Washington and Slow Progress at Sea

After 7 December 1941, President Roosevelt and his immediate advisers could not believe that the Japanese had attacked the fleet at Pearl Harbor instead of the Philippines. An ugly shock for the US Navy, the surprise attack on the fleet at Pearl Harbor caught American leaders completely off balance.[9] As a result, confusion and uncertainty reigned in Washington in the first months of 1942. As the Japanese overran the Philippines and other American outposts and scored victory after victory over British forces in Southeast Asia, US leadership struggled with mobilization and reorganization, and the tightening of ties with Britain.

Shortly after Pearl Harbor, President Roosevelt recreated the position of Commander in Chief, US Fleet (COMINCH) and selected Admiral Ernest J. King for the job. By signing an Executive order with last-minute changes, in part conceived by King, placing the Bureaus of the Navy under the chain of command, Roosevelt gave COMINCH command of the entire US Navy, an unprecedented amount of power. The order placed operational command of all fleet units, control of the Chief of Naval Operations (CNO) and his staff, and the Bureaus, as well as a degree of freedom from the Secretary of the Navy, in the hands of Admiral King. Shortly afterward, Roosevelt relieved the CNO, Admiral Harold R. Stark, sending him to command US Naval Forces in Europe, and added to King's responsibilities the actual position of CNO. This move meant that King, as a service chief and commander of all naval forces, could successfully resist pressure from all but the President himself. And Roosevelt was not a leader who readily stepped between powerful subordinates to settle a dispute.

To his position of institutional power, King brought great operational experience, a powerful mind, and an eccentric and unbending personality. Throughout his career, King was most sensitive to correction. He tended to argue with or request a transfer away from a senior officer who had counseled him.[10] He believed strongly that he alone knew what was best. To the extent that hard work and a brilliant mind allow, he often did, but when wrong or confronted with a challenging view, King proved totally unreceptive to the ideas of others. He argued with colleagues and senior officers; he dismissed subordinates coldly. In addition, he distrusted the people around him. King called Admiral Chester Nimitz, Commander in Chief of the US Pacific Fleet (CINCPAC) and a former Chief of the Bureau of Navigation and the Navy's personnel office, a "fixer." He distrusted the Army Chief of Staff, General George C. Marshall, and felt Marshall had shucked the onus of Pearl Harbor onto Admiral Stark. King admitted to "never liking" the officer who served as his Deputy Chief of Naval Operations for most of the war, Vice Admiral Frederick J. Horne. King thought President Roosevelt was "slippery," a man who always had "two strings in his bow." Not that Roosevelt was an easy man to work for, but King seems not to have respected or had full confidence in any senior figures he worked with during the war, save a small coterie of subordinates in his own headquarters.[11]

Without question, King was a brilliant naval officer and an exceptionally capable seaman. But he had a willful, mean, and brittle side to his nature that limited his effectiveness as a leader charged with bringing new people and new ideas to bear on problems of developing untraditional and unantici-

Lack of Preparation is Costly 45

Atlantic convoy at dusk. Scientific advice and naval operational experience combined to win the Battle of the Atlantic.

pated ways of waging warfare. King could innovate when he understood how new concepts fit into the traditional naval view, as his work on fast carrier groups showed. But he was not a leader who encouraged subordinates who had new ideas. In his new position as COMINCH, his institutional power buttressed the instinct of a brilliant though eccentrically stubborn mind. This flaw had an unfortunate effect on the campaign against the U-boat.

In the first months of 1942, King struggled to get the Navy out of the confusion of the aftermath of Pearl Harbor and into the fight. He had to invent and build from scratch a headquarters to run the operational aspects of the war, allowing the office of Chief of Naval Operations to continue to take care of administrative and logistics matters. In short order, he put together a staff consisting of divisions for War Plans, Operations, and Readiness and chose subordinates to fill important positions.[12]

While the bad news poured in and the work load exploded, King and his staff struggled to jump start the engines of war while simultaneously building their own organization. In football terms, they faced the equivalent of making up plays and passing out assignments after the kickoff of the big bowl game. Because of King's exclusive reservation of all executive authority, and the confusion in his overtaxed headquarters, no coherent and clearly stated American naval strategy for winning the Battle of the Atlantic would be developed until 1943.

Initially, Admiral King's staff had no organic section charged with analysis of operational results of antisubmarine warfare. In November 1941, the CNO, Admiral Stark, had created the Convoy and Routing Section that in May 1942 became part of the Operations Division of COMINCH. However, this Section was responsible for the organization, tracking, and routing of convoys, not the supervision of antisubmarine warfare.

Until the fall of 1942, a handful of officers on Admiral King's staff handled antisubmarine matters. These officers included King, his Chief of Staff, Admiral R. S. Edwards (formerly commander of submarines for King, when King

National Archives

Tanker SS *DIXIE ARROW* burns off Cape Hatteras 26 March 1942, victim of German U-boat menace. After Pearl Harbor, Admiral King and his staff struggled to jump start the engines of war and build an organization to meet this menace.

had been Commander in Chief of the US Atlantic Fleet (CINCLANT)), Captain George C. Dyer, and the officers in the Antisubmarine Section in the Plans Division. King gave Edwards responsibility for antisubmarine warfare, and Dyer played a central role. As Fleet Intelligence Officer, Dyer handled all special intelligence and ran Admiral King's compartmented situation room.

At the start of each day, for example, Dyer briefed Edwards on the antisubmarine situation. Dyer and Edwards had both grown up in submarines and had as good an appreciation for submarine tactics as anyone in the Navy. But none of the papers produced by these men in early 1942 seems to articulate a set of strategic objectives for the campaign against the U-boat.[13]

In informal meetings, two men, King and Admiral Royal E. Ingersoll, his successor as CINCLANT, improvised the strategy for the campaign against U-boats. King's desire to play a role of operational commander limited the authority of Admiral Ingersoll. Unlike the Army Chief of Staff, General Marshall, King commanded his Service. He was familiar with the antisubmarine problem in the Atlantic, because he had helped establish the convoy system in 1941. This system included execution of the President's policy of defending Allied shipping before war was officially declared, and ordering American submarines on combat patrol in the Atlantic a month before Pearl Harbor.[14]

Not only did Ingersoll have King looking over his shoulder, he had little control over task forces that fought the Battle of the Atlantic. Ingersoll was a coordinator who trained units, organized escorts for convoys and task forces, and monitored battles between escort groups and U-boats. Once they left port, however, task force commanders fought in accordance with rules and procedures for handling ships and naval units. They had great independence, but they followed very strict rules on how they must operate in given situations. While they had great freedom at sea, their reports went under the microscope back at CINCLANT and COMINCH.

This scrutiny caused the great irony of involving COM-INCH directly in operations. Given the communications of the day, COMINCH had an instant view of results. In relation to antisubmarine warfare, COMINCH took on the role of an operational headquarters as well as the headquarters involved with development of strategy. Pressures of time and pace competed with operational demands and the requirements of strategic planning. In 1942, King had a relatively small staff. Officers charged with antisubmarine warfare had other duties. Accelerating momentum of mobilization during day-to-day crises of running a war swamped them. Small wonder they had no time for the remedial work of developing a strategy while they found themselves at a dead run. They responded to the problem by pushing programs to build new ships and get them to sea with trained crews. Strategy went awry.

King and his staff believed that when available in the right numbers, traditionally trained and equipped surface escorts would defeat the U-boats. Somewhat like his counterpart, German Admiral Karl Doenitz, King saw his objective in terms of better tactics and more equipment, and not in the exploitation of technology to open new areas of military capability.[15] Ingersoll determined to sweat out the period of ascendancy of U-boats until the forces were ready to support convoying for all shipping. The US Navy continued to execute a strategy of "hold and build."[16]

King and, initially, Ingersoll believed that convoying in the Atlantic represented the best way of defeating the U-boat. King espoused a concept called "convoy vicinity." Surface craft and aircraft, either land-based or flying from escort carriers when they became available, would pick off U-boats as they were drawn to the merchant vessels, the bait. By enlarging the defensive area around convoys and providing more escorts, naval forces would inflict more and more casualties on the U-boats as they pressed their attacks.

King did not state an operational objective other than defeating the U-boat by defending convoys. No thought was given to seizing the initiative from the German submarines. King did not accept the value of the Royal Air Force's Coastal Command's campaign against the U-boat in the Bay of Biscay. In his unbending way, he opposed diversion of ships and aircraft from convoy defense as a waste of time and effort. He held tenaciously to this position until after the U-boat had been driven from the Atlantic, though they were driven largely by means other than "convoy vicinity."[17]

King never grew past his prewar experience discussed earlier and his belief in the primary role of the battle line in naval operations and the ancillary role of the submarine. His ideas had even more impact because of the Navy's peculiar command structure. In addition, the Eastern and Caribbean Sea Frontiers — basically administrative agencies with control over portions of the Atlantic off the US coast — reported directly to King, making their commanders both equals to Ingersoll. To get ships back under operational control of CINCLANT,

National Archives

USCGC *JOHN G. SPENCER* (WPG-36) in convoy in June 1943. The 327-by-41-foot, steam-powered *HAMILTON* Class Coast Guard Cutter displaced 2,750 tons and made 20 knots. Laid down 11 September 1935 at the New York Navy Yard, she was launched 6 January 1937 and commissioned 1 March 1937. After extensive antisubmarine operations in the Atlantic, Caribbean, and Mediterranean, the legendary cutter was converted to an Amphibious Force Flagship (AGC) and served in the Pacific from late 1944 through 1945. *SPENCER* was decommissioned to special status as an engineering training school on 23 January 1974; she was decommissioned 15 December 1980 and sold 8 October 1981.

once they chopped to the Eastern Sea Frontier, Ingersoll had to get COMINCH to give the order. Though CINCLANT had responsibility for training all antisubmarine units, COMINCH retained responsibility for antisubmarine warfare doctrine. Because CINCLANT had no official authority for antisubmarine doctrine, Ingersoll had to send his proposals to COMINCH for approval and then dissemination by COMINCH to his own task forces.

When CINCLANT staff officers wanted to create a manual for antisubmarine warfare for dissemination to the fleet, they not only had to write the book, they had to sell COMINCH on the idea and get COMINCH to publish it. When COMINCH published only enough copies of the manual for task group commanders, instead of one for each ship as recommended by CINCLANT, Ingersoll's men had to bootleg copies to individual ships. By requiring that COMINCH function as an operational headquarters in addition to its charge with strategic direction of the war, King ensured that confusion reigned in the name of centralization and uniformity. Not until May 1943 did King merge under one agent the responsibility for ASW doctrine, technological development, and training. As Ingersoll put it, "tactics and usages varied from place to place."[18]

In spite of convoluted command arrangements, Ingersoll's flexibility, skill, and informal brokering brought some continuity to American efforts in the Atlantic. While he constantly labored under an inefficient command arrangement, Ingersoll took the initiative to improve techniques for antisubmarine warfare without running afoul of his boss. Ingersoll had a passion for anonymity and avoided any public role as an operational commander. He travelled frequently to Washington to confer with Admiral King, most likely to keep himself abreast of what went on in the COMINCH staff as well as to push gently and tactfully for implementation of his own ideas. All the while, Ingersoll and his staff went about quietly doing whatever they thought needed to be done to defeat the U-boats, and in the process moved out on their own in several areas. To study antisubmarine warfare, coordinate and supervise training, develop materiel, and disseminate information, CINCLANT formed the Antisubmarine Warfare Unit in Boston on 7 February 1942.[19]

About a month later, the unit's new chief, Captain Wilder D. Baker, returned from a trip to England during which he gathered information from the Royal Navy. Impressed with the contribution being made to the British war effort by P.M.S. Blackett and his operational analysts, Baker went to John T.

Tate for help in recruiting a similar team of American academics. Tate recommended that Baker contact Massachusetts Institute of Technology (MIT) physicist Philip M. Morse, who had voiced his frustration on several occasions over the failure of the military to apply relevant scientific tools to development of the operational art.

From this small beginning grew an effort that gave the American Navy a tremendous advantage in its campaign against the U-boat and later against Japanese antisubmarine warfare units. Ingersoll and Baker understood that defeating the submarine menace meant developing the right tactics and weapons and rigorous training to make sure crews could use them. Ingersoll also formed an escort training school akin to HMS *WESTERN ISLES,* the Royal Navy's school for escorts. He saw his role as ensuring that functional commanders properly trained their crews, that the right ships were built and allocated to task groups at the proper time, and that the right tactics were developed and used.[20]

Despite the best efforts of Ingersoll, the scientists, King, and all of the US Fleet, the U-boats wreaked havoc throughout the first six months of 1942. The Americans used anything at hand to patrol the East Coast: yachts, private aircraft, even coast watchers from the Civil Air Patrol. Small patrol craft proved unsuited for extended antisubmarine operations. And like the British aircraft of 1939 and early 1940, American planes usually annoyed but seldom sank a U-boat. In a reverse Lend Lease, the British released to American control 10 corvettes and 24 coal-burning trawlers fitted out for antisubmarine work. But the Americans refused to institute convoying procedures. King argued that "inadequately escorted convoys were worse than none," a position long before proved incorrect by operational analysts in Britain. Finally, on 14 April 1942, the US destroyer *ROPER* sank U-85, the first kill of the war by an American fighting ship.[21] A number of factors began to weigh in favor of the American effort to defend its coastal waters. In April, King brought CINCLANT's Antisubmarine Warfare Unit into COMINCH, agreeing reluctantly to bring along Morse's scientists only after Vannevar Bush assured him that

COMINCH would have complete control over dissemination of the results of their work.[22] Slowly, American antisubmarine efforts began to jell. By June, the Navy had enough ships to put all shipping along the East Coast into convoys, though not before the US Merchant Marine sustained heavy losses; 20 percent of all independent shipping went to the bottom, as opposed to only 4 percent casualties among ships in convoy.[23] During this terrible period, the United States lost 5 percent of its total available shipping.[24] Losses peaked in June, when 140 ships went down. U-boats deployed in ever greater numbers; an average of 57 maintained station in the Atlantic up to September 1942. Monthly, they averaged 87 kills, losing only 5 U-boats, an exchange rate of 18 merchant ships for every German casualty. During this phase of the Battle of the Atlantic, U-boats survived an average of a year in combat, the longest life expectancy they enjoyed throughout the war. But as the waters along the East Coast of the United States became increasingly dangerous, Doenitz began to shift the efforts of the U-boats to the Caribbean.

The US Navy learned slowly. At this point in the war, the Royal Navy had an edge in experience that showed in results gained at sea. British ships damaged 25 percent and sank 10 percent of the U-boats they attacked; US Naval vessels damaged 12 percent and killed only 4 percent. American aircraft performed slightly better: Averaging 45 attacks a month, they damaged their quarry 20 percent of the time and obtained a kill in 2 percent of their attacks.[25] In July, Vice Admiral Edwards, King's Chief of Staff, felt that "prospects are far from bright." He predicted that without more escorts and more aircraft dedicated to coastal patrol, "we will in the not distant future be faced with a breakdown in essential sea traffic."[26] Recommending to King solutions to this problem, Edwards considered only production of armed escort ships, routing of convoy traffic, and building up "our own coastal air, as fast as possible."[27] He considered only increasing the Navy's ability to protect convoys. He did not consider the potential inherent in technological innovation.

III
R&D and Operational Analysis

While Admiral King and his staff struggled with problems of mobilizing the Navy and dealing with combat operations in the Pacific and the antisubmarine campaign in the Atlantic, John T. Tate's scientists in Section C-4 of the National Defense Research Committee (NDRC) of the Office of Scientific Research and Development accelerated their work to develop new weapons and equipment. Tate, who feared the Navy would not allow his scientists a major role in ASW, was relieved in March to receive an invitation from the Navy to expand his work in the antisubmarine arena. In early 1942, competition for scientific talent began to create friction between NDRC and the Naval Research Lab. This friction did not augur well for the future.

In addition, when scientists reported that in an attack with depth charges a ship had a 5 percent chance of killing a submerged U-boat, naval officers had hooted, maintaining that the chances of success were more like 70 percent. Now the Navy wanted the help of this section in training sonar (*so*und *n*avigation *a*nd *r*anging) operators. By conducting training at Woods Hole, Mass., and San Diego, the scientists could justify facilities and personnel to develop operational data they knew were necessary to derive tactics with a high probability of success in combat.[28]

The laboratories in New London, Conn., and San Diego expanded environmental studies intended to broaden understanding of the underwater habitat of the U-boat. Work on equipment fell into three general categories: location, tracking, and attack. Three items—10-centimeter radar, improved sonar, and magnetic anomaly detection (MAD) devices—promised better capabilities for locating German submarines. By March 1942, scientists installed the Mark IV MAD device in a Navy patrol bomber and demonstrated an effective range of 500 feet against a submarine. By May, the services ordered

240 MAD devices and the design phase of the Mark V gyro-stabilized* model was complete.

Scientists worked on a variety of improvements to sonar. These improvements included a more directional projector that also gave the depth of the target, better hydrophones (underwater microphones), and a way of putting a gate on the return signal to listen to reflections from targets at selected ranges from the escort. In addition, a gyro-stabilized projector awaited sea trials. In general, the devices met early skepticism from naval officers, who usually experienced a conversion phenomenon at successful field trials.[29]

To help solve the problem of tracking a submarine that had been forced to submerge, scientists developed an attack predictor that indicated to the conning officer** of a ship the best moment to fire his depth charges, given position and relative movement of his ship and its target. Trials finished in February 1942. Scientists had picked up a British suggestion about a sonobuoy*** containing a hydrophone and a radio transmitter that aircraft could drop around the suspected location of a submerged submarine. They produced a working model that by March demonstrated an effective range of three miles.

Given a reliable sonobuoy, aircraft could locate a U-boat, attack it, and, when it submerged, call for a destroyer and surround the area with buoys that transmitted the sound signature of the ocean around the submarine's last known location. Given a tight ring of sonobuoys, a U-boat could not penetrate the circuit without revealing its position and bearing to the aircraft. In this way, antisubmarine aircraft could track a submerged submarine while they waited for a surface escort. At the end of March 1942, having demonstrated the feasibility of the concept, scientists began working on shockproofing a prototype for further testing.[30]

---

* Maintained on a horizontal plane by means of a gyro mechanism.

** The officer in control of a ship's movements; to guide or pilot a ship is spoken of as conning.

*** A small receiver-transmitter normally dropped from aircraft to detect submarine noises and transmit them to the plane.

National Archives

Radio sonobuoys. A British suggestion, the sonobuoy contained a hydrophone and a radio transmitter that could be dropped from an aircraft near the suspected location of a submerged U-boat.

To improve the quality of attacks on U-boats, work progressed on a variety of antisubmarine weapons. By July, workers at the California Institute of Technology tested *Mousetrap,* a rocket-propelled, 40-pound depth charge with a streamlined case and a contact fuse.* Streamlining allowed a predictable underwater trajectory. Given a smaller weapon launched by a rocket, the weapons were light enough to be grouped on the foredeck of escort ships and launched in patterns. Using their trial data, scientists calculated for reluctant officials of the US Navy's Bureau of Ordnance that *Mousetrap,* firing a pattern of eight weapons, had a significantly better chance of hitting a U-boat maneuvering underwater than a pattern of conventional depth charges. It could be fired ahead before the

---

* With a contact fuse, the weapon exploded only when the charge actually hit the hull of the target.

cone of the ship's sonar passed over the U-boat and contact was lost, contrary to depth charges fired to the side of the ship or dropped off the stern. Also, *Mousetrap* projectiles posed no danger to the ship from shallow, premature detonation. Contact fusing had an additional advantage. Depth charges fused hydrostatically* exploded at a given depth, whether or not they fell close enough to a submarine to do damage. These underwater explosions roiled the water, causing a tremendous increase in ambient (surrounding) noise, making it harder for sound operators to regain contact with the submarine. With *Mousetrap,* an explosion meant a crippled U-boat. By May, the National Defense Research Committee began manufacturing the first 1,000 charges.

Scientists in California also redesigned conventional depth charges to make them sink faster with a more predictable trajectory under the water. Work also continued apace on acoustic mines or topedoes, now called *Fido*. Settling on the overall design, scientists at Harvard, working with engineers from Western Electric and General Electric, traded off improvements in acoustic steering with ways of making the device smaller, faster, and more lethal.[31] Pressed to get results, Tate and his colleagues estimated in June 1942 that their work in fiscal year 1942-43 would require more than $8 million. As it later turned out, the bill ran well over $13 million.[32]

Scientists in section C-4 also began to assist the Navy in training. Realizing that the sound operator—the sailor who manned the sonar—was the most important link in the chain of factors that allowed a successful attack by an escort on a submerged U-boat, a Selection and Training Committee began work on selection criteria for prospective sonar operators. Drawing on their research, they developed training programs that emphasized the physics of transmission of sound underwater, procedures for search and attack, and maintenance of equipment. They found their task complicated by the lack of valid and reliable techniques for search and attack and a tendency for the various commands involved in antisubmarine warfare to invent their own tactics. Scientists developing

---

* Set to detonate by water pressure.

training procedures discovered they had to adapt their curriculum, because tactics often changed before their eyes.[33]

After Captain Wilder D. Baker's invitation to organize a group of operational analysts for CINCLANT, Philip Morse set about recruiting his team and digging into problems of search and attack. In April, Morse began establishing files of data based on automated Hollerith codes developed by International Business Machine Company.* He found that the Navy had no body of data on antisubmarine attacks, and arranged for a colleague to go to England to gather information from P.M.S. Blackett's group.

In their early work, scientists of Group M found that in 40 percent of aircraft attacks on U-boats, the target remained on the surface. Some checking revealed that like the Royal Air Force in 1940, American aviators followed rules of engagement requiring fuse-settings on aircraft depth charges of 50 feet. To allow a better chance of a kill on a U-boat either on the surface or just under the surface, Group M recommended that fuse settings be changed to the minimum possible setting of 30 feet. This new setting resulted in an immediate rise in the percentage of successful attacks. When King brought Baker's new Antisubmarine Unit from CINCLANT to Washington in June, Baker used this new success as an argument to justify his claim that the antisubmarine campaign required nontraditional solutions that could best come from Morse and his small team of analysts.

Morse sensed that Baker had to put his career on the line to get his way. Actually, Baker had told King bluntly that the Battle of the Atlantic was being lost and had given his superior a number of recommendations to try to fix the problem.[34] Once in COMINCH, collectively titled the Antisubmarine Warfare Operational Research Group (ASWORG), scientists of Group M, known affectionately as "ASWORGs," provided recom-

---

* In computer technology, a code based on the punching of holes in cards at specified locations; from one to three punches may be made in each column of the card, and up to 80 column characters. The specific character is determined by the number and location of punches in that column. Named for Herman Hollerith (1860-1929), inventor of punched-card data processing and a founder of a firm that evolved to become part of IBM.

Torpedo comes aboard US submarine on loading skid.

mendations directly to the naval officers on the staff charged with antisubmarine warfare. Good ideas became the property of men in uniform and gained acceptability.

As Group M began to dig into operational issues, Morse saw a need for two categories of work. His analysts began to look at the problem of attack of a U-boat by an escort in terms of spherical geometry and probability. They also wanted tests on bombing errors and an opportunity to derive functions that described the relationship between the relative speed and depth of the U-boat and speed, altitude, and angle of approach of an attacking aircraft. This information could lead to an idea of optimum altitude of attack, lead, number, and spacing of bombs. As in their approach to other operational problems, the scientists started by attempting to analyze the process of attack, and then to derive a theory that allowed prediction of results.

They also began to look at associated problems of aerial search, to develop probability curves based on questions like:

- What was the probability of acquisition of a submarine on the surface at a given range, with an aircraft flying at a given height using visual observation?

- And subsequently of more importance, given a certain weather condition and range of visibility, at what altitude should an aircraft fly to yield the best chance of sighting a U-boat?

Once they developed a theoretical model, they turned to statistical summaries of actual operational reports to validate and improve their theory. In July, Verne O. Knudsen returned from his liaison visit with the latest insights from the operational analysis being done in England, as well as a data base of 529 recorded attacks.

Morse also moved to get a better grip on results of American experience in antisubmarine warfare. After a survey of available reports, and a determination that the US data were unreliable, he convinced a reluctant Captain Baker to push his superiors to allow his scientists to supervise the collection of data in the field. To make sure they had personalities that would fit into a military environment, he handpicked the first scientists, and made sure they understood that their reports would go first to commanders in the field. Morse wanted to avoid the impression that the ASWORGs really were keeping an eye on things for Admiral King.

At first, relations between the ASWORGs and their military counterparts were awkward. However, when airmen and escort crews saw that their operational reports really did matter at headquarters, they took a greater interest. The scientists also became engineering troubleshooters who assisted crews in understanding and getting the most out of their new equipment.

So his Group would stay aware of the realities of combat, Morse specified that his analysts return to duty in Washington after six months. He often found the operational headquarters reluctant to let their ASWORGs go; he constantly had to assure commanders that replacements would be as good as the men they were giving up. Group M provided an extremely important function in the Navy's simultaneous effort to develop doctrine and weapons while solving operational and tactical problems. Morse understood that

> the value of new equipment in warfare can only be judged in relation to the tactics and strategy for which it is to be used. . . . New tools and new tactics are inescapably bound together.[35]

By placing its men in the field, Group M not only ensured feedback of accurate and reliable operational data that enhanced the validity of their findings, the field work made possible the interaction in combat between trained scientists and sailors and airmen that suggested new tactics and specific requirements for new weapons. Scientists in the field became a "technical intelligence link between operations and development laboratories."[36]

Group M had published a *Preliminary Report of the Submarine Search Problem* in May 1942, before the move to COMINCH. The report hinted at the results that followed. The authors suggested gambit tactics for aircraft in which, after forcing the U-boat to submerge, airplanes circled just over the horizon observing the U-boat's suspected area with radar. When the unwary submarine surfaced, the circling aircraft would attack again, forcing resubmergence with depleted air banks and storage batteries. The aircraft then repeated the gambit, using the U-boat's new point of submergence as its new datum. Group M recommended combined attacks between air and surface units, suggested tactics to allow destroyers to regain sonar contact after attacks with depth charges, and indicated how to deploy successful barrier patrols. By July, ASWORG published detailed tactical instructions with diagrams of search patterns and search rates for ships. The scientists went further to suggest new operational procedures. While acknowledging the effectiveness of convoying, they stressed possibilities of combining capabilities to allow offensive operations:

> Recent operational experience indicates that closely coordinated groups of planes and ships are the most effective for offensive antisubmarine warfare. Quicker intercommunication arrangements, together with improvements in echo-ranging gear and depth-charge ordnance should make these combined groups deadly.[37]

By August 1942, ASWORG issued reports on doctrine and tactics that stressed consistency in a wide variety of tactical procedures, and began to lay the base for a coherent doctrine for antisubmarine warfare.[38]

Other scientists supporting the Navy's antisubmarine efforts came to similar conclusions around the same time about what needed to be done to defeat the U-boat. After his six-week visit to England to obtain reliable data for Morse, Knudsen reported to Tate his recommended priorities for effort. Knudsen argued that the "most effective use" of antisubmarine aircraft could save a million tons of shipping and should receive first call on resources. British naval officers felt the absence of "standard operating procedures for search and attack by escorts" constituted the greatest weakness in the American effort. Knudsen also emphasized changes in the training program for sonar operators to treat detection and attack as one function. He also stressed that everything possible should be done to expand the work on operational research.[39]

Still other scientists also had shared their concerns and insights with Tate, who in turn reported to Vannevar Bush. On his own initiative, Tate could marshal resources with Section C-4 to ensure coordination between work on the physics of the underwater environment and various programs to develop equipment and weapons. He also could help Morse obtain personnel and some of the equipment he needed to make ASWORG an effective contributor to the work of COMINCH staff.

However, Tate felt strongly the need for changes in management of the antisubmarine effort of the Navy. For any chance of bringing these changes about, he needed Bush's help. Tate reflected the general consensus among his colleagues when he argued for unity of command in antisubmarine warfare:

> There is no question that if planning and improving the conduct of antisubmarine warfare is to be kept abreast of the times, it is absolutely essential that the entire job be placed under unified, authoritative, and inspired leadership under the Commander in Chief of the U.S. Navy.[40]

The scientists wanted a close relationship between the derivation of operational doctrine and the development of equipment, and they pushed for an offensive aspect of antisubmarine warfare that exploited capabilities of aircraft. In addition, they began lobbying the Navy to get its house in order and to put someone in charge of the antisubmarine campaign.

IV
War Department Role

Another powerful individual shared the concern of the scientists about the Atlantic campaign. Early in 1942, Secretary of War Henry L. Stimson had worried about a "lack of aggressiveness" in the Navy's leadership.[41]

As Doenitz's U-boats continued their successes off the US East Coast, Stimson became more and more concerned with what he and some of his advisers found to be an absence of organization and continuity in King's headquarters. King's fetish for centralized control and his refusal to delegate any executive authority over operational matters prevented the efficient execution of programs like antisubmarine warfare.

- Only King could move forces between sea frontiers and CINCLANT's operational area.

- Only King had the authority to promulgate fighting doctrine and make changes in force structure in response to technological innovations.

In response to the uncertainty and organizational confusion that followed Pearl Harbor, King gripped ever more tightly the reins of command, not realizing that his policies and the force of his personality were choking the lines of communication. In Stimson's opinion, the situation did not improve over time. In April 1942, as he reflected on the news of the fall of Singapore and the threat of Japanese control of the Indian Ocean, Stimson's opinion of the Navy hit a new low:

> I have been more discouraged today over the situation with the Navy than I think I have ever been before. Here it is nearly two years since we came in here and the Navy is still badly organized and I do not feel any confidence in the men at the head of it.[42]

Stimson continued to worry about the Navy's inability to come to grips with the U-boat. He took his concerns to the President and found that Roosevelt shared them. However, when he recommended that the Commander in Chief take actions, such as relieving Vice Admiral Adolphus Andrews, commander of the Eastern Sea Frontier, "a terrible old fusspocket of a society man,"[43] Stimson found FDR reluctant to go over the heads of King and Knox. Stimson worked well with Navy Secretary Frank Knox, but believed strongly that his fellow Secretary did not have control of his department. Stimson grew to marvel at "how little he knows about the plans of his own people."[44]

Convinced of the central role of technological innovation in modern warfare, and concerned about the Navy's indecisiveness and insistence on a defensive operational strategy against the U-boats, Stimson resolved to alter the course of the antisubmarine campaign. A service secretary who interested himself in new weapons, Stimson observed, toyed with, and supported development of a wide variety of technological innovations. The DUKW (an amphibious two-and-a-half-ton cargo-carrying truck), radar, the proximity fuse, and the atomic bomb, to name a few, received Stimson's personal interest during the war.

Since late 1941, Vannevar Bush had periodically briefed Stimson on the mobilization of scientists to support the war effort, and on developments in weaponry. Bush argued that the airplane and radar presented the best potential for defeating the U-boat. He reported that the Navy had ignored the British antisubmarine experience and the successes of the Coastal Command in attacking submarines crossing the Bay of Biscay. These successes appealed to a strategist like Stimson, who believed strongly in the offensive.

After a tour of Panama Canal defenses in March 1942, and firsthand observation of radar, Stimson made scientist Edward Bowles his special consultant for radar. Bowles, a former student of Bush's and subsequently a colleague at MIT, brought to his new job an open mind, initiative, a scientist's understanding of electronics, and, most important, an engaging personality that won the confidence of Stimson, the Army Chief of Staff, General Marshall, and the Chief of the Army Air Forces, General Henry H. Arnold.

With Bowles on board, Stimson brought the Army Air Forces into the business of hunting and killing submarines.[45] Stimson personally ordered the Army Air Forces to organize a command to wage offensive operations against the U-boats. He wanted to strike them before they reached the convoys. On 30 May 1942, under a plan developed by Bowles, General Arnold formed the Sea-Search Attack Development Unit at Langley Field. SADU, as the new unit became known, had as its mission the development of tactics and doctrine for Army aviation units involved in antisubmarine warfare.

Bowles' concept involved analysis of results of actual patrols to derive a doctrine for a force consisting of long-range bombers equipped with second-generation ASV-10s (Airborne Surface Vessel Detection), the new 10-centimeter-wave radar. On 8 June 1942, Arnold formed the First Bomber Command, the striking arm of the Army Air Forces' new component. By the end of the month, Marshall's Deputy, Lieutenant General Joseph T. McNarney, rounded up 90 obsolescent B-18 bombers and had them fitted with the new ASV-10 radar.[46]

National Archives

General Henry H. "Hap" Arnold, right, Chief of the Army Air Forces, confers with Major General Louis E. Woods, commanding general, Second Marine Aircraft Wing, at Yontan Airfield, Okinawa, on 25 June 1945. An air strategist, General Arnold (1886-1950) advocated a separate Air Force to rank with the Army and Navy.

In July, as aircraft began acquiring and attacking U-boats, Stimson attempted to get the Navy to use First Bomber Command in a strategic role. King's staff had assigned various bomber squadrons to the Sea Frontiers. His concept of inviolate boundaries between Sea Frontiers and CINCLANT's area of responsibility prevented the flow of information and forces to meet a changing threat. For instance, aircraft flying for a Sea Frontier could not cross the Sea Frontier's boundary and patrol more than 300 miles into the Atlantic. King believed strongly that to order forces in and out of the operational areas of subordinates constituted a violation of the chain of command.

Stimson wanted an air arm able to strike U-boats wherever they concentrated, regardless of who owned the playing field. He wanted a functional capability not tied to geographical limits. He suggested to Secretary of the Navy Knox that all Army antisubmarine units work under a commanding general who reported directly to an admiral in COMINCH who had overall responsibility for antisubmarine warfare. Knox felt that "someone had been misrepresenting the situation" to Stimson.[47]

King resisted suggestions from outside the Navy. King replied that since the threat now lay in the Caribbean, why change command arrangements that had already chased the U-boats away from the Eastern Seaboard?[48] When King's Chief of Staff, Rear Admiral Edwards, suggested that a meeting between King and Marshall might prove useful, King made "quiet" inquiries and then quashed the idea, noting, "I don't think it necessary *or* advisable."[49] Not about to have anyone tell him how to run the Navy, Admiral King simply had dismissed Stimson's suggestion as unnecessary—the antisubmarine campaign was on track. King took this position in spite of his deputy's admission a few days later that "prospects are far from bright."[50]

King reported correctly that U-boats had begun to flow away from the East Coast and into the Caribbean. However, in addition to the implementation of convoying, aviation had played a major role in forcing Admiral Doenitz to make this decision. In July, August, and September, successful attacks by aircraft increased significantly.[51]

Stimson continued to push for a more offensive operational strategy for the campaign against the U-boat. He arranged to have 10-centimeter radar put into B-24 *Liberator* aircraft to create a longer-range capability for search and attack. He worked with Vannevar Bush on the formation of a Joint Committee on New Weapons and Equipment. Bush used the new committee to report to the Joint Chiefs of Staff the ideas of his scientists. The committee's report combined ideas that Morse and Tate had been developing throughout the spring and early summer of 1942.

National Archives

PB4Y (B-24 *Liberator*) on antisubmarine patrol over Bay of Biscay in December 1943. The 10-centimeter radar put into the *Liberator*s gave them a longer-range and more precise capability for search and attack.

The report laid down several principles that continued as mainstays of efforts of scientists to support the antisubmarine campaign. Large increases in capability depended on combining and synchronizing incremental improvements in equipment. Developments such as better sonar, attack predictors, more consistent depth charge patterns, and depth charges that sank more quickly on predictable trajectories when used together could triple or quadruple the probability of successful attacks by escorts. Likewise, second-generation microwave radar,*

---

* Most radars operate in the microwave region of the electromagnetic spectrum, between 1,000 and 35,000 megahertz (1 billion to 35 billion cycles per second). Microwaves thus are very short radio waves, from a fraction of an inch to a few feet in wave length.

along with better weapons for use by aircraft to attack U-boats, promised a completely new dimension of capability.

In addition, combining search capabilities of aircraft and the ability of escorts to hunt U-boats to exhaustion promised unprecedented results. To achieve these results, one central authority had to control seeding of prototypes in the combat environment, coordinate the simultaneous availability of airframes, radar and installation kits, and escorts, and manage the training of crews in tactics statistically derived from operational experience. The Joint Committee also recommended a more offensive operational strategy for antisubmarine warfare:

> Convoying remains the primary method of protecting merchant shipping. With the rapid introduction of new devices now available, there is every indication that the essentially defensive methods of the convoy can, however, be effectively supplemented by the offensive method of seeking out the submarine and destroying it, particularly within the range of land based aircraft.[52]

Bush brought the concerns of the scientists into the arena of policymaking. While Morse's ideas began to make an impact on COMINCH staff officers, Bush and Stimson used feedback from Tate and his colleagues to pressure the Navy at the strategic level of command. This debate provided both a stimulus and source of ideas for Secretary Stimson. More conferences with Bush convinced him that

> the Navy's resistance to the role of aircraft in antisubmarine warfare, its emphasis on a defensive strategy, and the lack of unity of command over the antisubmarine campaign leave me with a rather stiff problem of how to get another Department pushed along into the right channels on what is probably the most critical problem that now threatens the war effort.[53]

Stimson and the scientists took nine more months to force King's hand.

As summer waned in 1942, things looked difficult for the convoys. Doenitz now kept more than 100 U-boats at sea.

His submarines sank an average of 87 ships a month between January and September. By almost doubling his force, Doenitz made prospects for the Allies dismal indeed. Discounting the slow improvement in Allied air attacks against submarines, surface escorts demonstrated an effectiveness not much better than that of 1918. Barely enough ships were available to defend the sea-lanes that supplied the landings in North Africa and the buildup of forces in England. Crews of new ships had no time to train before CINCLANT had to throw them into the breach. New gear came on line slowly. The sinkings continued.

But because life for U-boats had become tougher in the western Atlantic, the crucial phase of the Battle of the Atlantic began in September 1942, as Doenitz shifted the focus of his operations back to the northern convoy lanes in mid-ocean. Convoying in the Caribbean and along the East Coast took away the easy targets that had compensated for difficulties of maintaining the long lines of deployment and communication from France to North America. Now the mid-Atlantic gap through which convoys had no air cover promised the most efficient hunting.

At this point in the war, the American antisubmarine campaign labored in heavy going and suffered from parochialism and King's heavy hand at COMINCH. "Hold and build" and "convoy vicinity" remained the bedrock of operational strategy. Scientists worked inside the Navy to press for improvements in training, equipment, and tactics. They worked outside it through the offices of Vannevar Bush and in concert with Secretary Stimson to push for unity of command and a more offensive campaign strategy.

However, in September 1942, as the focus of German efforts returned to the North Atlantic sea-lanes, American efforts lacked coherence. The enemy still held the initiative.

3
Convincing Admiral King

From September 1942 to the end of March 1943, U-boats steadily increased their tactical ascendancy in the Atlantic. Allied losses rose to unprecedented levels in March 1943, precipitating heated debate among Allied leaders. Secretary of War Henry L. Stimson and the Army Chief of Staff, General George C. Marshall, and senior British officials became convinced the US Navy was losing the antisubmarine campaign. They pushed very hard for a complete reorganization of the Navy's efforts. While resisting this outside interference, Admiral Ernest J. King, Commander in Chief, US Fleet (COMINCH), made belated changes to the command structure and allocation of forces.

The changes preempted King's critics and suggested a turn in the fortunes of the campaign. The scientists contributed in two ways. They provided strategic alternatives for debates at the highest level. And they derived for both the COMINCH staff and the War Department elements of an offensive operational strategy directed at seizing the initiative from the U-boats, while laboratories and contractors continued to develop new equipment and doctrine for use in combat. In March 1943, the momentum of the Battle of the Atlantic seemed to tip precipitously in favor of the Germans. But efforts of American scientists that began in 1940 had already led to the imminent deployment of weapons and tactics that

Henry L. Stimson, Secretary of War during the Roosevelt administration (1940-45). Stimson (1867-1950) supported aid to Great Britain and compulsory military training. He also served as Secretary of State under President Hoover (1929-33) and Secretary of War under President William Howard Taft (1911-13). As chief presidential adviser on atomic policy, Stimson made the critical recommendation to President Truman in 1945 to drop atomic bombs on Japanese cities of military importance.

proved decisive in the next round of the campaign. In the winter and spring of 1942-43, the US Navy consolidated its antisubmarine effort and prepared for a counterattack, a transition temporarily overshadowed by tactical successes of the Germans.

I
German Success and Innovation

As convoying spread along the East Coast and into the Caribbean, and the increasingly effective efforts of air patrols made hunting in American waters more dangerous, Admiral Karl Doenitz changed his concept of operations. The U-boats redeployed from their American hunting grounds to the convoy lanes to and from England that lay closer to German submarine bases in France. In the summer of 1942, convoys crossed the mid-Atlantic without the protection of air cover. The Germans marshaled their forces for the decisive attack on Allied shipping that they believed would begin in mid-1944, when they planned for production of U-boats to reach its peak. BdU had not changed its overall strategic objective; the entries in the BdU War Logs confirm this persistence:

> BdU is clearly convinced that the weight of the U-boat war must be carried out in the Atlantic, that only war against tonnage will be effective in the overall war and that any deviation from these fundamental concepts will only lead to damage of the total war effort.[1]

Through 1941 and 1942, the Germans continued to build the force to achieve this objective. Production of submarines created a fleet that kept more than 100 boats at sea, with 70 to 80 deployed to the Atlantic. Of the boats deployed to the Atlantic, approximately one-third actually were on patrol stations at any given time, with the rest in transit or in port. By

74   Slides Rules and Submarines/Meigs

National Archives

Atlantic convoy, seen from stern of escort vessel. Early in the war, convoys crossed the Atlantic without the protection of air cover.

December 1942, BdU had seven 1,600-ton submarines configured for refueling and resupply operations.

In March 1942, to extend patrols of U-boats operating off the Cape, South America, and in the Atlantic, BdU began using the new 1,600-tonners to man refuelling points at several locations. Reprovisioning at sea in effect doubled the length of a patrol of a Mark VII or Mark IX boat. Because of demands of other sectors, operations in support of the North Atlantic proved only marginally successful until the U-boats once again focused their main efforts on convoys moving to and from England. From September 1942 through June of the following year, BdU always had available between seven and nine of the 1,600-ton refuellers.[2]

From the hard training of 1938 and 1939 and the convoy battles of 1941, the U-boats had developed *Rudeltaktik* (wolfpack tactics) to a fine art. Doenitz now positioned his raiders in two groups, one at either end of the gap in Atlantic air coverage crossed by the convoys. He tried at all times to keep patrol areas of his submarines out of the range of land-based aircraft. Experience demonstrated the futility of attempting to shadow and attack convoys protected by air patrols.[3]

The western group of U-boats lay in wait for eastbound convoys laden with war materiel. Ships returning to North America made up the eastern group's objective. The submarines initially deployed in a patrol line across the suspected axis of the approach of a convoy. Doenitz repositioned the lines or ordered reconnaissance sweeps based on intelligence. Once a U-boat made contact, he ordered its mates to close for the kill. In spite of his emphasis on the tonnage war, Doenitz eventually concentrated more and more submarines to intercept convoys loaded with war supplies heading east. The operation resembled the gathering and casting of a fisherman's net. American intelligence analysts put it this way:

> The major convoy offensive might be described as a pulsation or rhythm: first, the convergence of U/B's from port (both Biscay and the Baltic or Norway) as they made for their waiting areas, then the formation of the patrol line followed by the reconnaissance sweep, and lastly contact and the vortex of operation. . . . After the operation came disentanglement and division. . . . Forming and reforming, they traced individual patterns and group patterns in a whole whose periodicity was determined by the convoy cycle.[4]

The term "wolfpack" misrepresents the way the U-boats actually worked their prey. Believing that "years of war experience" had demonstrated the futility of placing operational control in a task force commander at sea, Doenitz maneuvered his raiders from his headquarters in a most rigid, centralized way. He positioned U-boats on the patrol lines, directed them throughout their sweeps, and coordinated their attacks on individual convoys. Once ordered into the attack, German commanders were to continue to press home until the Admiral

National Archives

Navy Patrol Bomber (PB4Y) (Consolidated B-24 *Liberator*) on antisubmarine flight over North Atlantic. Admiral Doenitz changed his U-boat operations as convoying spread along the East Coast and air patrols became more effective.

called them off. They attacked individually. BdU allowed little or no local coordination of the battle, other than for actions taken by individual U-boat commanders reacting on their own initiative to cryptic reports sent by other boats involved in the fray. The wolves patrolled and attacked alone, each connected to BdU headquarters by the daily chain of Doenitz's admonition messages to the submarines and the frequent situation reports they had to send back. BdU badgered the submariners for results of combat operations and for frequent reports on locations and the tactical situation and on the status of fuel and torpedoes. This attempt to maintain centralized control later became a significant liability, when Allied cryptologists broke *Triton*, the German code used by BdU, in December 1942.[5]

At this point in the war, Doenitz enjoyed some significant advantages. In February 1942, BdU had added a fourth rotor to the *Enigma* machine used for North Atlantic communications. The new code proved impervious to the best efforts of Allied codebreakers for 10 months. In addition, penetration of British Naval Code Number 3 by German cryptologists tore the veil of secrecy from communications of American and British convoys. From July 1942, when the German cryptological unit *Beobachtungsdienst* (*B-dienst*) increased to 80 percent its ability to read messages in Code Number 3, until cryptologists at Bletchley Park[6] finally broke into *Triton*, BdU possessed the upper hand.[7]

Signals intelligence often allowed the planned encirclement and devastation of a convoy. In late December 1942, BdU coordinated the encirclement of southwest-bound convoy ON-154. Twenty-two U-boats of Group *Ungesturm* attacked the convoy for 3 days, sinking 14 of its 45 ships and damaging another. Occasionally, a chance sighting and timely intelligence combined to give the U-boats a success. In early 1943, Wolfpack *Delphin* caught convoy TM-1 in waters beyond the support of aircraft. Of nine tankers and four escorts in the convoy, the U-boats sank seven tankers. In sum, however, despite the ability of *B-dienst* to read most of the messages sent to and from Allied convoys, weather, chance, and Allied rerouting continued to make locating convoys a difficult task. Given BdU's best efforts, wolfpacks garnered only minimal results against the three convoys that had preceded ON-154.[8]

Successful attacks by the wolfpacks depended on good guesswork about placing a reconnaissance screen of U-boats in the path of the convoy. Timely intelligence made possible an accurate plot of the convoy route soon enough for them to concentrate for the attack. Once the pack closed in, success depended on weather and visibility, tactical surprise, and the presence of several especially daring submariners who accepted the risk of penetrating the escort screen to get among the merchant ships to take successive kills.

In spite of their successes, the Germans found adapting to the ability of the Allies to develop new antisubmarine capabilities increasingly difficult. This weakness indicated the trend of future events. Frequently, Doenitz wrote of his frustration over the effect of aircraft on the operations of his submarines. Activities of the Coastal Command of the Royal Air Force (RAF) over the Bay of Biscay caused increasing worry. RAF planes sighted almost every second U-boat and damaged a constant proportion of submarines crossing the Bay. Between July and September 1942, they sank five.

In the summer of 1942, the aircraft began attacking at night. Using radar, they located a U-boat, revealing their attack only at the last minute, when they turned on powerful searchlights for positive identification and accurate placement of bombs. Doenitz could not get the *Luftwaffe* to provide forces needed to contest the sky over the Bay effectively. He understood that improved tactics of convoy defense and closure of the mid-Atlantic gap in aircover by Allied "Very Long Range" (VLR) aircraft promised to make hunting convoys a more dangerous proposition.[9]

Accordingly, Doenitz began searching for technological innovations to counter the "ever increasing difficulties which confront us."[10] In the spring of 1942, the Germans captured an ASV (Airborne Surface Vessel Detection) Mark II meterwave radar. By summer, they had the new *Metox* R-600 radar receiver ready for the U-boats. Even though these devices were unreliable and fragile, the entire fleet had them by November. In June, Doenitz pushed the High Command to accelerate acquisition of a new type of U-boat, one with a streamlined hull and a radically different propulsion system that used hydrogen peroxide. Based on prewar work of engineer Helmuth Walther, the new submarine promised underwater speeds of up to 20 knots and an ability to operate submerged almost continually. At 18 knots submerged, a U-boat could outrun a destroyer escort. Increasing to 10 knots the sustainable underwater speed of a U-boat made placing a depth charge within the 18-foot radius required to rupture the hull much harder. In addition, the streamlined hull of the Walther design and the greatly improved capacity of its storage batteries promised to give it a 60-hour cruising life at six knots. This new design would make hunts-to-exhaustion far more difficult for escorts.

Atlantic convoy in the rough seas of the mid-Atlantic, where the gap in Allied air cover was closed by the development of very-long-range aircraft, making the hunting of convoys by U-boats more dangerous.

Doenitz wanted greater underwater speed and endurance for operational as well as tactical reasons. From the operational perspective, speed allowed an ability to concentrate U-boats from greater distances, and thus to offset the ability of faster convoys and merchant ships to outrun the wolfpacks. Given the Allies' extensive use of evasive routing, greater speed simplified the problems of controlling and coordinating attacks by shortening the lead time required to gather a wolfpack, once intelligence located a convoy.

In addition, it meant that for a given number of submarines in a patrol area, more U-boats could be massed in time at the critical point. The power of the new submarine and the efficiency of its streamlined hull had another beneficial effect. Increased power and greater ease of movement through the water yielded greater top-end speed. The charge of storage batteries decays exponentially with the rate of the load. Thus, for a given power rating, streamlining has a geometrical effect on extending the time a submarine can operate on batteries at low speeds. If a U-boat could maintain 10 knots submerged for long periods of time, it could shadow slower convoys regardless of air cover.[11]

In November, Doenitz convened a meeting of engineers to discuss production of the new submarine. Allied defenses further convinced him of the need for a boat that could operate underwater continuously. But in his discussions with the engineers, he discovered that the emphasis on production of conventional submarines had preempted work on a new powerplant based on hydrogen peroxide. As a compromise, the German Navy's engineering experts suggested putting twice the battery capacity of a conventional U-boat into the Walther's streamlined hull. But a final decision on production was delayed.

The Germans fielded other innovations. A cartridge that gave off a cloud of bubbles when released underwater, producing a false sonar target, *Pillenwerfer*, found its way onto the U-boats. BdU scientists continued to improve the killing power of the German submarines. They sorted out problems with magnetic pistols in their original torpedoes. They also developed a new torpedo, the *Federapparat* or FAT torpedo, that ran in circles, giving U-boats a standoff weapon that could be fired into a convoy from relatively long range and then looped through the formation for a higher probability of a hit than a torpedo with a straight trajectory. German engineers also began working on an acoustically guided torpedo, which gave excellent promise as a defense against escorts. A U-boat under attack would be able to take out its attacker and then exploit the hole in the escort screen.

Throughout the fall and winter of 1942, German engineers perfected these new weapons. But they had started late in the game. The German effort could in no way match the integrated research and development programs in England and the United States.[12] The German acoustic torpedo had greater speed and range than the original American model, but the Allies' communications intelligence made possible deployment of countermeasures that were ready for use when the Germans introduced their new weapon. The Germans often fielded weapons individually more advanced than those of the Allies. But while American scientists looked at ways of expanding the envelope of operational capabilities by exploiting the interaction of the submarine system and its environment, with the exception of the Walther submarine, the Germans usually worked only to improve known tactical capabilities. The modified Walther submarine, for example, proved superior to any Allied design, but a critical delay occurred between the events of 1942 and the initiation of its production.

In the fall of 1942, Doenitz could count on several advantages that supported a cautious view that the U-boat could win the Battle of the Atlantic. Production of U-boats increased steadily. And though three of every four U-boats that sailed during this period left port under command of officers on their first patrol, the second "happy time" off the East Coast of the United States had provided an experienced core of battle-hardened men. In addition, the *Rudeltaktik* proved itself in combat and had the confidence of crews. German research and development establishments were working on new weapons that seemed to promise not only to make U-boats more invisible and more deadly, but also to checkmate improving and bothersome capabilities of Allied escorts and VLR aircraft. Finally, *B-dienst* regularly provided in its reports on communications intelligence a cloudy, though operationally current and vital, picture of movements of Allied convoys. Through the winter of 1942 and into March 1943, the Allies watched the effectiveness of U-boats steadily increase.[13]

From September 1942 into March 1943, Allied convoys operated under several disadvantages. Shortages of fuel kept them relatively close to the shortest track to and from Great Britain. Though VLR B-24 *Liberators* had begun patrol, the one squadron available could not cover the gap in air cover between Newfoundland, Greenland, and Ireland. Weather that grew nastier with the onset of winter favored the U-boat and

This merchantman, torpedoed in the North Atlantic early in the war, demonstrated that Allied convoys operated under several disadvantages, including shortages of fuel and air cover and nasty winter weather.

cut down on flying hours logged by patrol aircraft. German submarines used moderately bad weather as cover for their attacks. More than one-third of their attacks came in sea state* 4 or higher. Escorts made only one-eighth of their attacks in these conditions.

The general shortage of destroyers and destroyer escorts also made life less dangerous for the wolfpacks. With only an average of six escorts per convoy in 1942, escort commanders could not afford to weaken their force by detaching units for coordinated hunts. Often, the escorts had to satisfy themselves with forcing the German submarine to break contact and submerge. Defenders could only jab; they could not linger for

---

* Numerical or written description of sea roughness; the higher the number the rougher the sea.

deadly combination punches. In addition, as a convoy came under attack and ships took torpedo hits, escorts frequently had to assist with rescuing survivors or to hunt down ships that ran off on their own in the confusion of the fighting. Surprisingly, however, many convoys crossed the Atlantic unscathed. In 1942, the Allies ran 246 convoys averaging 31 ships each. Only 127 ships were lost in more than 7,600 ship-sorties made in convoy.[14]

II

Small Losses . . . Big Impact

From the fighting of the fall of 1942, several lessons emerged. Success in antisubmarine operations depended on training and habitual association, and to get the most out of new equipment required the integration of new weapons into tactics based on the investment of hard work.[15] Scientists quickly found much of their time consumed as engineering troubleshooters and trainers who conducted remedial seminars in the field on basic functions and maintenance of equipment. Finally, the British continued to push steadily for unity of operational command over the Battle of the Atlantic, arguing that until it existed, lapses in coordination and inefficiencies of execution would continue to hamper combat effectiveness.[16]

Admiral Royal E. Ingersoll, Commander in Chief of the US Atlantic Fleet (CINCLANT) played a crucial role in the antisubmarine campaign. He helped to get the American part of the *Operation Torch*[17] invasion fleet across the Atlantic without alerting the Germans. In part because convoys used a less secure British code and US Navy combatant units used a more secure cipher machine than other Allied ships, the Germans missed the electronic signals that might have revealed this massive movement of ships. Ingersoll had the thankless task of pulling destroyers from the already weakened escort groups to provide protection for the invasion fleet.

Courtesy Mrs. Arthur C. Nagle

Admiral Royal E. Ingersoll, US Navy, Commander in Chief, US Atlantic Fleet, watches as *Operation Torch* **Task Force stands out from Hampton Roads, Va., enroute for North Africa on 24 October 1942. Note light cruiser in distance.**

Successes of wolfpacks with convoys like SC-107, in which the U-boats sank 15 of 42 ships, actually helped the Allies move the invasion fleet. Doenitz preferred to focus his U-boats on the crowded North Atlantic routes. He had better luck there intercepting convoys than in the less heavily travelled waters off Gibraltar. As the *Torch* fleet moved, a chance encounter between U-boats on patrol and a convoy bound for England distracted Doenitz and his raiders just as the invasion fleet slipped past. Blind luck made possible one of the great operational surprises of the war.[18]

But most of Ingersoll's effort involved the production of the Atlantic lines of communication. He and his staff worked long and hard to improve the operations of units hunting and killing German submarines. He knew that "few ships were thought to be dangerous to a submarine." The Antisubmarine Warfare Unit in Boston had produced, in June 1942, the first how-to-fight manual for escorts, and continued to put into the hands of ships' captains and division commanders doctrinal materials that emphasized drills and procedures. These publications drew their findings from operational experiences reported to CINCLANT, experiments with new equipment, and investigations of operational analysts. Ingersoll also continued to develop the school for training escort crews. Located in Bermuda, it finished the shakedown training of crews of newly comissioned ships and ran refresher training for escorts that had for a time been withdrawn from the rigors of the battles for the convoys.[19]

In spite of the best efforts of the navies of Britain, Canada, and the United States, the trend at year's end continued against the Allies. Production of U-boats allowed Doenitz to increase the size and number of his Atlantic wolfpacks and, in addition, to begin to place large patrols in distant waters off the Cape of Good Hope and into the Indian Ocean. BdU counterattacked the *Torch* landings only after the Allies had landed and the Royal and US navies consolidated their defenses. The Germans succeeded in sinking a handful of ships at a loss of 15 submarines. In spite of this Allied victory and American and British consolidation of control over the Eastern

Mediterranean and the Southern Atlantic, the decisive battle in the North Atlantic lay in doubt.[20]

III

Turning Point

Whatever the tactical and operational lessons of the antisubmarine campaign, in January 1943 the Allies agreed they were losing the war against the U-boat. At the Casablanca Conference,* senior leaders called for a number of changes.

- The Royal Navy and Royal Canadian Navy took responsibility for the northernmost convoy routes and set up new timetables for convoys.
- The number of specially equipped B-24s allocated to Newfoundland to cover the mid-Atlantic gap was increased to 140.
- The direction-finding and radio-interception net that played the vital role in locating U-boats and facilitating evasive routing was extended.
- The leaders called for use of the new escort carriers as soon as possible.

Admiral King came away from Casablanca with a new view of the importance of the Battle of the Atlantic. Until this meeting, his main priority had been to defend the Navy's campaign in the Pacific against the increasing demand for resources for the European theater. After Casablanca, he seemed convinced that defeat of the U-boat should take at least a temporary first priority.[21]

---

* Anglo-American summit meeting in Casablanca, Morocco, 14-23 January 1943; decision was made that Sicily, not Sardinia, would be the next step after the victory in North Africa. The conference gained political notoriety because of President Roosevelt's publicly announced demand for the "unconditional surrender" of Germany, Italy, and Japan. This policy may have prolonged the war, but it solidified cohesion among the allied nations.

Discussions at Casablanca brought to just beneath the surface several operational issues that caused controversy between American and British naval authorities.

As a means of killing U-boats, the British relied heavily on Coastal Command's attacks against their crossings of the Bay of Biscay. In the fall, the German use of the *Metox* radar signal receiver cut the number of successful attacks by British aircraft. However, the British worked hard to deploy aircraft with new radar operating on shorter wave lengths. This new radar promised a greater range, a better discrimination of targets, and a way around the Germans' warning receiver. P. M. S. Blackett's operations analysts reported that 40 of the Very-Long-Range (VLR) B-24 *Liberator*s operating against the Bay of Biscay could sink 1 of every 6 U-boats making the crossing. They argued that attacking U-boats in the Bay promised a great effect on the morale of German submariners, who had no choice but to run the gauntlet. Making BdU pay one submarine for every five on patrol stood a good chance of breaking the German will to fight. It certainly promised to make life marginally easier for the convoys.

King resisted pressure from the British to take part in air operations against U-boats, arguing that the RAF should concentrate on the submarine bases in France. He thought searching for submarines in the open sea was a waste of time. He allocated all his B-24s to the Pacific and looked askance at efforts of the Army Air Forces' 1st Bomber Command to develop a doctrine for long-range antisubmarine attack. However, British scientists passed their results to their colleagues in the National Defense Research Committee (NDRC), the War Department, and COMINCH. The American scientists were believers.[22]

Division of the Atlantic at Casablanca into northern and southern zones of responsibility put the Royal Navy in command of the vital lifeline to Britain and represented a half step toward unity of command.[23] Coincidentally, King received subtle pressure from yet another quarter. King's ideas about the organization for, and the way to execute, antisubmarine warfare did not have the support of the more junior officers on his staff. Many shared the belief that since antisubmarine warfare presented the major problem in the Atlantic, CINCLANT should be given command of the battle,

> CINCLANT does not have sufficient control over all of the available ships and aircraft to execute most effectively our antisubmarine effort.[24]

King's staff also took issue with his position on aircraft:

> All of the working hands concerned with antisubmarine warfare are in full agreement on this question, but the assignment and priorities of long-range aircraft originating on much higher levels, have so far prevented the availability of these planes in anything like adequate numbers.[25]

Officers with responsibility for day-to-day operational issues in the antisubmarine campaign appreciated the strategic significance of VLR B-24s configured as submarine killers. They advocated coordinated groups organized to operate against known concentrations of U-boats. They knew in 1943 that the major problem in the antisubmarine campaign concerned "effective use of current weapons rather than development of new ones."[26] The challenge lay in getting new weapons from test benches into the hands of sailors and skippers trained to get the most out of them.[27]

The VLR aircraft proved a difficult problem. With all its B-24s allocated to the Pacific Theater, the Navy relied on the old PBM-3c (Patrol Search Plane) for antisubmarine operations. This aircraft did not have the payload to carry radar and depth charges to make it an effective submarine killer. As for long-range antisubmarine patrol, the Army's 1st Bomber Command offered the only option and "dependence on the Army for such purely naval operations was embarrassingly imperative."[28]

No doubt much of the interest on the COMINCH staff in technological innovation and antisubmarine potential of the airplane came from the general knowledge and experience officers had developed on their own. However, scientists like John T. Tate and Philip Morse also played a role in building this consensus. In October 1942, COMINCH began bimonthly antisubmarine warfare conferences. Alternating their focus from consideration of air-related to surface-related issues from meeting to meeting, participants covered a broad range of topics at each session. Chaired by the senior representative from COMINCH, usually Captain J. M. Haines, the conferences served as clearing sessions for a wide variety of topics, from reports on the status of trials, to problems with training devices, to requirements for personnel in the training pipeline. The discussions fostered a convergence of ideas of working scientists and operational analysts and their counterparts in uniform. In these sessions, the scientists' ideas about training and doctrine began to have an impact.

As the new year began, a number of factors worked to the advantage of the American antisubmarine effort. American aircraft began to become a factor in the antisubmarine campaign. In the last six months, 5 percent of their attacks sank U-boats and 23 percent inflicted damage.[29] The chiefs of the Navy's shipbuilding program continued to promise new destroyer escorts and the arrival of the first escort carrier in April. In December 1942, cryptologists at Bletchley Park broke the four-wheel *Enigma* code, *Triton*. Bit by bit in the ensuing months, they increased their familiarity with the code and gave to a handful of decisionmakers at COMINCH and CINCLANT a clearer picture of the operations of U-boats:

> It was like trying to watch the U/B's through a condition of changing visibility. At intervals the clouds would open and one could see the present situation, but not completely, for much of the present . . . could be seen only in the immediate past.[30]

In spite of this view, in the new year the U-boats brought on the critical stage of the Battle of the Atlantic. After a slow start in January and February, sinkings began to increase. In March, Doenitz successfully guided his wolfpacks onto four convoys in a row. SC 121, HX 228 and 229, and SC 122 lost

National Archives

Escort carriers (CVEs), such as USS *BOGUE* (CVE-9) shown here, gave North Atlantic convoys protection from U-boats in mid-ocean beyond range of land-based planes. *BOGUE*, which displaced 9,800 tons, was completed in 1942. Her flight deck measured 492-by-112 feet; she could accommodate 30 planes and could make 18 knots.

a total of 38 merchant ships and an escort. Worldwide losses to all causes accelerated from two a day in January to five a day in March.[31]

The situation now became desperate and, as wolfpacks began their most successful attacks on North Atlantic convoys, the Allies convened the Atlantic Convoy Conference in Washington. As the conference conducted its deliberations, the U-boats ravaged merchant ships crossing the Atlantic in a manner not seen since World War I: 42 ships in convoy and 16 stragglers, more than a half-million tons of shipping, went down. These losses represented one-twentieth of the ships attempting the round-trip across the Atlantic. On the other side of the ledger, in the first 21 days of March, the Germans lost only 10 submarines.

The conference resulted from a British consensus that winning the Battle of the Atlantic required major changes in strategy and organization for combat.[32] Admiral King opened the meeting with a statement of his own, and thus the American naval position on antisubmarine strategy:

> I see no profit in searching the ocean, or even any but a limited area, such as a focal area. All else puts to shame the proverbial search for a needle in a haystack. . . . Let me say again, by way of emphasis, that antisubmarine warfare for the remainder of 1943, at least, must concern itself primarily with the escort of convoys.[33]

King held to the strategic concept he had originally begun to develop in his strategic thinking at the War College and later: Make convoy escorts strong; and extend "convoy vicinity" and bleed the wolves as they attacked the bait, the merchant vessels. He still believed in a defensive strategy based on attrition of the enemy's fighting force. He meant to break the U-boat arm by positioning superior power on sea-lanes.

The British strongly disagreed. Admiral Sir Percy Noble, chief of the British delegation, argued that "the submarine menace, to my mind, is becoming every day more and more of an air problem."[34] The British wanted to attack U-boats at every point. They wanted aircover for the entire convoy route from Newfoundland to England. They lobbied for more VLR B-24s for their campaign in the Bay of Biscay. They advocated groups specially organized to attack known concentrations of submarines before the U-boats could approach the convoys. The British came to the conference determined to achieve several changes in antisubmarine operations. Advocating unity of command under a single naval officer and a single communications system to tie together all command and control, they also pushed for a coordinated effort for research and development regarding antisubmarine technology and settled for a set of agreed-upon priorities for development.

At the conference, the British had the official support of the American scientific community, in the participation of Edward L. Bowles, scientific adviser to Secretary of War Stimson. Bowles provided arguments for an offensive strategy that maximized the potential of long-range bombers.[35] The British did not get everything they wanted. They made final arrangements for assumption of responsibility for northern convoy routes in April. King never relinquished personal command of all antisubmarine operations for the Navy; nor did he accept the idea of an offensive strategy, at least officially. Informal cooperation between American and British scientists already linked development of weaponry. For every priority expressed in the final report of the conference, the scientists had projects well under way. Inclusion of these priorities in the report meant that they were recognized as official policy.[36]

Most important, the conference put tremendous pressure on Admiral King. Now, with the most senior British naval authorities in open opposition, pressure from "Former Naval Person" Winston Churchill would follow soon. Since January, King's subordinates at COMINCH had been circulating ideas on how to reorganize command and control of the antisubmarine effort. Pressure from the British merely made getting the changes accepted easier for them.[37]

Admiral King received a not-too-gentle nudge from another quarter, the War Department. Increasingly concerned about the antisubmarine campaign, Secretary Stimson asked Bowles to study how to defeat the German submarines. Drawing on the work of P.M.S. Blackett's analysts, and with the cooperation of Philip Morse, head of operational analysis for COMINCH, Bowles put together a paper entitled, "The Acute Problem of Ocean-Borne Transport and Supply."

Arguing that the Army should be the proponent for protection of supplies headed for Europe, he advocated creation of a strategic Air Arm to conduct independent offensive operations against U-boats wherever they might concentrate. Operating under "operational control" of COMINCH, but under the command of an Army aviator, this organization would strike U-boats anywhere, without regard to boundaries between Sea Frontiers and various fleets. In short, by gaining responsibility for protecting war supplies, and vesting unity of command in an aviator who would have the most effective submarine killers at his control, Bowles attempted to circumvent the inefficiencies Admiral King's ideas forced on American operational strategy:

> The conclusion that an Army man should be entrusted with the primary responsibility for the safety of the supply of our overseas troops is inescapable. . . . Past difficulties have in no small measure stemmed from a failure to realize the effectiveness of air attack on the U-boat. We are entering an era in which the airplane and its complement of new weapons and navigational weapons will, if used intelligently, enable the destruction and demoralization of the submarine almost wherever he may be.[38]

Henry L. Stimson and Vannevar Bush, head of President Franklin D. Roosevelt's Office of Scientific Research and Development (OSRD), took the issue to the President. Most significantly, perhaps, Stimson received the support of Harry L. Hopkins, President Roosevelt's emissary and closest personal adviser during World War II. Stimson also wrote letters to Navy Secretary Frank Knox and his Under Secretary, James V. Forrestal. Intending either to take over the airborne campaign against U-boats or settle for forcing the Navy into recognizing and exploiting the new capabilities of VLR aircraft, Stimson mobilized his staff. Calling it the "outstanding issue of the war," Stimson instructed General Marshall to take the matter to the Combined and Joint Chiefs of Staff:

> Whereas the Navy has confined its efforts to attacking submarines only (1) when they attack a convoy, and (2) when they are discovered by haphazard patrolling, Bowles proposes a system which will attack them all over the ocean. . . . This whole matter is so important that I have been studying it carefully myself and am prepared to take

the thing up with the President if the Navy proves too obdurate in respect to cooperation.[39]

Marshall needed little prodding from his boss. He had become increasingly fed up with the Navy's antisubmarine campaign and believed that "the problem of combating the submarine menace has been insufficiently coordinated and has not been singled out for direction on the highest level." [40]

In February, the first two squadrons of VLR B-24s equipped with 10-centimeter radar had turned in excellent results over the Bay of Biscay. Recommending the new concept of a unified command to the Joint Chiefs of Staff, Marshall expressed his deep concern "with the matter of the present organization and technique for the employment of aircraft in the anti-submarine effort." Admitting to the difficulties of an antisubmarine "Air Arm" operating under unified command, Marshall stated that "unless we take drastic action in this matter we fail of our duty." [41] With the criticism implicit in this statement, the gauntlet landed at King's feet. This comment was highly unusual for the Army Chief of Staff, a soldier of great discretion and discipline, who eschewed public criticism of superiors and subordinates alike both during and after the war.[42]

King and his key subordinates saw the issue as a struggle for roles and missions. Determined that the Army not interfere in naval business, they based a delaying action on traditional philosophies of naval command and played on FDR's reluctance to intervene. In each fleet, the naval structure contains functional commanders responsible for readiness and training, but who have no control over the forces under a task force commander. The Commander of Cruisers and Destroyers Atlantic supervised materiel readiness and training of the Atlantic Fleet's cruisers and destroyers, but had no authority over ships subsequently allocated to a task force or those under temporary operational control of one of the Sea Frontiers.

The age-old distinction for the functional commander limited his authority when it met an operational boundary. King could rely on the acceptance of this tradition of command by the former Secretary of the Navy, President Franklin

D. Roosevelt. By ostensibly concurring in Marshall's suggestion, and agreeing that the new Air Arm was to be a functional command like any other in the Navy, Roosevelt placed Stimson and the Army Chief of Staff in the position that they must convince a President normally reluctant to go over King's head to approve an unprecedented form of command arrangement. By making the issue look like an argument over unity of command, King delayed and minimized the chance of presidential intervention, as much to protect the Navy's exclusive control of antisubmarine warfare as to protect the Navy's continuing strategic role as a "long-range striking force." For, in the words of one of his key subordinates, "We could very properly be told next that we could use our carriers only in defense of the fleet." [43] Winning the submarine campaign was not as important as preserving roles and missions.

Even under this pressure, King maintained a public stance of pained opposition. But the furor allowed a recasting of COMINCH's campaign strategy and a reorganization of its antisubmarine effort.[44] On 6 April, King appointed Rear Admiral F. S. Low as Assistant Chief of Staff, Antisubmarine. When Low left King's staff a year earlier for an operational command, he was convinced that the Navy's organization for antisubmarine warfare had fundamental flaws. On his return, he spent two weeks studying the whole problem and on 20 April submitted his "Appreciation" to King. He stressed training of the antisubmarine force, recommended that VLR aircraft and surface forces not required on convoys be deployed against "focal areas of concentrations," and recommended the "earliest possible installation" of new devices from MAD and retro-bombing (rocket-retarded bombs) to synthetic training devices. The ideas of Morse, Bowles, and Ingersoll appear in cryptic form in many of Low's recommendations. Low managed to include all the elements of offensive operations without using the language of an offensive strategy that was anathema to his superior. King approved the memorandum on 23 April and less than a month later signed a letter to the fleet entitled "Antisubmarine Measures," establishing training guidance for all antisubmarine units. On 20 May 1943, King established Tenth Fleet as the Navy's organization with responsibility for antisubmarine warfare. Later, he admitted privately to Bowles that the War Department's campaign had forced his hand.[45]

Admiral King still argued that defense of convoys promised the most effective means of defeating the U-boat menace, but a number of factors made it possible for his subordinates to push successfully for an offensive strategy. Naval cryptographers now had almost complete access to radio messages of the German Navy. And direction finding had expanded to units at sea. Finding concentrations of U-boats no longer involved searching vast stretches of ocean. Admiral R. S. Edwards, King's capable Chief of Staff, husbanded the consensus that had grown among members of the COMINCH Staff all through the first 14 months of the war. From Admiral Ingersoll to the chiefs of branches in King's own staff came a steady pressure for an offensive against the U-boat.

Recalled by King from a command in the Pacific, Rear Admiral Low had a charter to bring order to the contentious problem of defeating the U-boat. The British, Secretary Stimson, the President, Admiral William D. Leahy, the President's Chief of Staff, and Dr. Vannevar Bush, Director of the Office of Scientific Research and Development, had all pecked at King. In March and April, Leahy sent King a personal note, and, on receipt of King's reply, an identical second note indicating, in the oblique way so typical of FDR, the President's displeasure. King knew the signs. He wanted the helpers out of his kitchen.[46]

The pressure of events, confusion in the Navy's antisubmarine program, and a desire to preempt further intervention by senior political officials led Admiral King to accept an idea brought along by Edwards since January. King decided to create an operational headquarters for the campaign against the U-boat. Because of its wide-reaching mission and Admiral King's authority, Tenth Fleet now took the central position in the American antisubmarine effort.

IV

Role of Tenth Fleet

Admiral King kept Tenth Fleet in COMINCH because he wanted to be able to resist further outside interference in the antisubmarine war. The knowledge that the exploitation of communications intelligence would play a large role in subsequent operations also made a difference. Placing Tenth Fleet under Ingersoll meant either CINCLANT had to move to Washington, or accept an increased danger of compromise because of the extra layer of communication. Transmission to another location and processing by a second staff meant more links in the chain. Sending orders directly to fleet units from COMINCH promised greater efficiency and security. Nor could King settle on an officer to put in command of Tenth Fleet. Eliminating all other options, he decided to keep himself as commander, with Low as his chief of staff. This decision made Low the central figure in American antisubmarine efforts, with the authority to usurp CINCLANT when he felt necessary.

Tenth Fleet brought together all the disparate elements concerned with antisubmarine warfare. King commanded Tenth Fleet in theory, but in actuality Low ran it. Low formed the command around the Convoy and Routing Section of the Operations Division, which controlled all convoy traffic and evasive routing. The Antisubmarine Measures Section, proponent for developing doctrine and materiel, included Philip Morse's operations analysts. Low also took control of Admiral King's "Chartroom" and made himself the main customer of Op-20-G, the communications intelligence analysts, by removing the *Ultra Secret* intelligence summaries from circulation in the Operations Division and directing they come to him.

Low formed an operations section in Tenth Fleet, and took on a Scientific Council as a sop to Vannevar Bush, who wanted scientists involved in developing strategy. Low never planned to use the Council; he did not trust Bush. Low wanted to protect King from more of what he called flank attacks from Bowles and the politically dangerous OSRD Director, Bush. Planning to work through more cooperative scientists like Tate and Morse, when he needed scientific advice, he put Bush's name on the letterhead for ceremonial reasons only. In Morse and the operational analysts who had grown up in COMINCH and CINCLANT, Low had a source of scientific expertise on doctrine and technological innovation that was politically safe and, from an institutional perspective, relatively loyal. In Low and his new authority, Morse's analysts gained primacy over the Navy's antisubmarine doctrine and the strategy for developing new technology. Supported by Edwards and known by all to have King's blessing, Low performed organizational surgery unthinkable six months earlier.[47]

In establishing Tenth Fleet, King responded to pressures from Stimson and the British as well as concerns expressed in his staff during January, February, and March. He could argue that unity of command over antisubmarine operations now existed. Because he commanded Tenth Fleet, its authority over antisubmarine operations cut across the Navy's functional and geographic boundaries. Low originally wanted to place Tenth Fleet under CINCLANT, but this idea had a short life. King was too sensitive to the possibilities of pressure from the War Department and the President. Though he did not involve himself in day-to-day operations, he wanted Tenth Fleet in COMINCH for political reasons. In addition, King's new command preempted the many voices concerning antisubmarine warfare that were beginning to fill the air: There would be only one fighting doctrine.

Seventeen months after the onset of hostilities, more for political than operational reasons, the US Navy finally formed an organization with responsibility for formulation and execution of the operational strategy for the antisubmarine campaign. Admiral Low soon found that the weapons for a decisive counterattack lay at hand.

V
Payoff for Scientific Work

The final set of factors that allowed the defeat of the U-boat came from scientists in the scientific community, who by March 1943 had developed doctrine and weapons that proved decisive in the spring and summer of 1943. This offensive took place before the Navy's shipbuilding program delivered the large numbers of destroyer escorts and escort carriers that became a common sight later in the war. The attacks of May 1943 that drove U-boats from the convoy routes came from British-controlled forces that continued to defend the North Atlantic, aircraft that kept the pressure on in the Bay of Biscay, and a handful of escort carriers that went after Doenitz's refuelling operations. These forces used new weapons and procedures that had just emerged from the laboratories of the scientists and the workshops of the operational analysis groups and their counterparts in uniform.

Debates over campaign strategy and antisubmarine doctrine developed two groups of thinking, and scientists contributed to both. Many naval officers concentrated on defensive aspects of the campaign. This group included in particular officers involved with procurement of resources, the naval campaign in the Pacific, and strategic debates with the British. King and his Chief of Staff, Admiral Edwards, hung on tenaciously to their idea of convoy vicinity, minimizing convoy losses by providing the strongest possible air and surface escorts. This thinking led the Navy's major thrust to create forces to defend convoys. The scientific community supported but did not lead this effort. The scientists also helped develop the doctrine and weapons that made possible the offensive operations advocated by the second group of officers, who wanted to maximize the utility of the airplane.

In support of better defensive tactics, the scientific community helped map out defensive tactical doctrine and better weapons for search and attack. The first functional aspect, acquisition, had three phases. High-frequency direction-finding equipment on land and at sea warned of the presence of a wolfpack of German U-boats and gave approximate locations. Radar picked up the U-boats as they made their approach to set up their attacks. In early 1943, analysts watched the average acquisition range increase from the previous year's average of 2,700 meters (1.67 miles) to nearly 7,000 meters (4.3 miles). Sonar provided the close-in means of holding on to the enemy and guiding the final attack.

Ideally, a convoy received warning of the presence and general intent of a wolfpack and then used whatever aircover it could to pick up the U-boats as they trailed their prey in daytime. At night, as radar became more of a fixture on escorts, defending destroyers and Coast Guard cutters located the attacking U-boat and closed to lock on with sonar for a deliberate attack. This concept had some disadvantages, however. Aircraft could only fly in daylight and then only in good weather. Navigation proved difficult. Only 60 percent of the aircraft sent to provide air cover for convoys arrived on station before fuel or weather forced them to return to base. In spite of new radar and sonar coming into the fleet, one-third of attacks made by escorts on U-boats began with a visual sighting. Increasingly, naval officers became aware of the difficulties posed by the inability of crews to maintain and operate their new equipment properly.[48]

While operational personnel in the Navy played significant roles in sponsoring doctrine for defense, scientists played the central part in sponsoring and developing concepts for offensive action. Building on the experience of the British, they wanted to use aircraft, and, when enough ships became available, groups of ships and aircraft to take the strategic initiative from U-boats. Morse and his colleagues pointed out that in World War I, by sinking from one-eighth to one-fifth of U-boats on patrol, the Allies forced German submarines from the fight. They predicted that similar loss rates would have the same result in 1943. Accordingly, they pressed for offensive operations against critical nodes of the U-boat system. In short, they stressed, use aircraft to attack known concentrations of U-boats before they got to the convoys, and bleed the submariners as they crossed the Bay of Biscay. The deadlier gauntlet to the patrol areas undermined U-boat crew morale, making BdU more susceptible to a quick change of fortunes in the Atlantic hunting grounds.[49]

The shortage of destroyers, destroyer escorts, and escort carriers made these operations dependent on long-range bombers equipped to locate and attack submarines on the surface and then continue the attack after the U-boats had submerged. The National Defense Research Committee (NDRC) sought to improve on capabilities developed for the Biscay campaign. Even the latest VLR B-24s with 10-centimeter radar had no bombsights and demonstrated bombing errors along the line of attack of as much as 800 feet. Once the U-boat submerged, the bomber became ineffective. Now American scientists sought to use magnetic anomaly detection (MAD) devices and radio sonobuoys to make aircraft into platforms that could hunt and kill submerged submarines. By providing retro-bombs and acoustic torpedoes, they made the airplane a weapon that could strike into the deep. Study of the problem of aerial search and attack also led them to push for the immediate employment of navigational equipment like LORAN * to allow aircraft to mass at a given location at sea quickly and accurately.

In addition to pushing the limits of offensive and defensive capabilities forward, Philip Morse's scientists in the Navy's Operations Research Groups began to paint an accurate picture for the COMINCH staff of the dynamics of the battle with the U-boats. Morse controlled scientists who worked not only in COMINCH but in the Antisubmarine Warfare Unit in CINCLANT, its counterparts in the Sea Frontiers and Naval Operating Bases in Brazil and Trinidad, and in antisubmarine

---

* *LOng-RAnge* electronic *N*avigation. A system of electronic navigation, in which time difference in reception of pulse signals originated simultaneously at master and slave stations is used to locate the ship or aircraft as being on a charted hyperbolic curve that is the locus of all possible positions that would observe the identical time difference—the intersections of two such lines gives a fix.

US *BOGUE* (CVE-9) on 3 November 1942. *BOGUE* joined Atlantic Fleet in February 1942 as nucleus of pioneer US antisubmarine hunter-killed group; she got her first U-boat on 22 May 1943, when her aircraft sank U-569 on her fifth Atlantic crossing. Early versions of these so-called "jeep" carriers were converted from oiler and mercantile hulls. Her designation was changed to CVE (from ACV) on 15 July 1943; she was named for a sound in North Carolina. *BOGUE* was stricken in 1960.

agencies of the Army Air Force. The ASWORGs in COMINCH began to process their recorded data in December, with a newly acquired IBM machine that used Hollerith cards.

With this statistical tool, they drew important conclusions about what worked in combat. They found that the larger, more seaworthy, and faster escort ships had a better chance of catching U-boats by surprise on the surface. They proved that coordinated attacks by two or more surface vessels or by a ship working with aircraft had twice the likelihood of success as an attack by a single ship. Good quality attacks depended on several factors, such as the absence of diurnal gradients in the water,* initiation of attack from a radar sighting, and experience and quality of the sound operator. They published doctrinal studies on the best tactics for search and attack of submarines by ships or aircraft, and the most effective procedures for screening convoys.

They also worked on doctrine for the employment of new weapons, applying statistical inference to the questions of how best to employ MAD devices, retro-bombs, and other prototypes. Their reports also began to isolate reasons for failure in unsuccessful attacks and of equipment before and during attacks. They showed, with hard numbers, the importance of good maintenance and constant, realistic training of operators and conning teams.[50] For instance, they revealed that the battered convoy SC-121 had been defended by escorts with half their radar and HFDF (High-Frequency Direction Finding) gear out of order. Many of these conclusions may seem commonplace today. But in the confusion of what was in many quarters perceived as a possible defeat in the antisubmarine campaign, Morse and his analysts became one-eyed men in the valley of the blind.

While Tate, Bush, and Bowles pushed for improvements to doctrine and strategy, and Morse and his analysts helped the COMINCH staff to cut through opinion and emotion to see the causal factors at work in the antisubmarine campaign, the laboratories of the universities and industrial contractors began to turn out new weapons ready for use. In the area of acquisition, the Navy had 11 British HFDF ("huff duff") finders on hand by April 1943. American manufacturers geared up to produce 45 redesigned models a month by 30 September 1943. A number of American escort ships had 10-centimeter radar. The Navy now pushed to get them on all its escorts and continued to develop a version of the newest 3-centimeter radar for shipboard use. In February 1944, new shorter-wave radar began searching for U-boats over the Bay of Biscay and soon after along the convoy lanes.

---

* Also diurnal inequality: the difference in height or time of the two high or low waters each day; or the difference in velocity of either of the two flood, or ebb, currents each day.

National Archives

Radar equipment in USS *BOGUE* (CVE-9), 14 October 1943. While several US escort vessels had 10-centimeter radars by September 1943, the Navy pushed to get them on all escorts and to develop the new 3-centimeter radar for its ships. In February 1944, ships with the new shorter-wave radar began searching for U-boats in the Bay of Biscay and along the convoy lanes.

Radar for aircraft had developed somewhat more quickly than radar models for ships. The Army and Navy already had tested the latest sets in aircraft. From an aircraft flying at 200 feet, radar had demonstrated acquisition ranges of 3 to 5 miles against a submerged submarine with only 10 feet of periscope exposed. NDRC contracted with Sperry and Philco for more than 6,000 airborne radars of both 10- and 3-centimeter wave lengths. In addition, the ability of Division 14 to continue to produce new radars of increasingly higher frequency gave strong confidence of a constant ability to preempt German countermeasures. To help ships and aircraft navigate accurately to points of known concentrations of the enemy, LORAN stations began operation. Coverage extended to much of the North Atlantic and Caribbean, and 300 receivers for ships and 30 for aircraft reached the services. After several hours of training, crews had a capability to fix their positions with an error of 4 miles at a range of from 1,200 to 1,500 miles from transmitting stations.

A variety of new weapons moved beyond prototype status. Division 6 of NDRC developed a number of improvements for the Navy's echo-ranging and sound gear, including circuits for more accurate determination of range and azimuth,* noise reduction, and a filter that allowed the operator to focus on a particular range and on a discrete frequency band. Scientists at Harvard and New London perfected automatic echo-ranging gear.** This development involved work on a beam projector that remained trained on the target regardless of its movement relative to the ship. It included a new sonar that radiated energy in a 360-degree pulse and electronically isolated energy reflected from the submarine and displayed the information on a cathode ray tube. This latest development offered the potential of greater mechanical simplicity and ease of operation, as well as a possible first step toward a system that internally solved the attack problem and fired weapons at the submarine. New faster-sinking depth charges, the Mark 9 and

---

* The angle measured clockwise between the direction north and the other direction being described.
** Equipment that would track the target automatically without input from the operator.

Mark 11, and projectors to fire them began appearing on ships. *Hedgehog* and *Mousetrap*, projectors that fired clusters of small depth charges ahead of the ship, found their way onto American escorts and patrol craft. Though they had not participated in enough attacks to yield statistically significant conclusions, they had seen combat.[51]

Scientific developments opened new capabilities for the long-range bomber. The Mark IV magnetic anomaly detector (MAD) device was on hand. The National Defense Research Committee (NDRC) had a contract for 100 models of a Mark VI version that achieved better accuracy by using 2 sensors in wingtips instead of 1 towed array. In field trials, MAD equipment now demonstrated reliability rates of more than 90 percent and operating ranges of between 500 and 850 feet. The Navy placed Mark IV MAD devices on all its patrol blimps. A MAD-equipped patrol squadron, VP-63, assigned to CINCLANT's antisubmarine development organization, AirASDevLant, worked to perfect operational doctrine for the new system. Division 6 had produced 51 of the new Mark VI sets in the laboratory, and the Bureau of Aeronautics pushed to get contractors to deliver 300 by August.

Radio sonobuoys went into production, with an order for over 6,000 buoys and 500 receivers. Division 7 worked to improve a new Low Altitude Bombsight that demonstrated a reduction of bombing error along the azimuth of attack from 800 to 125 feet. NDRC had a prototype Magnetically Assisted Bombsight that linked into MAD gear on an aircraft and signalled exactly when to punch off a new type of bomb, the retro-bomb. The retro-bomb actually was a *Mousetrap* warhead fitted with a rocket motor to counter the relative motion of the airplane. It fired rearward from racks on the wings or bomb bay doors of an aircraft to drop vertically in a large pattern around the aiming point. The pattern then descended with a high probability that one of the contact-fused warheads would hit the submarine. Most importantly, the Mark 24 acoustic mine, actually a torpedo, had seen successful field trials and production was imminent. By midsummer, the airplane promised to become a deadly submarine killer.[52]

The consensus between the NDRC scientists and the COMINCH staff officers brought about another new direction. Morse's analysts reported more problems maintaining and operating sound and radar equipment in early 1943, as the new equipment began to find its way into the fleet. They and their counterparts in uniform recognized a need for further improvements in training and sustainment. NDRC expanded its interest in training aids from those applicable to the schoolhouse on shore to those that could be deployed on board ships and aircraft to allow realistic sustainment training during routine operations when not in contact with the enemy.

Antisubmarine warfare involves long hours of boring searching. Often an aircraft or an escort came across a U-boat weeks or months after the crew's last training. Atrophied skills and the excitement of the chase often combined to cause a bungled contact or attack. Crews needed training aids they could take to the field. Accordingly, in addition to continuing its work on selection and training of individuals and on large-scale training aids for training bases, NDRC worked hard at perfecting a number of training devices that could go to sea. These devices included a suitcase-sized trainer that allowed two officers to run through successive attacks, one playing the submarine and one playing the escort. Scientists also developed a module that fitted into the sound console on a ship and allowed supervisors to simulate attack problems for crews electronically, on the same gear they used for combat.

Further, to ensure the new equipment remained operational once it arrived in the fleet, NDRC let a contract with Columbia University for 75 to 100 field-service engineers. Intimately familiar with the workings of radar and sonar gear, these scientists and engineers worked in the units deployed in operations. NDRC had them supervising maintenance, conducting remedial, hands-on training, debugging problems, and reporting back on required modifications or possibilities for new applications.

Slowly, the work of late 1941 and 1942 began to pay off in new doctrine, new weapons, and better procedures for helping sailors and airmen get the most out of their new gear.

Radar on ships, the silent weapon of World War II. Radar for aircraft was developed more quickly than radar models for ships. Scientists became one-eyed men in the valley of the blind in the confusion of what was seen as a possible defeat in the antisubmarine campaign.

The months from September of 1942 to April of 1943 had seen a twofold transition in the antisubmarine campaign. Aided by excellent training of his crews, a comparative advantage in communications intelligence, and an ability to direct U-boats to weakly defended parts of the increasingly crowded North Atlantic sea-lanes, German Admiral Doenitz had brought the Allies to a crisis. They could not continue to sustain the losses of March 1943.

But unbeknownst to Doenitz and to many Allied leaders, several factors began to weigh in the favor of the Americans and British. After January 1943, Allied admirals read German messages in the German Navy code *Triton* anywhere from 2 to 14 days after transmission. Pressures from the British, Secretary of War Stimson, and General Marshall, perhaps Admiral Ingersoll, and subtly from members of the COMINCH staff forced King to accept changes needed to put the American antisubmarine effort in order. Finally, as the Allies struggled to devise a counterattack against the U-boat, American scientists provided an analytical framework and produced a variety of new weapons that greatly expanded the range of possibilities for counterstrokes.

4

Campaign Against the U-Boat

THE YEAR 1943 SAW FUNDAMENTAL CHANGES IN SUBSURface warfare. Tenth Fleet brought order to the American antisubmarine effort. In May, the Royal Navy and the Royal Air Force (RAF) forced a turning point in the Battle of the Atlantic. They drove the U-boat away from Atlantic sea-lanes and made it vulnerable to counterattack.

While the British continued to defend the North Atlantic, Tenth Fleet and the Commander in Chief, US Atlantic Fleet (CINCLANT) took weapons fresh from the laboratory and attacked the German submarine fleet as it recoiled from its defeat at the hands of the British. While the Royal Navy defended the convoy lanes and scoured the Bay of Biscay, the US Navy used newly forged capabilities to attack the Germans' vulnerable logistic system. Simultaneously, both sides began a new phase in their campaign in subsurface warfare. Out of desperation, the Germans searched for countermeasures to the Allies' tactics and accelerated development of a new class of submarines. But the German effort to develop a submarine capable of total underwater warfare came too late.

Realizing the potential for countermeasures to their new weapons, the Americans in turn began to work on a second generation of equipment and on new combinations of capabilities. Word of the successes of the scientists also reached the Pacific Theater, where American submariners had begun looking for ways to cut their losses to the Japanese Navy. By December 1943, the emphasis of Divisions of the National Defense Research Committee (NDRC) shifted from location and destruction of German U-boats to protection of American submarines.

I
Tenth Fleet Brings Unity

Formation of Tenth Fleet meant that, for the first time, the American campaign against the U-boat enjoyed a degree of unity of command. Though the dispute between the War Department and the office of the Commander in Chief, US Fleet (COMINCH) sputtered on into the summer, Secretary of War Henry L. Stimson and General George C. Marshall, Army Chief of Staff, soon noted changes in the Navy's organization, and King's acceptance of the potential of the airplane for offensive antisubmarine warfare. The argument lost importance as the Secretary of War satisfied himself with having forced the Navy to accept many of his ideas as their own. The Army Chief of Staff laid down his cudgels, content to concentrate on the Germans rather than the Navy.

Gladly agreeing to turn over the very long range (VLR) B-24 *Liberator* of the 1st Bomber Command, in return for an equal number of *Liberator*s from the Navy's quota of production, the Chief of the Army Air Forces (AAF), General "Hap" Arnold, enthusiastically returned the newly regained B-24s to his own main focus of effort, the strategic bombing campaign against Germany.[1] From the start a reluctant supporter of Stimson's diversion of aircraft to killing U-boats, Arnold openly fussed and fretted about ever getting on with the AFF's raison d'être. This agreement took the Army out of the antisubmarine business and actually allowed the Navy to develop

National Archives

Planes are ready to take off at dawn from the flight deck of USS *SANTEE* **(CVE 29) to hunt German U-boats in the Atlantic in November 1942.** *SANTEE,* **which displaced 6,534 tons and made 18 knots, was launched 4 March 1939 as** *ESSO SEAKAY.* **She was acquired by the Navy 18 October 1940 and her conversion from oiler to aircraft carrier was begun in the spring of 1942.** *SANTEE* **was commissioned an ACV (escort carrier) 24 August 1942.**

operational doctrine without the worry of encroachment on its roles and missions.

Tenth Fleet's mission gave it a broad mandate. With the task of searching for and destroying enemy submarines, protecting allied shipping, supporting other antisubmarine forces, exercising control over convoys and routing, and correlating training and materiel development, Admiral "Frog" Low had an open charter. Ironically, King allowed violation of the authority of the Sea Frontiers and the Atlantic Fleet. It was understood that while operational control of forces would be exercised through the Sea Frontiers or CINCLANT,

> Special operations may be under immediate operational control of C1OF [Commander, 10th Fleet] where there will be no interference with area commands.²

This line from one of Edwards's memoranda about the design and final approval of Tenth Fleet concerned the Navy's codebreakers. Op-20-G focused on the Atlantic Theater and produced the compartmented intelligence that combined results of radio direction finding with information from deciphered German radio traffic. Reports carried the classification *Ultra Secret*, or *Ultra* for short. When Op-20-G signaled an opportunity to attack U-boats, Low planned to bypass CINCLANT and send the orders directly to the task groups involved. King sanctioned this violation of command procedure, which he had argued so vehemently with Stimson and Marshall to protect.

A crusty, no-nonsense officer, Admiral Low enjoyed the confidence of both King and Edwards. Somewhat opinionated, tough, an alter-ego to King, Low knew his way around the COMINCH staff. In 1942, he had left COMINCH for an operational command, convinced of the inadequacy of the organization for antisubmarine warfare. On his return, with King's blessing, he set about making things right. Building on the work of Edwards, he circulated to the staffs concerned with ASW a draft memorandum outlining his and Edwards's ideas. To a man, branch chiefs responded that the program needed unity of command, a strong emphasis on training, and an effort to coordinate research and development and get the most out of members of Philip Morse's Antisubmarine Warfare Operational Research Group, the ASWORGs.³ Low wasted no time putting the ideas of his new subordinates into practice.

As he cobbled together the organizational components of his new organization, Low took a grip on operational aspects of the campaign. He met with Ingersoll. He reviewed and began to overhaul doctrinal publications pertaining to antisubmarine warfare. He ordered the intelligence staff, under Commander

K. A. Knowles, to analyze the product of Op-20-G and publish a "proper" antisubmarine bulletin that focused on future trends. To bring order to the previously uncoordinated agents in antisubmarine warfare, he began to exercise a strong coordinating role and, when necessary, command. To his credit, Low had a strong sensitivity to dangers of usurping the traditional chain of command. He only bypassed Ingersoll on two issues: Initiation of "special operations," and control of research and development as it applied to tactical doctrine.

To provide the closest possible relation between technological innovation and development of techniques for fighting, Low and Edwards formed the Antisubmarine Development Detachment Atlantic (ASDevLant). Nominally under control of CINCLANT, ASDevLant had two branches, one concerned with conducting antisubmarine warfare from the air, and the other responsible for operations by surface escorts. Charged with experimenting with equipment to determine its practical value and its best tactical use, while stressing coordinated employment between air and surface units, AsDevLant became Tenth Fleet's operational laboratory. Continuing to rely on his Antisubmarine Warfare Unit in Boston, Ingersoll concerned himself with ensuring that the Fleet's system for training worked properly. The unit worked closely with ASDevLant.

To afford him immediate control over the operational exploitation of new technology, Low made sure he had direct access to ASDevLant. He wanted a hand in ensuring that the right techniques were brought forward in the most efficient manner. While CINCLANT could develop training and help to refine tactics, procurement and development meant coordination with Bureaus and agencies outside the Navy. This degree of coordination required the authority vested in King's office.[4] By June 1943, the first patrol squadron in the Navy equipped with *Catalina* bombers (PBYs) with magnetic anomaly detection (MAD) devices, reported to work for AirASDevLant to develop MAD bombing techniques. Now, for the first time, sailors and airmen in uniform worked together under a mandate and the institutional sponsorship of the Commander in Chief, US Fleet.[5]

Formation of Tenth Fleet and provisions for coordination and control in the firm hands of a competent operator like Low had several significant effects. Formerly, to become policy, findings of ASWORGs had to have a sponsor in uniform, like Captain Wilder D. Baker, to guide them up the chain of command. Now, Low took a positive interest in what Morse's operational analysts had to say and became a supervisor who demonstrated wisdom, toughness, and an ability to maintain the friendship of the scientists. Once Low accepted the ASWORGs' conclusions, they went out to the Fleet bearing the signature of Admiral King.[6]

Low also brought greater efficiency to decisionmaking in the antisubmarine war. All interested agencies reported to him. No longer did a captain in the Readiness Division, for example, have to work indirectly with a captain in the Operations Division to get their ideas to a very busy Admiral Edwards. They worked for Admiral Low, and he had the authority to make decisions and the political acumen to ensure they received the nod from King.

Finally, Ingersoll benefited from the change. Though he lost some of his freedom for maneuver in influencing development of new weapons, and had to put up with occasional tactical instructions from COMINCH to units under his command, Admiral Ingersoll now had an ally in court in Washington who supported his ideas about the need for an offensive campaign. Since he still controlled training for all units in the Atlantic Fleet, he could ignore Tenth Fleet's doctrinal pronouncements when he felt it was necessary. Though certain critical orders came from COMINCH to the Task Groups to move to attack U-boat concentrations at this or that location, Ingersoll made sure that his commanders had complete latitude in how they went about their business.[7]

CINCLANT and Tenth Fleet soon developed a sound working relationship. Greater efficiencies in decisionmaking, the close integration of intelligence, scientific expertise, and tactical know-how, and the presence of an operational chief of staff, able to move outside King's narrow view of a defensive strategy, soon combined to improve American antisubmarine efforts.

U-118 sunk by planes from USS *BOGUE* 12 June 1943. While critical orders came from COMINCH to Task Groups for attacking U-boats at certain locations, Admiral Ingersoll gave his commanders latitude for how they went about their business.

For some time, a frustrated Admiral Ingersoll watched escort carriers proceed through commissioning and shakedown cruises and then move off to the Pacific or to duties ferrying aircraft to North Africa. King assigned interception of German blockade runners off Brazil to his old confidant, Admiral Jonas Ingram. This effort took priority over defense of convoys. Ingersoll itched to go after U-boats with new "Jeep" carriers. After the Casablanca Conference, and as something of a cosmetic gesture favored by President Roosevelt and Prime Minister Winston Churchill, King and his British equivalent commissioned the Allied Antisubmarine Survey Board to evaluate combined antisubmarine efforts. The Board had recommended using carriers to cover convoy routes, and provide an offensive capability to take the fight to the U-boats.

British pressure at the Atlantic Convoy Conference in March forced King to agree to allocate an Escort Aircraft Carrier (CVE) Group to protect North Atlantic convoy lanes, once the British took over complete responsibility for the western half of the North Atlantic. Continuing pressure from Ingersoll, most likely made more effective by dismal results of March, made King promise that the Atlantic Fleet would get the next CVE Group.[8]

Low seems to have had no doubt about how to conduct an offensive campaign. King's directive about antisubmarine measures included wording identical to Stimson's earlier proposals. The new language opened the door for an offensive campaign. Forces not required for convoy defense of "Support Groups" would

> be used either to augment escort groups or to operate in areas of submarine and/or convoy concentrations as appropriate.[9]

Low made this language somewhat more clear:

> The first charge on A/S forces was to deliver the convoys safely. . . . The second charge was offensive action against known concentrations of U-boats.[10]

He planned to attack the weakest point in Doenitz's system of deployment, the 1,600-ton refuelling subs or "milk cows." As escorts in the Atlantic grew increasingly proficient at their business, more and more U-boats had to return early for repairs. Turnaround time increased, cutting into the number of boats on patrol. Keeping the remaining undamaged U-boats at sea was critical for BdU.

In January 1943, Doenitz put 87 of his 148 available submarines to sea. After the hard fighting of March 1943, BdU could only send 90 of 156 available boats on patrol. Doenitz depended on the 500-ton U-boat as the mainstay of his fleet. But its limited operational range required a concerted effort by reprovisioning subs to maximize the number of submarines available for wolfpacks. In January, Doenitz's three available

National Archives

U-boat under attack, 3 July 1943. The 500-ton U-boat was the mainstay of Doenitz's fleet, but required several refuelling submarines as seagoing logistics bases.

refuellers performed 23 link-ups. In May, BdU increased the number of refuellers to six, and 54 U-boats received provisions at sea. Low planned to attack the seagoing logistic base of the U-boat operation.

This course of action had several positive features and one very considerable risk, underscored by the British. Destruction of Doenitz's ability to refuel at sea promised not only to reduce the number of submarines on patrol in the Atlantic, it would also limit the number of submarines on patrolling stations in the Caribbean and off South America, and off Africa. Attacking rendezvous points of refuellers also offered the prospect of multiple, unsuspecting U-boats compelled to risk time on the surface looking for each other. However, argued the British, too much success might get the Germans to searching about for reasons, and risk compromising the source of the *Ultra Secret* communications intelligence.

American cryptologists had just recently matched an order in British Naval Cipher Number 3 to divert a convoy with an order transmitted hours later by BdU to redirect a wolfpack to prove that the Germans were reading the messages to the convoys. Discovery that codes had been compromised came quickly, once cryptanalysts began sorting through the right clues. The Germans could make similar comparisons. But the Americans were determined to take advantage of the weakness presented by Doenitz's logistic system. King argued to the Admiralty that breaking the back of the U-boat fleet was as worthy of risking *Ultra* as any other war aim.[11]

In retrospect, one can make an easy judgment about this decision that fails to take into account the mood of the hour. King had embarked on a very risky course. If attacks on the German refuellers fell in a pattern that followed too closely the pattern of deployments ordered by BdU, the Germans might look too hard for underlying cause. Scrutiny might lead them to discover the transparency of their codes and cost the Allies their main advantage over the Germans, an advantage that benefited not only naval operations but ground and air operations as well.

On the other hand, the invasion of Europe required clear seaborne lines of communication across the Atlantic. In April 1943, victory over U-boats seemed uncertain. Stimson, Ingersoll, and Low and their offense-minded colleagues in Navy blue all chafed to seize the initiative from the wolfpacks. Crushing the U-boat system meant clear passage to the European beachhead and the opportunity to concentrate the bulk of American naval power in the Pacific. From the American perspective, the benefit may well have seemed worth the risk. King and Low, however, did not understand how close the Royal Navy had come to forcing the critical point in the North Atlantic. Nor could they at this point appreciate the value provided by access to BdU's radio nets in the Baltic, the testing area for new German weapons for subsurface warfare.

By May, the US Navy developed the analysis of communications intelligence into a fine art, providing a picture of

Bombing of submarine by aircraft. Patterns of attacks might have led the Germans to discover the transparency of their codes, costing the Allies an advantage that benefitted naval, ground, and air operations.

the operations of U-boats that made possible an effective counteroffensive. Established in December 1942, the "Secret Room" operated close to but isolated from the main Operations Center, the Sub-Tracking Room. Other than King, Edwards, and Low, only a handful of full-time intelligence personnel had access to the room, where a small team analyzed several different kinds of raw intelligence.

American cryptologists identified each U-boat by the "hand" of its radio operator: the idiosyncratic pattern of his dots and dashes, and the electronic signature of the signal produced by the submarine's transmitter. This identification, combined with the results of direction-finding and information gleaned from interception and translation of actual radio messages, yielded the intelligence on which evasive routing and attacks on the milk cows were based. Op-20-G's mixture of communications and signals intelligence, the Admiralty's daily summaries of similar British data, and a detailed knowledge of BdU's order of battle combined to produce a graphic and analytical picture of wolfpack operations. This looking glass, while sometimes murky, gave a view of current intentions and dispositions of German submarines and their status of fuel and torpedoes, as well as German Admiral Doenitz's orders and plans for the campaign. It also helped yield a detailed understanding of effects on U-boats of various Allied weapons and tactics, along with indications of the arrival and nature of German countermeasures. Later, transmissions of the Japanese attache in Berlin also gave up detailed information about the Germans' reasearch and development program.[12]

II
New Weapons Mean New Tactics

Along with the reorganization at COMINCH and the grudging emergence of an offensive operational strategy, another factor, the appearance of new weapons and the tactics they made possible, increased the probable effectiveness of an American counterattack. Once these weapons displayed a capability in the field environment, uniformed officials saw their potential value and pushed for further development. The National Defense Research Committee (NDRC) had husbanded new technologies by granting contracts for research and then continuing development of prototypes. Through a continual process of test and redesign of prototypes to a point where they stood ready for engineering development by an industrial firm, scientists took equipment rapidly from successful field trials to the assembly line. Scientists often built the first lot of gear by hand and worked with fighting units to install the equipment in aircraft or ships, which immediately began combat operations with it.

A two-step process of research and development had evolved. Under NDRC sponsorship, the best available physical scientists worked closely with officers with fresh operational experience in a repetetive process of testing and redesign that produced a final prototype. Then NDRC contracted with a manufacturer for production. Engineers from contracting firms suggested improvements to designs, but by and large the manufacturer only took on production of designs given by NDRC. In this way, operational need and possibilities afforded by the electromagnetic spectrum, the physical environment, and available technology dictated the form taken by weapons. Institutional prejudice and mythology, profit motive, or vested interest based on sunk costs or institutional origin played little role.

By May, MAD, the acoustic torpedo, retro-bombs, and the sonobuoy reached the final stage of development. The first Mark VI MAD device performed its initial tests in a B-24 *Liberator* in April 1943. NDRC froze the design in May. Installation was scheduled for carrier-based torpedo bombers for completion in September. In June, the Army Air Forces' 1st Sea Search Attack Unit reported to the COMINCH Antisubmarine Conference on the best tactical combination of radar, MAD, and depth bombs. The Joint Committee on New Weapons and Equipment recommended the Joint Chiefs of Staff continue to push ahead development of two programs: MAD linked with retro-bombing, and the Mark XXIV acoustic torpedo.[13]

The Mark XXIV acoustic torpedo had passed its final trials. And General and Western Electric and the Bureau of Ordnance rushed to turn out service torpedoes. The sonobuoy also had passed the threshold between prototype and production. In April, Navy blimps tested AN/CRT-1A* sonobuoys and MAD gear together against a fleet submarine soon to

---

* Most electronic equipment has no popular name. All equipment in the Electronics Nomenclature (AN) System begin with AN/, followed by three indicator letters, signifying kind of installation, type of equipment, and purpose. Thus, AN/CRT-1A−AN/ = listed in the Joint Electronics Type Designation System; C = air transportable; R = radio; T = transmitting; 1 = model number 1; and A = modification A of model 1.

US Navy blimp over Atlantic Coast convoy. Patrol blimps were equipped with Mark IV MAD devices, giving them 90-percent reliability on ranges from 500 to 850 feet. Successful tests involving a blimp and a state-of-the-art submarine led to full-scale production of sonobuoys.

deploy to the Pacific for combat operations. This particular submarine, USS *HARDER*, and her skipper, Commander Samuel D. Dealey, became legends in the submarine corps through daring, grit, and competence. *HARDER* made a practice of taking on and sinking Japanese destroyers. Dealey discovered that K-49, an unlovely blimp, had located his new, state-of-the-art submarine by listening to her main motors and reduction gears and the operation of her trim pump as she cruised between 130 and 150 feet at speeds of 2 to 4½ knots. The tests led to an order for full-scale production of the sonobuoys.[14]

Sightings and attacks over the Bay of Biscay again picked up and reopened an old wound that worried and frustrated Doenitz and his submarine captains. In May, Coastal Command's aircraft sighted every submarine running the gauntlet at least once. Every few trips home cost a crew that had successfully weathered the convoy battles at sea. Now a new radar reached production stage. SJ (antisubmarine) radar with a 3-centimeter wavelength demonstrated a range of 6 miles against a surfaced submarine from an aircraft flying at 500 feet. The ASWORGs had proved that the probability of success in an attack depended on warning time afforded a surfaced submarine. SJ-1 radar had the capability to allow low-flying aircraft to pounce even more quickly on the prey by instantly beginning an attack, without having to drop from a higher altitude. It also promised to counter the next generation of German search receivers.

In addition, the system of LORAN stations moved toward commencing operations in July. By helping ships and aircraft to pinpoint their locations better in any weather, LORAN offered more efficient control of forces attacking concentrations of U- boats. It also made it easier for pilots to find their way home.[15]

In the meantime, NDRC and the US Navy's Bureau of Ordnance had not neglected the actual weapons for killing submarines. When dropped on target, the nine-charge pattern of Mark 8 depth charges had a 25 percent "best case" probability of killing a submarine, compared with the 7 percent chance of a similar pattern of the old Mark VI depth charges. A whole new range of depth charges, Mark 9s and Mark 11s, and new firing devices based on proximity and influence fusing began to come into the fleet. Along with ahead-firing weapons like *Hedgehog*, improved depth charges increased the effectiveness of surface escorts once they locked onto a submarine and made an attack.

Morse's Group M continued to knit these weapons into a set of tactics and procedures that generated actual capabilities at sea. They used their analysis of operational data to point out where to invest research to create capabilities. For instance, they pointed out the poor record of low-level attacks from the air and demonstrated the need for a bombsight for aircraft attacking from under 500 feet. Understanding that the technological trick to a new weapon could be unraveled once the enemy saw how it was employed, the scientists ensured that work on the counter for a new weapon paralleled development of the weapon itself. In March 1943, before the new acoustic torpedo went to the field, they initiated the development of a countermeasure for the Mark XXIV. To highlight the need for better training for sound operators and conning teams, Group M also quantified the sources of error in attacks, demonstrating a 5-to-1 ratio between human and mechanical errors. These error ratios included the accuracy of the point of attack and the depth setting on charges.

The Operational Research Group made a direct contribution to tactical doctrine through its studies of the relation between the success of an attack and the method of target acquisition, the ship's speed, and the quality of sound-ranging conditions in the water. The work of the ASWORGs also showed that large convoys sustained proportionally fewer losses than smaller ones and that once a certain ratio was reached between escorts and merchant ships, adding escorts to a convoy had no effect on the losses it could expect. Operational analysis showed which tactics had the best probability of working. These findings made their way into the fleet through two channels: deliberations of the COMINCH Antisubmarine Warfare Committee, now chaired by Rear Admiral Low, and the direction sent by Admiral Ingersoll's Antisubmarine Warfare Unit to schools run by the Atlantic Fleet's Training Command.[16]

III
Defeat of the U-Boat

Accustomed to the tactics and weapons of surface escorts, capabilities symmetrical to their own profile of operations, the Germans anticipated improvements in known ways of killing submarines. To counter these anticipated improvements, they redesigned the Mark VIIC/41, 500-ton U-boat and developed the Mark VIIC/42, a submarine with a stronger pressure hull and more powerful engines. The VIIC/42 added 2 knots of surface speed and 3,500 nautical miles of range. Designed to dive deep to wait out depth charge attacks, it had a test depth of 300 meters (984 feet).[17]

Doenitz changed the tactics of the wolfpacks from nighttime to daytime attacks and began ordering U-boats to fight back from the surface when surprised by aircraft. But NRDC had helped the Navy to deploy capabilities asymmetrical to those known to the German Navy. This development yielded two effects. Until the Germans discovered and deployed an effective countermeasure, the rate of destruction of U-boats accelerated and the German fleet had to absorb unanticipated, frightening losses. Confronted with casualties that had no apparent explanation, BdU became frantic; Doenitz and his wolfpacks lost their will. Psychological disruption followed an unexplained acceleration in physical destruction. Rapid increases in the rate of attrition, combined with an inability to understand the cause, had a devastating effect at the operational level of command, where the commander must constantly ensure his ability to dominate future trends.

In May 1943, the Royal Navy and the RAF's Coastal Command inflicted losses on U-boats that forced Doenitz to pull his forces back from convoy battles. Faced with unprecedented losses, he ordered his U-boats to adopt a new operational strategy of silence and stealth, while he pushed German industry to develop countermeasures to Allied weapons, along with a whole new generation of submarines.

The critical convoy battles of May centered on the well-known routes from Halifax and New York to Britain. Convoys set out with plodding regularity on their slow irregular course across the Atlantic. Having recovered from damage inflicted by the heavy battles of March, U-boats moved to the patrol areas in the greatest numbers seen so far. In May, Doenitz kept an average of 81 boats at sea in the North Atlantic, supporting them with 6 refuellers. But the Allies began to deploy units that made the lot of the U-boats more difficult. The British increased the number of "Support Groups"

National Archives

HMS *BITER*, British escort carrier, in 1942. *BITER* and her sister escort carriers HMS *ARCHER*, HMS *AVENGER*, and HMS *DASHER* were converted from merchant ships by the US Navy and delivered to the Royal Navy in the spring and summer of 1942. At war's end, *BITER* was assigned to France and renamed *DIXMUDE*.

available to augment convoy escorts on the Atlantic run. These task groups of destroyers and corvettes moved to reinforce escort groups when wolfpacks threatened a convoy. Three Escort Carriers, HMS *BITER*, HMS *ARCHER*, and USS *BOGUE* now plied the sea-lanes, looking for U-boats. In addition, several new VLR squadrons added their weight to patrols over the Bay and the Iceland Gap. In March, they started operating with 10-centimeter radar and in May began to carry the Mark XXIV acoustic torpedo. The Allies had considerably strengthened the net through which U-boats had to pass to do their killing. The Royal Navy's defense of convoys and the constant attrition caused by the RAF's 3-centimeter-radar-equipped VLR aircraft now took the measure of the wolfpacks.

The battles of April and May 1943 opened inconclusively. Doenitz established four patrol lines by 1 May. Two lay off Newfoundland, backed by a third south of Greenland. Submarines positioned themselves to intercept eastbound convoys to Britain. The fourth group waited north of and between the Azores and Spain to attack shipping that ran between Gibraltar and England. In the last half of April, the fighting gave inconclusive results: 258 ships in 6 convoys made crossings to Liverpool. U-boats sank only three merchantmen, at a cost of four U-boats. The US Coast Guard Cutter *SPENCER*, a B-24 *Liberator* of RAF Squadron 120, and HMS *HESPERUS* scored individual kills, while a coordinated attack from HMS *PATHFINDER* and aircraft from HMS *BITER* sank the fourth. Bad weather and other factors frustrated attempts of wolfpacks to mass on individual convoys. Doenitz ordered his captains to shift from attacks at night to submerged, head-on strikes in daylight. U-boats found their work tougher, but the battle still hung in the balance.[18]

The crisis for the U-boats followed quickly. On 21 April 1943, convoy ONS-5 left Liverpool bound for Halifax. In heavy weather from 2 May to the morning of 6 May, 40 U-boats attacked the 42-ship convoy. In confused night fighting, U-boats sank 11 ships in convoy and 2 stragglers. But the U-boats paid dearly: Seven went to the bottom and two more took heavy damage. Long-range aircraft accounted for two of the submarines. With ramming, *Hedgehog*s, and depth charges, surface escorts sank the rest.

Putting together their best cryptological effort of the campaign, the Germans attacked the next eastbound convoy, HX-237, with a 12-boat wolfpack. Aircraft kept them at bay, and they only sank three stragglers, losing two U-boats to coordinated attacks of escorts and aircraft that damaged three more. Dropping back and regrouping to pick up SC-129, the next convoy through, the U-boats attacked again. Of 25 to 30 submarines, 2 were lost and 10 damaged. The pattern continued for the rest of the month, with aircraft for the most part keeping the U-boats from closing on the merchantmen. When submarines did penetrate the defensive screen, escorts

National Archives

Effects of fire from US Coast Guard Cutter *SPENCER* (WPG-36) are visible in this closeup photo of a German U-boat, made in the spring of 1943. The sailor standing by the midships stanchion disappeared a moment after this picture was made. The U-boat had been trying to sneak into the center of the convoy. U-boats found their work tougher because of bad weather and better search methods, but the battle still hung in the balance.

pounced. Unlike conditions in 1942, however, escort groups now had enough ships to allow destroyers and corvettes to remain with submerged U-boats, conducting successive attacks to exhaustion.

The game had changed. Convoys now slipped through with hardly any casualties, while U-boats experienced a steady toll of losses.[19]

In mid-May 1943 another factor, the acoustic torpedo, made its presence felt in the campaign. On the morning of 14 May, a US Navy PBY5A flying aircover for convoy ONS-7 sighted and attacked a U-boat 14 miles out from the convoy. After dropping his torpedo, the pilot reported a

> circular burbling disturbance of surface of water resembling large air bubble seen 200 feet ahead of swirl (left by the submerging U-boat) 20 seconds after mine entered water.

With its crew probably thinking they had successfully evaded the PBY, U-657 became an unsuspecting victim. Within a week, bombers had dropped 11 of the torpedoes. On 29 May, Admiral Ingersoll received instructions to "designate ACV [Auxiliary Aircraft Carrier] for immediate equipping with Mark 24 mines." He ordered USS *SANTEE* to take on the new weapons and prepare to escort convoy UGS-10 to Gibraltar on 10 June.[20]

On 17 May 1943, Doenitz ordered the wolfpacks to change tactics. Because air cover had taken away the submarine's ability to use its advantage in surface speed to pull ahead of a convoy to set a nighttime ambush, he directed his captains to fall away after the initial attack on a convoy and concentrate on stragglers and preparation for the next convoy.[21]

To no avail. U-boats came away empty-handed from their assault on convoy SC-130 with five more losses of their own: three to long-range aircraft and two to escorts. Two convoys followed, the first escorted by USS *BOGUE*, the second by HMS *ARCHER*. The U-boats made no kills; the escort carriers made one each, *BOGUE*'s aircraft with depth bombs, *ARCHER*'s with a new rocket with a solid head designed by the scientists to punch holes in a surfaced U-boat's hull. Before *ARCHER* set out with convoy HX-239, a frustrated Doenitz radioed to his command:

> Now if there is anyone who thinks that combatting convoys is therefore no longer possible, he is a weakling and no true U-boat captain. The battle in the Atlantic is getting harder but it is the determining element in the waging of the war. . . . Do your best with this convoy. We must smash it to bits.[22]

Admiral Ingersoll presents Navy Cross to a flyer on flight deck of USS *SANTEE* (CVE 29) on 5 April 1943.

And two days later:

> I expect of you that you will continue your determined fight against the enemy and that against his wiles and technical innovations you will pit your ingenuity, your ability, and your obdurate will.[23]

Ingenuity, ability, and will the U-boat skippers had in good measure. But ordering them to press on against capabilities they did not perceive or comprehend meant certain defeat. A week later, after his U-boats failed to inflict any damage on convoy HX-239, Doenitz called for a retreat. Attributing the defeat to superiority of the *ortung* (locating by radio) of the Allies and the ubiquitous air cover that could strike U-boats anywhere, he radioed:

> The situation in the North Atlantic now forces a temporary shifting of operations to areas less endangered by

Campaign Against the U-Boat   133

National Archives

HMS *ARCHER*, British "jeep" carrier, in 1942. *ARCHER* **and her sister escort carriers had small islands on their starboard sides and diesel engines with no funnels; combustion products were discharged on either side of the flight deck.** *ARCHER* **was built by Sun Shipbuilding Co., Chester, Pa., and launched 14 December 1939; she was converted from a US Maritime Commission C-3 cargo hull. She carried 31 aircraft and had one catapult.**

aircraft. . . . These decisions comprise a temporary deviation from the former principles for the conduct of U-boat warfare. This is necessary not to allow the U-boats to be beaten at a time when their weapons are inferior, by unnecessary losses while achieving very slight success.[24]

Doenitz now redeployed his submarines away from convoy lanes into the South Atlantic and to waters off Gibraltar, Brazil, and Africa. From 14 April to the end of May 1943, 912 merchant ships crossed the Atlantic in convoy. In their attacks on convoys, the German U-boats sank only 23 ships, at a cost of 29 submarines lost to surface and air escorts. In the same period, operations of air patrols over transit areas leading from U-boat bases and off the American coastline netted nine more. Doenitz lost 50 U-boats worldwide in the 6-week period ending 31 May. Of these, the Royal Navy received credit for 17 5/6 U-boats; the RAF for 15 1/3. Surface elements of the US Navy sank 2; US naval aviation 4½. Other Allied forces, mines, collisions, and unknown causes accounted for the remainder. Losses to all causes drove his fleet of operational U-boats from May's total of 121 to 62 in June. The tonnage war was over.[25] Having lost the initiative to the Allies, Doenitz had to find new weapons and methods that would support a counterattack.

A number of factors contributed to the Allies' victory. Communications intelligence, radar, and the improved weather of May allowed aircraft to strip from the U-boats the operational and tactical invisibility they had enjoyed up to early 1943. A host of new weapons, many developed by the National Defense Research Committee, allowed Allied airmen and seamen to attack with more deadly efficiency, once they acquired a target. Of these new weapons, the Mark XXIV torpedo showed the greatest promise. For the most part, however, the Allies owed their success to the skill and persistence of support and escort groups of the Royal Navy, and aircrews of the RAF who, with a handful of VLR squadrons from the US Navy and the AAF's 1st Bomber Command, broke the will of the German submarine fleet in the North Atlantic.[26]

IV
Tenth Fleet and Scientists Consolidate Advantages

On both sides of the Atlantic, perceptions of a change of fortune on the battlefield brought a reexamination of programs for research and development. In the United States, senior scientists in the NDRC and Group M understood the ephemeral qualities of capabilities they had created. Bush, Tate, and Morse began to implement broad programs to develop countermeasures. They understood that once German scientists knew a weapon existed, they could quickly isolate the scientific principle on which the device worked and produce a

National Archives

Convoy in North Atlantic. The Allies owed their success in the North Atlantic in 1943 to better communications intelligence, radar, improved weather, new weapons, and above all to the skill and persistence of support and escort groups of the Royal Navy and aircrews of the Royal Air Force, who broke the will of the German submarine fleet.

counter. Often, the uniqueness of a weapon lies not necessarily in understanding the knowledge of the basic scientific principles it exploits, but in the technological tricks of electronic and mechanical engineering that make it work.

Once scientists and engineers discover that a principle can be exploited feasibly, they usually can run down an engineering solution, especially if the solution involves saving lives and winning battles. Security for capabilities asymmetric to those of the enemy require protection not only of technological secrets of how the weapon actually works and the manufacturing processes for its production, but, equally important, of the very fact that it exists at all. The scientists and, in short order, Rear Admiral Low understood this. They acted quickly in accordance with the corollary that, given use of the new weapon carries a high risk of exposure of its capability, the best chance of maintaining the asymmetry lies in having at hand, before the enemy deploys his countermeasure, devices to check the whole range of likely options he may follow. They also understood that the most difficult capabilities to counter combined multiple and unique ways of acquiring the enemy, delivering the weapon, and killing the target.

In April 1943, Bush instructed his subordinates to focus attention primarily on the question of "how our research programs should be altered or emphasized in view of possible enemy trends."[27] After the change of momentum in the Battle of the Atlantic, Bush traveled to England in July to confer with military and scientific heads of the British antisubmarine effort. British military officials questioned Bush about specific weapons and techniques, for instance, to enable an aircraft to attack a surfaced U-boat from outside the range of antiaircraft armament Doenitz began deploying in the summer of 1943.

Requests about how to improve specific weapons came up in meeting after meeting. Bush responded with solutions to the problem of killing submarines that combined technologies. He suggested aircraft carrying sonobuoys, radar, MAD devices, retro-bombs, and acoustic torpedoes. This equipment gave the pilot the capability to find the surfaced submarine and, if it had just submerged when he attacked, how to use the acoustic torpedo. If the U-boat had been submerged for some time, the pilot searched with sonobuoys, making a final exact fix with MAD and attacked with contact-fused retro-bombs. Given this way of looking at the problem, addressing specific German tactics or counters required modification of only one or two capabilities of the system. Avoiding the U-boat's antiaircraft fire meant reprogramming the Mark XXIV acoustic torpedo to run straight for 1,000 meters (a little more than half a mile) before it began its search, or adding antipersonnel bombs to be dropped from high altitudes to convince the submarine to submerge. Combining capabilities made the antisubmarine aircraft or escort a robust and redundant system for search and attack.[28]

Depth charge hunts U-boat off stern of US Coast Guard Cutter *SPENCER* (WPG-36). Combining capabilities made the antisubmarine aircraft or escort a robust and redundant system for search and attack.

In 1942, John Tate had returned from his visits to British laboratories and naval staffs with new insights for scientific support of the war effort. Profiting from this meeting of military and scientific minds, he brought new ideas back to the NDRC. For a variety of reasons, Bush did not play a direct role in the next phase of the wartime antisubmarine effort. Low and King did not trust him. Though an irritant to Bush's ego, this lack of trust did not materially effect things. NDRC's senior people met routinely to cross-level information. Lateral channels designed into the NDRC by Bush and Conant existed throughout the organization, to ensure that results or requirements from one division found their way to the appropriate branch of another. The scientists also had an excellent informal system for disseminating information. The same personal and professional contacts that served for the peacetime sharing of purely academic ideas and findings worked equally well in wartime, if the parties trusted one another. Though Bush had to work indirectly through Rear Admiral Julius A. Furer, the Navy's Coordinator of Research and Development, many other senior scientists had access to Low and other naval officials in COMINCH, CINCLANT, and the Navy's Bureaus.

A variety of initiatives came from individuals concerned about countermeasures. Morse advocated a better understanding of possible counters to acoustic torpedoes. Tate and Furer emphasized work on noisemakers released by submarines to give a false target indication to sound operators. Low soon became a factor and reflected concerns of the senior staff about German responses to a variety of Allied weapons, from new radars appearing on U-boats to German acoustic torpedoes. ASDevLant also became a force in development of countermeasures. Group M analyzed operational data to develop theoretical solutions to tactical problems. ASDevLant tested them in a field environment.[29]

Another element worked in the Allies' favor. Communications intelligence gave hints about the direction of German work on future weapons for antisubmarine warfare. When a new German submarine began tests in the Baltic, Allied codebreakers reported whatever information the submarine or testing headquarters put in the electromagnetic spectrum. In addition, airwaves gave up the presence of new countermeasures as BdU sent them to sea. Instructions to U-boats on new radar, *Pillenwerfer*, a false sound target that gave off gas bubbles underwater, and *Aphrodite*, a balloon with reflectors to make it look like a submarine on radar, came into COMINCH. Low also watched every twist and turn of the German effort to comprehend each new generation of Allied radar. From March through the summer of 1943, the Germans struggled to understand the Allies' advantage in radar. Not only could Low monitor to some degree the progress of the Germans' research effort, he kept up-to-date on reports from the field that drove BdU to develop their statements of require-

U-664 sunk 9 August 1943. Communications intelligence gave hints about German work on antisubmarine weapons. Also, from March through the summer of 1943, the Germans struggled with the Allied advantage in radar.

ments. With a hint to Morse or Tate on "data from prisoner of war reports," he then could spur the American scientists in the right direction.[30] Leads and direction given by Low pushed the development of FXR, a noisemaker towed by a ship to divert a German acoustic torpedo, and spawned a variety of studies from Group M that detailed tactics for use against new German weapons and techniques.[31]

In October, concerned that U-boats might have deployed an aircraft search radar of their own, Low sent a specially configured B-24 *Liberator* to the Eastern Atlantic to measure and record electronic emissions from U-boats. He specified to CINCLANT the rules for employment for the aircraft.[32] In a unique position to coordinate the combination of operational experience with the recommendations of scientists and a detailed knowledge of German intentions and perceptions in the arena of countermeasures, Low became the guiding force in directing the thrust of American scientific development as it affected antisubmarine warfare. Advised by Morse and Tate, he helped keep the American program for the most part one to two steps ahead of the Germans.[33]

V

The Germans Respond

In spite of the advantages of communications intelligence, keeping ahead of the Germans proved difficult. Germany possessed scientific and engineering establishments unsurpassed by any other nation. Her problem seems to have involved not the availability of a broad base of scientific and engineering developments from which to choose, but establishment of priorities and coordination of operational needs with available technology. As Doenitz cast about in the frantic aftermath of the May 1943 defeat, he found many projects that lay fallow in the early years of the war from which to develop his new weapons. To the effort to counter Allied radar, he added emphasis in two other directions.

- He intensified the effort to restore tactical and operational invisibility to the U-boat by accelerating construction of the new Walther submarine.
- To check increasingly successful tactics of air and surface escorts in defending convoys, he pushed work on decoys, antiaircraft weapons, and acoustic torpedoes.

In early 1943, the Germans captured pieces of the British 10-centimeter radar from a bomber shot down over Rotterdam. But until engineers completed the analysis and reconstruction of the British radar, they continued to deploy and improve the *W.anz g1*, a receiver capable of sensing very short radar pulses that had a lower electromagnetic signature than

German Admiral Karl Doenitz, left, congratulates U-boat crews late in the war. Admiral Doenitz succeeded Adolf Hitler as German head of state for a few days after Hitler's death on 30 April 1945.

Metox. Initial patrols of submarines equipped with this device passed unmolested across the Bay. The Germans deployed a second-generation, virtually emission-free device, the *W.anz g2.* Not until *W.anz*-equipped U-386 reported a nighttime attack did they reopen the question of radar frequencies. By the end of 1943, *Naxos* appeared as a counter to the 10-centimeter sets.[34]

In addition to radar receivers, BdU commissioned another approach to avoiding Allied radar. The *Schnorchel* (snorkel) *

---

* Breathing device for submarines; charging the batteries for underwater propulsion remains a basic problem of submarines powered by internal combustion engines. Generators for charging batteries are powered by diesel engines, which require air; the submarine had to surface and was exposed to detection. The snorkel allowed the charging of batteries while the submarine cruised just beneath the surface, by permitting air intake and emission of the engine exhaust.

appeared in a Dutch patent in 1933 and then lay forgotten. In March 1943, Doenitz discussed the difficulties of battles for convoys with Dr. Hellmuth Walther, designer of the Mark XVIII submarine. Walther came up with the revolutionary idea that for maximum speed underwater, the submarine should be shaped like a fish. Walther suggested the snorkel as a way to help restore submarines' invisibility. Doenitz at once saw the utility of the idea and ordered a program to develop the underwater breathing apparatus. By August 1943, tests with training submarines had validated Walther's concept. Orders went in immediately for snorkels for the Mark VII-class U-boats. Production began in late 1943.[35]

In June, Admiral Doenitz ordered a new change in production of the new generation of submarines by accepting modifications to Walther's original design. The new boat displaced 1,453 metric tons (1,601 short tons) submerged, and was designed for 17 knots on the surface and 24 knots maximum under water, with a cruising range of 18,500 nautical miles at 8 knots. It had the potential of running rings around convoys and their escorts and completely avoiding aircraft. But the closed-circuit combustion process based on hydrogen peroxide proved too difficult to manufacture, given German priorities and resources allotted in 1942. On 19 June 1943, Doenitz approved a change in design recommended by Walther's subordinates and seconded by the "K" Office, the German Navy's Head Office for Warship Construction.

The new submarine had much of the capability of the Walther design, but relied on conventional power systems. Designated the Mark XXI, the new boat incorporated the 2,000-horsepower MAN (*Maschinenfabrik Augsburg-Neurnberg*) diesel engines of the Mark VIIC/42 for surface cruising; for fast underwater operation, the new boat boasted a pair of 2,050-horsepower electric motors and a pair of smaller and quieter electric motors for silent running. A redesign of the hull gave room for storage batteries with three times the capacity of conventional U-boats. This compromise between capability and engineering feasibility retained many advantages of the Mark XVIII. The MAN diesels gave it a planned top speed of 16 knots on the surface, but the big electric motors had the potential of pushing it along at 18 knots submerged. Battery capacity promised 48 hours of underwater operation at the relatively silent speed of 6 knots. Even this reduced capability promised to embarrass surface escorts. But the Mark XXI proved a difficult infant.[36]

Not satisfied with the proposed schedule of production that would start large-scale manufacture in March 1945, a frantic Doenitz lobbied Minister of Armaments Albert Speer. He realized that since Speer controlled seven-eighths of Germany's war production, only his help could increase the Navy's share of national resources desperately sought by other services. In a decision unpopular with the Navy, Admiral Doenitz turned responsibility for naval armaments over to Speer. In July 1944, Doenitz pressured Hitler for a larger authorization for steel and for the rights to draft technicians who would have to come from other services. He did not get everything he wanted. Hitler only reaffirmed the steel quota and authorized a smaller allocation of technicians than requested.[37]

Not all the news displeased Doenitz; however, Speer had made progress on the manufacturing front. Accepting Doenitz's appeal for an augmented production schedule for new U-boats, Speer called in the Director of the *Magirus Werke*, Otto Merkur. Experienced in manufacturing heavy vehicles and an expert in assembly, Merkur devised a production system based on prefabrication. Steel firms all over western and central Germany, some not familiar with U-boat construction, built sections of the new boat. They then shipped completed sections, milled to within plus-or-minus 2.5 millimeters (not quite a tenth of an inch) in diameter, to shipyards. Using a schedule of delivery coordinated to the day, the yards added engines and other components and assembled the sections. Final welding of pressure hulls went on around the clock in special blacked-out hangars. Up to half the effort invested by these yards went into construction of facilities and gear to handle the sections. The investment in efficiency paid back a reduction of approximately two years in lead time in delivery of the first Type XXI operational submarine.[38]

National Archives

The snorkel, shown here in a three-quarter view on *U-3008*, a Mark XXI boat, was an air-intake-and-exhaust funnel. It permitted engines to run while boat was submerged, enabling it to recharge batteries without having to surface. The snorkel presented a small radar target.

Campaign Against the U-Boat   145

Like work on new designs for submarines, German development of acoustic torpedoes began in the years before the war and languished for want of sponsorship. In 1940, tests of a torpedo optimized for use against merchant ships saw trials. It had a lower speed of 20 knots and greater acoustic sensitivity than models designed to home on noisy propellers of warships. Final modifications of the design followed operational trials of February-March 1943, and a torpedo suitable for use against ships moving at 7 to 13 knots arrived ready for operations on 1 July. The losses of May convinced Doenitz that he needed a model for use against escorts. He demanded that development establishments have the new version ready by 1 October 1943. As the tactical situation worsened, he moved the deadline to 1 August. Contractors delivered 80 new models on time. Capable of 24½ knots, the new acoustic torpedo, *Zaunkoenig* or T5, had a range of approximately 5 kilometers (3 miles) against ships making 10 to 18 knots. It saw its baptism of fire in September 1943, nine years after initial development of its acoustic system and five months after Doenitz demanded results. Compare this time frame to *Fido*, pushed along by US scientists in the fall of 1941, accepted in principle by the US Navy in December 1941, and launched to make its first kill in May 1943.[39]

BdU developed other devices to fool Allied means of killing U-boats. *Aphrodite*, a balloon with attached reflectors, enabled a U-boat to release a false target to cover its movements. German engineers improved *Pillenwerfer* to allow it to work at depths of 200 meters (656 feet). They did not seem to understand that Allied sonar operators quickly learned to distinguish between signals reflected from the stationary cloud of bubbles and those from a moving U-boat that exhibited a Doppler effect.* The Germans also developed

---

* Doppler is an apparent change in pitch (frequency) of sound or radio wave caused by a change in effective length of travel between the source and point of observation; it is caused by a speed differential between the source and the observer. A Doppler effect in antisubmarine warfare gives some indication of target motion and thus helps to confirm or classify a sonar blip as a submarine.

noisemakers that either reproduced the sound of a U-boat or set off a series of explosive charges to interfere with the sound gear of the escort.[40]

Starting in April 1943, after reports began coming in about cases of U-boats driving away attacking aircraft with antiaircraft fire, Doenitz began to order his submarines to fight the aircraft from the surface. BdU began developing improvements to antiaircraft weapons on the boats. First adding quadruple 20-mm mounts and later sailing with combinations of 37-mm and 20-mm weapons, U-boats began fighting back against aircraft. In June, German submarines began crossing the Bay of Biscay in teams. When attacked, they circled, putting up a hail of fire to keep their attackers at bay. Doenitz ordered these changes for two reasons. He believed that this tactic offered a solution to the problem of air attack, and he knew that the submarine became most vulnerable when she began her crash dive. For the 30 seconds to a minute that it took to get safely beneath a covering layer of water, the submarine offered a slow-moving, defenseless target. U-boats knocked down some Allied aircraft and damaged more, causing a flurry of activity aimed at increasing firepower of patrol planes. But changes in Allied tactics came quickly, and pairs of aircraft soon proved more than a match for U-boats. By staying up to fight, they merely increased the chance that one of the aircraft would get in for a well-aimed attack. The percentage of successful attacks by aircraft doubled in the last half of 1943; 25 percent resulted in sinkings, 40 percent in damage.[41]

While Doenitz had revised his tactics for the campaign and redirected construction of submarines to allow total underwater warfare, Low and CINCLANT counterattacked. The first cruises of USS *BOGUE* operating exclusively with convoys gave lackluster results. This lack of real success led to the decision that once the convoy reached safety on the eastern side of the Atlantic, the escort carrier (CVE) groups should be released to operate offensively against known concentrations of U-boats. Ingersoll felt all along that attacking wolfpacks as they concentrated made more sense than patrolling over the convoy.[42] In mid-June, Ingersoll heard from Washington:

> Assume you are giving consideration of escort carrier support groups in such manner that when a known submarine concentration has been cleared by a convoy . . . such group may then operate independently against the concentration.

Low later wired that he would release special information "that will enable you to more quickly and positively" maneuver the escorts.[43]

As the US Navy prepared to go on the offensive, Doenitz made or continued to make mistakes that increased the effectiveness of the American effort. In June and July 1943, he pulled all his U-boats out of the Atlantic and doubled the number positioned to attack sea-lanes to Gibraltar, for which the Americans had assumed responsibility in March. He also attempted to shift submarines around Africa to the Indian Ocean. Potential targets increased in the very area the counterattack was to take place. BdU continued to demand from all submarines detailed reports on tactical situations and the status of fuel and torpedoes. They disseminated the rendezvous for refuelling two weeks ahead of the actual date of execution, giving the escort carriers plenty of time to react. When a refueller went down, it set off a number of reactions. U-boats low on fuel had to return to base or meet with other attack submarines to take on fuel. Other refuellers had to change their schedules to take up the load. The changes caused a torrent of new messages from BdU to the submarines involved and, inadvertently, to COMINCH and the Admiralty. Changes in campaign strategy and insecure communications combined with the new tactics of remaining on the surface to fight it out with aircraft. Dangers for U-boats increased. Fighting off a lone patrol bomber proved far easier than beating off teams of aircraft from the escort carriers, which could summon up help in the form of more aircraft or one or two of the CVE Group's five destroyers. In addition, BdU failed to recognize the offensive tilt in American antisubmarine operations and continued to develop operational strategy in a vacuum.[44]

The offensive began in July 1943, when USS *SANTEE* (CVE-29) left convoy GUS-9 and began attacking Doenitz's

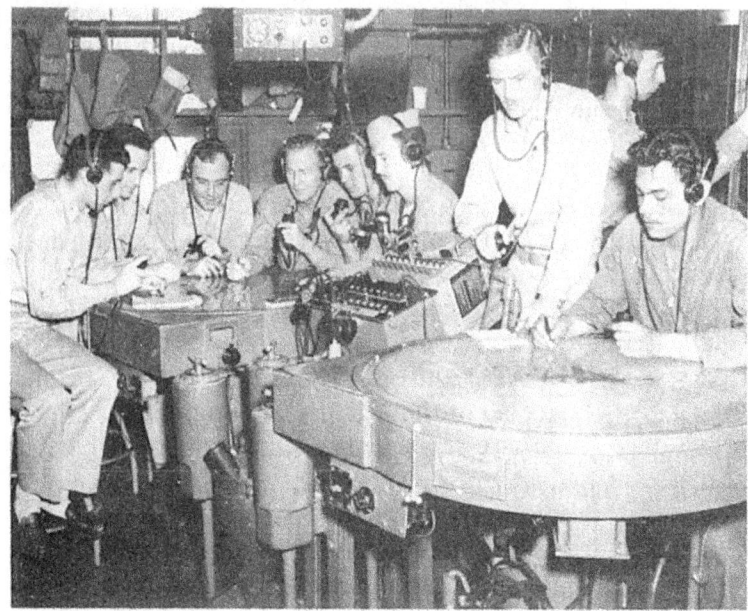

National Archives

Members of a CIC (Combat Information Center) team in the escort carrier USS *SANTEE* (CVE-29) vector a plot from posits determined by a combination of air patrol and ship radar. Successful operations by aircraft from *SANTEE* proved the worth of new acoustic torpedoes.

Group *TRUTZ* off the Azores. Much rode on the results of *SANTEE*'s foray. Ingersoll wanted to outfit another CVE with acoustic torpedoes, and was told not to until the weapon proved itself in *SANTEE*'s operation. After solving difficulties with mounting racks on its aircraft, *SANTEE* began to score. From 14 to 24 July, she sank U-509 and U-160 and damaged U-373. After picking up convoy UGS-10, she killed again on 30 July, sinking U-43. Low, who had personally monitored reports from *SANTEE* and whose initials appear on the assessments, immediately authorized the equipping of USS *CARD* (CVE-11) with Mark XXIVs.[45]

Subsequently, Ingersoll gave the CVE Groups wide latitude to follow up on leads given by special intelligence to attack refuellers and concentrations of submarines forming to intercept convoys. For the remainder of 1943, CVE Groups escorted their convoys across the Atlantic and dropped off to concentrate on wolfpacks. Teams of carrier planes, one armed with bombs to force the U-boat to submerge and one armed with *Fido* to chase the submarine under water, took a high toll of U-boats. In July, the Allies sank 37 U-boats, 52 percent of the force at sea. CVEs accounted for six of the total. By August, five escort carriers operated in the American sector, three equipped with acoustic torpedoes, the other two scheduled to pick them up on their next US port call. Three Navy patrol squadrons were getting magnetic anamoly detection (MAD) devices to expedite service tests. With new confidence in the Mark 24 came increased interest and support for the Mark 32, an acoustic torpedo with active homing. By the end of August, Doenitz began to realize the damage done to his refueller fleet, now reduced to zero from June's total of six. U-boats began a "mass return" from their patrolling stations.[46]

In September, into a tactical environment dominated by the increasing strength and skill of CVE Groups defending convoys, effectiveness of the Biscay Campaign, and offensive action of the American escort carriers off the Azores, Doenitz launched his counterattack. Though the Allies had replaced Cipher Number 3, BdU had good intelligence on movements of more than 80 percent of the convoys.[47]

BdU ordered the U-boats back into the North Atlantic to attack convoys bound for England. Armed with more powerful antiaircraft weapons, new decoys, and the T5 acoustic torpedo, they were to shoot their way through air patrols when stealth failed. Then, as surface escorts reacted, they were to use the T5 to blow holes in the escort screen, enabling members of the wolfpack to infiltrate the convoy. On 19 September, the 21 submarines of Group *LEUTHEN* attacked convoys ONS-15 and ON-202.

In three days of fighting, U-boats scored a partial success. Attacking mostly at night, using conventional and acoustic torpedoes, they sank three escorts and four merchant ships and damaged a fourth escort and two other merchantmen. The 24 attacks with the *Zaunkoenig* T5 acoustic torpedo caused the damage to the escorts. Claiming 10 destroyers sunk and 3 more probables, an ecstatic Doenitz wired to the fleet that the battle had been the greatest victory against the escorts so far.[48] He ordered a concentration on the next eastbound convoy and issued instructions for the attack. No longer could U-boats jump ahead in daytime to prolong the battle for the convoy. U-boats could only count on several nights of operations. They must decimate escorts on the first night and return to go after the merchant ships on the second.[49]

These operations continued through October, but losses soon convinced Doenitz that his counterattack had failed. The German Group *ROSSBACH* attacked convoy SC-143 and sank only one escort and one merchant ship. BdU now expanded its attempts to employ technological factors in the battle. Three U-boats carried teams equipped to intercept Allied signals, to get a better picture of Allied antisubmarine tactics. In this battle, *Naxos*, the new radar receiver for the 10-centimeter radar, appeared for the first time. But the counterattack lost momentum. Doenitz no longer could move his reconnaissance screens quickly to match Allied diversions of convoys. Air patrols cut deeply into his operational mobility. BdU had to preposition groups of submarines in the projected path of the convoy; but the U-boats often failed even to make contact. *Zaunkoenig* did not dominate the fighting, partly because the Allies had already deployed towed noisemakers, and partly because after so much uncertainty, German skippers seemed unenthusiastic about risking their lives to try out a new device. U-boats made only 16 attacks with the T5 acoustic torpedoes in October and November, sinking 1 ship. In the 6 months following *SANTEE*'s first attack with the Mark 24, escort carriers spent 28 days employed offensively in the Atlantic. Of their 60 attacks, 40 percent sank U-boats. German casualties in October jumped to 26 boats lost: 6 to escort carriers, 13 to air patrols, 5 to surface ships in individual or coordinated attacks, and 1 each to a submarine and a coordinated attack between air and surface escorts. Despite new weapons, the price for almost negligible Allied losses had become too high.

In November 1943, Doenitz once again pulled his submarines away from convoy lanes, ordering tactics of stealth and submergence until new weapons for total underwater warfare became available. The Royal Navy's defense of the convoys, the Biscay campaign, and the counterattack of CVE Groups had broken the will of the U-boat arm.[50] Pinned down by air patrols, unable to mass effectively against convoys, hunted by escort carriers, tracked daily by "Secret Rooms" in COMINCH and the Admiralty, half commanded by skippers on their first cruise, the U-boats could only wait and hide.

5
American Submarine Campaign in the Pacific

IN 1942, AS THE US NAVY STRUGGLED IN THE ATLANTIC to overcome its inadequate prewar preparation for the campaign against the U-boat, American submariners in the Pacific Theater wrestled with their own problems. Like their counterparts in the surface fleet, submariners had learned the wrong lessons from their prewar training.

Time was needed to allow them to discover their errors and to overcome them by inventing new tactics and ensuring their use throughout the Pacific Theater. While submariners had done a better job of developing new equipment than their counterparts in the surface navy, shortages occurred and some gear—torpedoes in particular—failed the test of combat. In addition, for the first year of the war, the US Pacific Fleet spent all its energy checking the Japanese advance and wresting back the operational and strategic initiative. Depending on the state of the campaign, American submariners often found themselves diverted from their offensive against Japan's economic lifelines and strategic lines of communication.

Slowly, as the offensive campaign gathered momentum and losses demonstrated the need for better offensive capabilities, commanders in the Pacific sought assistance from

USS *PETO* (SS 265), a *GATO*-class fleet submarine, on Pacific war patrol in May 1945. The *GATO*-class submarine, developed between the wars, was twice as large as its German counterpart, the Mk VII, and provided a platform for a continuing range of improvements.

the scientific community. When asked to help, scientists quickly adapted research to develop better techniques for antisubmarine warfare and exploited them for new ways of protecting US submarines from Japanese counterattacks.

I
Legacy of Prewar Years

American submariners possessed a major advantage in the excellent fleet submarine developed between the wars. At 1,525 tons, the *GATO*-class submarine was twice as large as its German counterpart, the Mk VII. It could make close to 20 knots on the surface and, for short periods, 8 to 9 knots submerged. The original *GATO* boats had an operational range of 12,000 miles and a test depth at the center axis of 300 feet. Most importantly, the *GATO* class possessed internal room for a continuing range of improvements. New weapons added during the war included radar sets of successively shorter wave length, such as the SD, a meter-wave set that warned of the presence of aircraft but gave no bearing; a later development, the SJ, a centimeter-wave set that pinpointed aircraft and ships with a bearing and range; and the ST, a millimeter-wave set.

The *GATO*-class boat also took on new types of sonar and associated warning devices, decoys, new torpedoes, and a night periscope that included an ST antenna. Later, designers also changed the design of structural components and fuel bunkers to give increases of test depth to 400 feet and range to 16,000 miles. When the time came to add new capabilities to the submarine without compromising the offensive potential of its combat load or crew, the *GATO* provided a platform with room for development. By supporting, in peacetime, the marginal cost of extra room, power, and battery capacity, the Navy had ensured the wartime capacity of its submarines to accept improved capabilities.[1]

Unfortunately, the operational insight of the Navy's senior officers responsible for training and doctrine did not match the foresight of submarine designers. As is often the case in military affairs, problems encountered in the first year of the war stemmed directly from operational patterns of prewar years. American submarines did not have as severe doctrinal shortcomings as their surface counterparts, who in 1940 had no idea of the probabilities of surface attacks on submerged U-boats. The submariners had worked out a doctrine for surfaced and submerged attacks. However, this doctrine suffered from the lack of realism of the peacetime training environment.

This problem stemmed from the pattern of prewar training exercises. Tactical exercises for submarines attacking naval task forces became increasingly more complicated between 1925 and 1940. Complexity and difficulty combined with training restrictions to teach the wrong lessons to a generation of submariners. From slowly zigzagging cumbersome groups of ships, the target became a more difficult combination of capital ships covered by aircraft and surrounded by surface screens with active sonar that could move much more quickly than the submarines themselves.

In prewar training, American submariners learned of the hazard of attacking surface task forces by daylight. Well before King's opposition to the efforts of Stimson and Marshall to get more aircraft into the business of killing U-boats, American submarine skippers learned the hazards of attacking surface ships protected by air cover. They developed a technique based on a submerged approach and the launching of torpedoes on a sonar bearing. They also learned that the speed of targets and the threat from airpower meant that a target missed was a target lost. In addition, the unrealistic requirements of peacetime exercises at night, in which submarines had to attack with their running lights on, led to the acceptance of the ineffectiveness of night attacks. Even in 1940 and 1941, as German U-boats tore into convoys, using darkness and weather to cloak their actions, the US Navy continued to classify night practice as developmental. Only 23 of a possible 69 submarines fired night practice. All these lessons had to be unlearned during the war.

Where Doenitz's prewar training instilled confidence and boldness in German submariners, American training instilled caution and the expectation of high losses. It also led to a US doctrine that had to be recast and rewritten by a handful of innovative, risk-taking skippers, literally while conducting combat operations. This difference between German and American experiences probably is due to the fact that Doenitz developed his U-boat arm primarily as a force for destruction of the enemy's merchant marine. The Germans believed their U-boats had war-winning potential. Though well versed in the strategic requirement for unrestricted submarine warfare, their American counterparts found themselves continually employed and trained as auxiliaries to operational capabilities of the main battle line of the surface fleet.[2]

Fleet Admiral Chester Nimitz, USN, shakes hands with members of the crew of a US Pacific submarine while presenting awards during ceremonies in June 1945. At left is Vice Admiral Charles A. Lockwood, USN, Commander of US Submarine Forces in the Pacific.

II

Caught Off Guard

Despite several years of anticipation and buildup to war, the onset of hostilities in the Pacific caught the US Navy off guard, not only tactically at Pearl Harbor and in the Philippines, but operationally: Its submarine fleet was not prepared to sustain the operational tempo of theater-wide offensive operations. As the war began, of the score of submarines at Pearl, only three were ready to begin war patrols. This small number indicates the confusion and disillusionment of the frantic early months of 1942. There were not enough of the *GATO*-

class boats; and the submarine arm, like the rest of the Armed Forces, was not ready for war when it broke out. A year was needed before US submarines broke free of operational diversions that kept them from concentrating on their potentially most significant strategic contribution to winning the war — the offensive against Japan's ability to bring natural resources to its industrial center and to move military supplies and units to the defensive periphery of its empire.

After declaring unrestricted submarine warfare a day before he received authority from Washington, Admiral Thomas C. Hart, Commander in Chief, US Asiatic Fleet, attempted to mount an offensive campaign. But pressures from the Dutch and General Douglas MacArthur to use submarines to help blunt Japanese maritime spearheads kept the boats in the Southwest Pacific tied up in defensive operations. On these assignments, Hart's skippers proved again and again the futility of attacking landing operations with submarines alone. The Japanese always provided air cover and a very active surface screen in these shallow waters, which had confined manaeuvering room. A similar pattern took shape at critical choke points, narrow straits, and sea-lanes, throughout the theater, which the Japanese guarded with heavy air and surface patrols.

To make matters worse, US units evacuated the Philippines and withdrew to Australia. In the time they could have used to concentrate on offensive operations, American submarines continually stayed on the run from one defensive task to another or on resupply or evacuation missions.[3] Submariners had to perform repairs on the hop; staying just ahead of Japanese spearheads, they spent their short stays in port rigged for quick dives. As the Japanese moved into the Philippines, the submariners lost approximately 200 torpedoes when MacArthur declared Manila an open city without coordinating ahead of time with Hart. The submariners also began to experience problems with their torpedoes, a major difficulty that would persist for more than half the war.

Later, as the American campaign consolidated its base in Australia, and the United States prepared to defend against further advances by the Imperial Forces, the pattern of diversion to tasks other than offensive campaigns against Japanese sea lines of communication continued. Many skippers tended to spend a good deal of time running submerged to avoid the perceived threat of enemy air and surface patrols and possible contacts with enemy submarines. They also tended to eschew use of their SD radar. They believed the Japanese could cut bearings on the radar set and thus chart the positions of their submarines, a procedure that was far more difficult with a long-wave set, like the SD, than they realized. These tactics greatly reduced the area a submarine could sweep on patrol, and thus reduced the probability of acquiring targets. Scientists later would define this probability as search rate.[4]

Tactical deficiencies and the subordination of offensive submarine campaigns to specific defensive operations in pursuit of the overall strategic aim in theater remained a fact of life for submariners until early 1943. Subordination of offensive submarine campaigns against the Japanese merchant marine to tasks required by a defensive phase was not, as some have charged, due to a failure of imagination.[5] Both Admiral Chester Nimitz, Commander in Chief, US Pacific Fleet (CINCPAC), and MacArthur made stopping the Japanese offensive their first priority. MacArthur's attitude about New Guinea is well known. Nimitz's strategic view is less well documented. CINCPAC saw his mission in terms of a defensive-offensive campaign:

> The Mission is formulated as follows: While protecting the territory and sea communications of Associated Powers east of 180° and raiding enemy communications and forces, to reenforce and defend Oahu and outlying bases; in order to retain, and make secure, a fleet base for further operations. When the fleet is strong enough, to take the strategic offensive.[6]

Nimitz understood the value of choking off Japan's overextended sea lines of communication. However, he also believed his forces must first deny the Japanese high command the operational and strategic initiative in theater. He had to force them to the defensive and buy time for the arrival of new forces before he would be able to dictate to the

National Archives

Admiral Chester W. Nimitz, Commander in Chief of the US Pacific Fleet (CINCPAC) and Pacific Ocean areas during World War II. In 1944, Nimitz (1885-1966) was promoted to Fleet Admiral, a new rank established by Congress. Admiral Nimitz headed all US and Allied forces in the northern, central, and southern Pacific, except US Army Air Forces bombers that raided Japan from the Marianas.

Japanese when and where and over what objectives the decisive battles would be fought.[7]

Throughout 1942, as submarines available for operations almost doubled, the diversions of boats needed for the offensive against Japanese lines of communications continued. Submarines screened carrier raids. When the Japanese Navy began to mass its forces for the battle of Midway, Nimitz pulled submarines from offensive patrol and put them on reconnaissance screens to intercept attacking units. When the situation at Guadalcanal became critical in the fall, submarines again were pulled back to help check the Japanese Navy's attempt to reinforce their forces on the island.

Carrier raids had mostly a psychological effect, but the battles for Midway and Guadalcanal were turning points in the Pacific campaign. Japanese losses at Midway eliminated the Imperial Navy's ability to conduct offensives directed at destroying US naval power. Guadalcanal, a battle fought on the far limits of Japanese lines of communications by marginal forces on both sides, broke Japan's ability to defend at any point on the periphery of its empire. It marked the first of many ruptures in the defensive rings around the Home Islands. The last-ditch fighting in New Guinea and Midway and the seizure of Guadalcanal and holding it against all counterattacks stayed the offensive momentum of the Japanese campaign in the Pacific.[8]

By keeping the US Navy on the defensive, the Japanese avoided the necessity of diverting resources to a concerted antisubmarine campaign. So long as Japanese offensive thrusts dictated the pace and focus of operations, and kept Allied forces from regrouping for counterattacks, the Empire's internal sea lines of communication were safe. Either by design or because they were lulled into a false sense of security early in the war, the Japanese did not establish a system or headquarters for control and protection of their merchant shipping. While combatant task forces, critical bases, and choke points had antisubmarine screens and air cover, merchant ships moved throughout the Co-Prosperity Sphere individually, without antisubmarine protection. Once the momentum of the Japanese offensive stalled, and the Imperial Navy no longer could dominate the strategic initiative, the Empire's strategic lines of communication lost their only defense against a concerted submarine campaign by Commander, Submarine Force, US Pacific Fleet (COMSUBPAC).[9]

Japanese sampan seen through periscope of US submarine in Luzon area of Philippine Islands on 17 January 1945. Sampans, driven by motor and sail, did much of the local convoying of Japanese supplies.

Despite not having understood the nature of the threat the American submarine arm posed to its war effort, the Japanese Navy had developed a wide variety of antisubmarine equipment and platforms. The Japanese possessed airborne magnetic anomaly detection devices and good sonar equipment. In addition, they mounted sonar and depth charges on a wide variety of vessels, from "sampans" (small, flat-bottomed skiffs) to a number of different classes of frigates and destroyers.

In the early stages of the war, the frequency of Japanese air patrols provided a major hazard for American submarines. But, like the British and Americans, the Japanese failed to integrate these tactical capabilities into a defensive system under a unified, operational command and control system that could direct combat power against the threat posed by a submarine campaign. The Japanese failed to correct this problem until 15 November 1943, when it was too late.

In terms of the US submarine campaign in the Pacific, 1942 proved to be an inconclusive year for both the American and Japanese navies. Requirements of supporting a strategic defense, torpedoes that ran too deep and failed to explode, timid skippers (40 were relieved of command), and bad doctrine, all sapped the effectiveness of efforts of American submariners. Though American submarines did sink a sixth of the Japanese merchant marine—a result touted by President Roosevelt at Casablanca—Japan's construction program replaced the bulk of the losses. The year of 1942 and experience of "exploratory patrols and limited freedom of deployment" frustrated and disillusioned US submariners.[10] On the Japanese side, Midway and the campaign in the Solomon Islands forced Japan from the strategic offensive onto the defensive, overall a major development. But the senior leadership of the Japanese Navy did not yet perceive a threat from the American submarine arm that later compelled them to revise their operational strategy and task organization.[11]

As German U-boats chalked up their greatest successes in the Atlantic campaign, American submariners in the Pacific turned in inconclusive results. However, just as Midway and Guadalcanal signaled the turn in the road for the surface component of the US Navy, they marked the beginning of the acceleration of the US submarine campaign.

III

Strategic Offensive

The first seven months of 1943 saw a major change in the direction of the American submarine effort. Released from the requirement to husband scarce forces to support the defense against Japanese advances, Nimitz turned to the strategic offensive against Japan: COMSUBPAC now could concentrate US forces on the campaign against Japan's sea lines of communication. Production of new submarines meant more submarines were available for patrol, especially at Pearl Harbor. Slowly, problems with torpedoes were sorted out and new, more aggressive tactics began to take hold.

The shift to the offensive by the Americans and the vigorous Japanese defense intensified the fighting. As more US submarines began to penetrate deeply into the defenses of the Japanese Empire, exposure to counterattacks of Japanese antisubmarine warfare patrols increased. With the heightened pace of operations, the rate of losses of US submarines doubled. At the same time, the accidental death of the original COMSUBPAC brought to Pearl Harbor from the Southwest Pacific a new commander, Rear Admiral Charles A. Lockwood. Upset by increasing losses and what he perceived as an improvement in Japanese antisubmarine techniques, Lockwood began to rejuvenate the American submarine campaign.

Prior to Lockwood's arrival, Nimitz had not issued written orders for submarine operations in the Pacific. For the first months of his tenure, Lockwood had received instructions during informal conferences with CINCPAC. As Nimitz began to rely less on submarines for defensive purposes, the mission for the submarine arm took a new emphasis, one now recorded in a more orderly process than allowed by the first chaotic months of the war:

> (1) To inflict maximum damage to enemy ships and supply by offensive patrol at focal point.
> (2) To plant offensive minefields in suitable waters. . . .
> (3) To perform other tasks as might be required from time to time by the tactical and strategic situation, or based on intelligence which might come to hand.[12]

By June 1943, Lockwood published SUBPAC's first operations plan, *OPLAN 1-43*, and began preparations to operate in the Sea of Japan. In response to pressure from Admiral King, he began developing the American counterpart to "wolfpack" tactics and searched for better ASW (antisubmarine warfare) countermeasures.[13] While the close personal contact with Nimitz continued, the thrust of the submarine campaign changed direction to aim directly at Japan's overextended strategic lines of communications.

Like Low, Lockwood proved to be the epitome of the officer best suited for the operational level of command. He had personal experience with the combat environment and detailed familiarity with equipment used by his submarine commanders. When problems developed with torpedoes, first at his base in the Southwest Pacific in 1942 and later at Pearl Harbor in 1943, he personally supervised firing trials that allowed the diagnosis that uncovered problems and made further denials by the Bureau of Ordnance impossible. He took great pains to ensure that successful techniques invented by his subordinates became part of operating doctrine of his command. And he personally made sure that new equipment going into his submarines worked as advertised. He also had a superb informal network of loyal submariners back into critical offices in Washington.

By the spring of 1943, Lockwood began exercising this network, asking for help in countering losses of his submarines to Japanese attacks. He worried about the possibility of new and better ASW gear in the hands of the Japanese, improvements in Japanese air operations, and the difficulty his commanders experienced operating in close proximity to base areas like Truk and Palau. He encouraged his commanders to try new tactics, leading to innovations by risk-takers like Commander Dudley W. "Mush" Morton, skipper of the legendary fleet submarine USS *WAHOO*, who began loitering at known convoy departure points instead of near well-defended base areas.

When targets came into view, Morton discarded prewar training lessons and attacked repeatedly at night, using "end around" tactics. These tactics consisted of attacking, breaking off, and then running on the surface, using extended periscope and SJ radar to regain contact. Radar and the extended periscope allowed Morton to keep his submarine below the horizon, while racing ahead of the target to get into a new firing position.[14] Slowly, new tactics and doctrine forged in the heat of combat, continued marginal improvements to torpedoes, younger, more aggressive skippers, and a steadily increasing number of boats available for patrols began to have

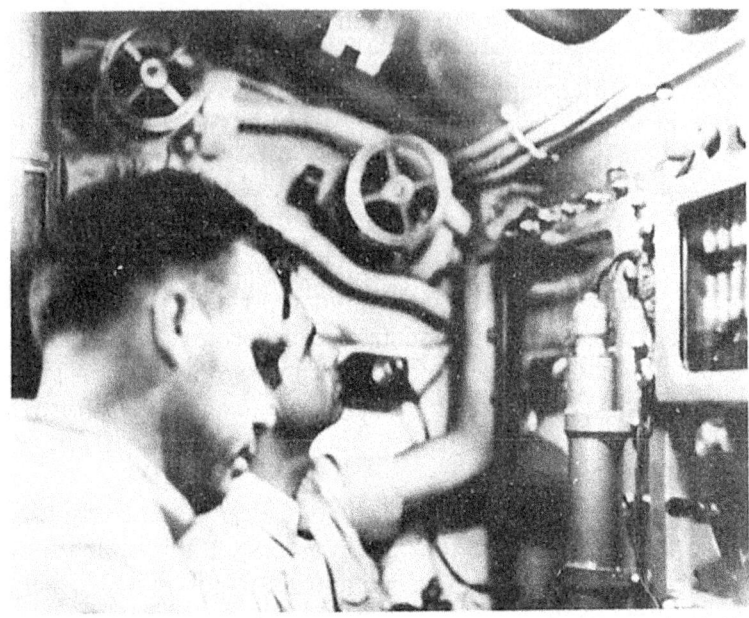

Lcdr. Dudley W. "Mush" Morton, commanding officer of USS *WAHOO* (SS 238), and another officer, probably Lt. Richard H. O'Kane, stand watch in *WAHOO*'s conning tower during action with a Japanese convoy north of New Guinea on 26 January 1943. Several ships, including the transport *BUYO MARU*, were sunk during this action.

an effect. In addition, Lockwood's requests for help in countering Japanese antisubmarine warfare techniques fell into the capable hands of Rear Admiral "Frog" Low.

The connection between Low and Lockwood, the result of a number of serendipitous factors, proved extremely beneficial. Low was a perfect ally, one particularly able to cut across bureaucratic boundaries. Already familiar with contributions of scientists to campaigns against U-boats, he provided instant access to NDRC Divisions working for the Navy. In addition, his relationship with Morse's ASWORGs gave him an appreciation of how similar techniques could be used in submarine warfare, as well as antisubmarine warfare. Plus,

Pacific Fleet submarines returning from patrols are moored at Pearl Harbor in September 1945. US submarines are credited with sinking 4.7 million tons of merchant shipping and 525,000 tons of combatant shipping during World War II.

Lockwood had unwittingly gained a degree of autonomy Low did not possess. Edwards, a submariner, had successfully resisted attempts to establish a submarine command headquartered in Washington, convincing King that operational control of submarine warfare belonged in the field.

Lockwood gained a good deal more latitude to use his initiative in developing new tactics and capabilities than did other component commanders, whose efforts were scrutinized directly by COMINCH. In April 1943, Lockwood began rattling the traces of the informal network of submariners that led back to COMINCH and to the office of the Chief of Naval Operations (CNO). Captain John B. Griggs, commander of Mare Island, the administrative and logistic base for the Pacific submarine effort, served as a conduit of information on personnel, efforts to get the Bureau of Ordnance to solve torpedo problems, and developments in new equipment. The network also included Captain Merrill Comstock in the Office of the Vice Chief of Naval Operations. Griggs worked on nuts and bolts problems; Comstock provided a conduit to Low and Edwards.

In response to Lockwood's requests for help in developing new equipment and new tactics to counter Japanese ASW techniques, Comstock and Low arranged for John Tate and several colleagues to travel to Pearl Harbor for a conference. Low knew what was required and who to send. His clout in COMINCH meant quick circumvention of clearance procedures that kept unwanted "visiting firemen" out of Nimitz's hair.[15] Lockwood's meeting with the scientists led to a reorientation of the entire effort of Division 6 of NDRC. Already intimately familiar with problems of finding and sinking submarines, scientists at Columbia and the University of California had developed a body of research and expertise that made possible a quick transition to developing ASW countermeasures.

To help facilitate his entrée to Lockwood, Tate arrived at Pearl with a personal letter of recommendation from the Commander, Submarine Forces, US Altantic Fleet. He discussed with COMSUBPAC what NDRC could do to help the submarine campaign. Pleased with what he heard from Tate and his scientists, Lockwood was impressed with their practicality and willingness to help. Specifying that nothing added to a submarine should detract from its primary mission of "aggression against enemy ships," Lockwood gave Tate a list of priority requirements and asked for instructors and study groups to perform "analysis of operational information which may point the way to us for improving our methods of attack."[16] On his return to Washington, Tate submitted a proposal to NDRC for work to be done, and began, with the help of Low and Morse, to provide in COMSUBPAC a group of analysts equivalent to Morse's ASWORGS in COMINCH.

The combined efforts of Tate, Low, and Lockwood touched off a flurry of activity. Tate began recruiting scientists to help with what now became "prosubmarine" warfare. Tate had no problem enlisting the support of the OSRD Director, Vannevar Bush, who had just returned from England full of ideas about "counter antisubmarine measures." Low also helped out. He suggested to Edwards and King organizational changes that could make Lockwood more effective, such as promoting him to vice admiral and making him commander of all submarines in the Pacific. Low also kept Bush out of the game, recommending to King that involving Bush and his Advisory Council of the most senior scientists would only waste the time of the people who had to do the actual work.[17] The submariners also had ensured sponsorship at the highest level. One of the submarine "mafia" had staffed a letter for King's signature, advising the Bureaus that "the development of counter antisubmarine measures is considered a matter of grave urgency" and listing in very specific fashion the types of equipment needed.[18]

By the end of 1943, this activity resulted in a major reallocation of resources to support and an organizational structure for integrating research and development and operational analysis into operational capabilities for US submarines. The lessons learned in the antisubmarine campaign in the Atlantic resulted in fast, effective action to launch a prosubmarine program. The organization for prosubmarine warfare was at the outset more efficient than the one developed to support the campaign against the U-boat in the Atlantic. Lockwood eventually drew on the services of two groups of operational analysts. A Submarine Operations Research Group (SORG) in Washington studied long-term issues; a SORG in Pearl Harbor concerned itself with problems of an immediate tactical nature. Both groups eventually used IBM machines to process data gleaned from debriefings of submarine crews. Scientists at Columbia and California had already forged close working relationships with submarine squadrons at New London and San Diego. The scientists helped the submariners with glitches in equipment or with derivation of training techniques. In turn, the submariners gave the scientists a wide range of operational advice and insight. Scientists

USS *SPIKEFISH* (SS-404) surfaces at sea during a Pacific patrol on 24 September 1944. Scientists helped submariners with glitches in equipment, while in turn submarine personnel gave scientists a wide range of operational advice and insight.

at New London and San Diego quickly developed a host of new warning devices and countermeasures for submarines from antisubmarine technology already under development.

This close working relationship proved to be a critical factor in the success of the prosubmarine effort. Once the work got under way, the laboratories of Division 6 produced prototypes of equipment, and the Bureaus contracted for the manufacture of new gear and integrated it into boats coming off production lines. The scientists entered the picture again, assisting in final field tests of newly modified submarines, developing tactics and doctrine for employment of the new equipment, based on the work of the SORGs, and deriving training materials and curricula, to be sure that when crews deployed for combat, they could get the most out of their new weapons.[19]

Even though many decisions still had to be run through King, Lockwood had great autonomy in his relations with the senior scientists of Division 6. Having kept Bush out of the picture, Low ensured that institutional concerns would not hinder the effort. With Lockwood linked to scientists trusted by the Navy, decisions concerning prosubmarine work avoided the political controversy that had surrounded the debates of 1942, over the use of Army Air Forces aircraft to hunt U-boats. No question was heard here of which service would control the technology or new operational functions that might spin off from it. Lockwood was free to ask for whatever promised greater combat capability. He had to overcome only two disadvantages: the distance of his headquarters from Washington; and coordination with the relevant agencies in COMINCH, the CNO's office, and the Bureaus. Since, short of King, Lockwood was the senior decisionmaker on prosubmarine matters, no central agency had to overcome objections raised by officers on the staff in Washington, who had an aversion to technological risk. Autonomy came at a price in the ability to push things through.[20]

By the end of 1943, the prosubmarine effort was in full swing. Tate had shifted the emphasis of his Division in a few short months. In August 1943, the Columbia Research Laboratory allocated one-fifth of its resources to prosubmarine work. By January 1944, the lab was dedicating three-quarters of its energy to new projects. As the work multiplied and the program to support Lockwood took off, Low bowed out and arranged for the scientists to report directly to submarine warfare divisions in COMINCH and the office of the Vice Chief of Naval Operations.[21]

NDRC began work on a number of weapons that were to make an impact on operations.

- In addition to SJ radar, already deployed by August 1943 on a number of boats, developmental work started on a

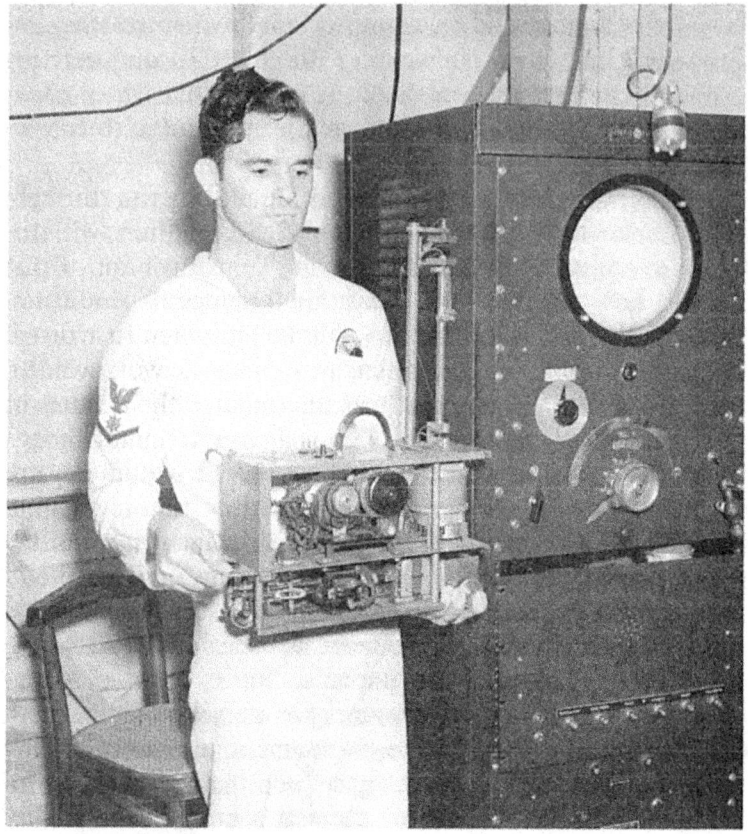

Echo-ranging device, shown here by a Quartermaster Third Class in the US Navy, was known as SESE (for Secure Echo-Sounding Equipment) and served as a "silent" fathometer.

night periscope containing the antenna for a new radar, the ST. This millimeter-wave set promised better discrimination and accuracy.

• To throw off sound operators from the acoustic signature of a submerged submarine, scientists started to perfect sonic decoys or noisemakers.

• To allow submarines to penetrate minefields protecting important harbors and access points to critical sea-lanes, the echoscope, an FM sonar originally developed to hunt U-boats and kept alive by the scientists, was demonstrated to Lockwood. He requested accelerated procurement.

• *Fido*, the Mark 24 torpedo that proved so effective against the "milk cows" in the Atlantic in the summer of 1943, became the basis of work on a smaller acoustic torpedo, the Mark 27. *Cutie*, as the new torpedo became known, allowed submarine skippers to strike back at attacking Japanese destroyers.

• Scientists also accelerated work on a wide variety of devices for indication and warning. These devices included the SESE (Secure Echo-Sounding Equipment), a "silent" fathometer; the TDM (Torpedo Detection Modification), a torpedo detection device; and, to allow a skipper to turn away from the point at which the last enemy attack was made, the DC and DI series of depth charge indicators, which gave the direction of the detonation of depth charges dropped on the submarine.[22]

Operational analysts began work on a significant contribution to submarine tactics soon after they began preliminary analysis of available operational data. Many observers in SUBPAC attributed increased losses to Japanese ability to vector aircraft onto emissions of a submarine's SD radar. By statistical analysis of scanty information concerning unsuccessful Japanese attacks on American submarines, the operational analysts proved that the most likely cause of US losses was not attacks from aircraft, but more probably from ambushes by enemy submarines lying in wait. This finding later helped save American submariners from some of the superstitious behavior exhibited by German U-boat skippers, who frequently turned off their radar warning devices because they believed that allied aircraft were using emissions to vector onto their location.[23]

This work by SORG also accelerated development of the TDM, the torpedo warning device that allowed a submarine to pick up the sound of an incoming enemy torpedo. In this case, operational analysis guided developmental priorities. SORG results also showed the value of camouflage painting schemes, and highlighted the relation between the success of

National Archives

The pointed bow of USS *SEA DRAGON* (SS-194) rises from the depths as the Pacific submarine approaches the flaming carcass of a Japanese ship she attacked in June 1945.

attack and range. Attacks launched in 1941 and 1942 at less that 1,500 yards proved almost half again as successful as attacks made at greater range.[24]

In all these areas, the work of the SORGs made positive contributions to the development of new operational capabilities in the Pacific submarine fleet.

IV

Results of Prosubmarine Program

By November 1943, Lockwood's emphasis on encouraging the best tactics, demands for ASW countermeasures, and the work of the scientists began to bear fruit. More submarine commanders began to employ "end around" tactics. Night attacks increased, as the SJ radar made its way into the fleet and as operational sets were modified to accept Plan Position Indicators (PPIs), scopes that showed a polar plot of the location of the target in relation to the submarine. The radar allowed acquisition of targets at longer ranges and in conditions of poor visibility. The PPI facilitated the approach and positioning of the boat for attack. SORG studies — as well as the desire of Lockwood and his subordinates to invent more effective offensive techniques — resulted in a good deal of experimentation with tactics.

To ensure that the word got out to the fleet about changes in tactical doctrine, SUBPAC began publishing a *Submarine Warfare Bulletin* similar to the *Anti-submarine Warfare Bulletin* published by Tenth Fleet under the auspices of COMINCH. By year's end, Lockwood had 73 *GATO*-class boats at Pearl Harbor to support the increased effort against the Japanese merchant marine. And in its November 1943 *Tactical Information Bulletin*, COMSUBPAC announced the isolation of the last of the problems causing torpedo duds, the faulty design of the firing pin holder in the Mark 6 exploder. Now crews could expect that when they fired torpedoes accurately on target, they would log a kill.[25]

The end result of these developments was a steady rise in sinkings of Japanese ships. The rate doubled in 1943 over 1942's rate. In November 1943, Japanese losses peaked to more than 250,000 tons, reaching a total for the war of 2,500,000 tons. This loss finally forced the leaders of the Japanese Navy to re-examine their organization for antisubmarine warfare. Belatedly, they established a Surface Escort Force, under the direct command of Combined Fleet. Consisting on paper of eight escort convoys and a Naval Air Group, the command received only enough ships to organize four task forces. To make defense of sea-lanes even more difficult, as American attacks drew closer to the Home Islands, the Japanese Navy General Staff diverted ships and planes to defensive operations and counterattacks. Thus these efforts by the Japanese Navy to redirect its resources and place more emphasis on the

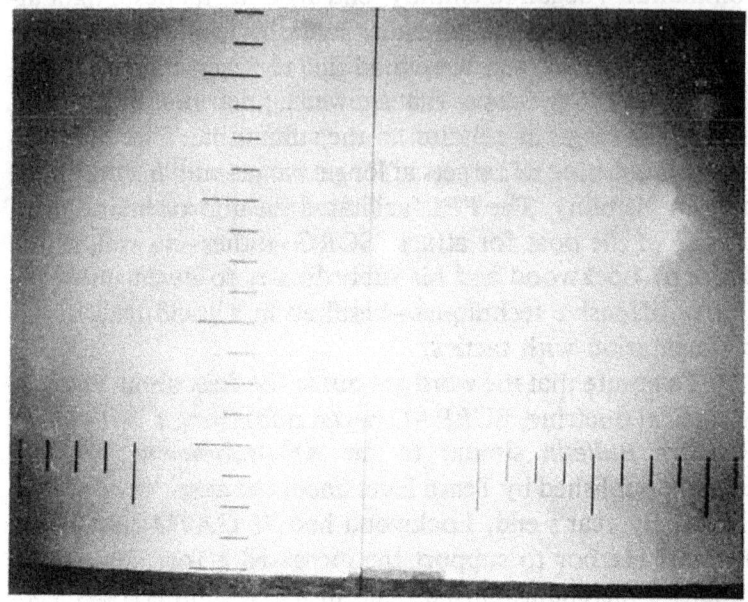

Japanese aircraft carrier seen through the periscope of USS *HADDOCK* (SS-231) in the Pacific in April 1943, is either *OTAKA* (*TAIYO*), *UNYO*, or *CHUYO*. Loss rates of Japanese shipping doubled in 1943 over the rate for 1942, forcing Japanese Navy leaders to re-examine their organization for antisubmarine warfare.

antisubmarine warfare campaign represented too little force applied too late.

The year 1944 would bring the full brunt of combined results of the work of Lockwood and his subordinates and the scientists. In Nimitz's words, the submarine concentration in the active area was beginning to "shape up." American submariners were about to come into their own as a major naval weapon.[26]

Progress was made in the dark months of 1942 and the frustrating first half of 1943. Complications slowed solutions of problems. But eventually, through determination, initiative, competence, and bravery, the submariners themselves forged new tactics and ironed out deficiencies in existing equipment through which the scientists brought new capabilities on line. In addition, the scientists' studies on and insights into certain operational issues, their skill in designing prototypes, and their assistance in sea trials and in the training establishments helped produce a number of new weapons and tactical insights that increased combat effectiveness and saved ships and crews. This combination led to results in 1944 and 1945 that had a devastating impact on the maritime operations of the Japanese Empire.

In the Atlantic, in the meantime, the Germans, after their losses of October 1943, no longer attempted the aggressive *Rudeltaktik* that had threatened to choke off Britain's lifelines. As the next chapter will show, the Germans were faced with an unacceptable and unexplainable attrition, loss of their most aggressive captains, and a general decline in morale.

6
Victory in Subsurface Warfare

BdU AGAIN CHANGED TACTICS IN 1944, PLACING ITS hopes on the new class of submarine designed to conduct continuous underwater warfare. While lowering the vulnerability of U-boats to Allied radar by mounting snorkels on them, Admiral Karl Doenitz pushed construction of the new class of submarines as fast as the condition of German industry would allow.

In addition to their advantages in numbers and superior weapons for locating and sinking submarines, the Allies found a new dimension to communications intelligence. As the Germans began to cooperate more closely with the Japanese Navy, messages between Berlin and Tokyo in Japanese codes long broken by American cryptologists described in great detail new developments in BdU's technological and maritime strategy. In addition, the American National Defense Research Committee (NDRC) also continued to contribute to the antisubmarine campaign, but the emphasis shifted to work in support of the submarine offensive in the Pacific.

Convinced that the war had been won, scientists began to dismantle the NDRC divisions that had so quickly brought weapons from the laboratory into operations at sea. They turned their contracts over to the Navy, and by mid-1944, the

180   Slide Rules and Submarines/Meigs

National Archives

K-gun fires a depth charge (upper right corner of photo) from the Coast Guard Cutter *SPENCER* **(WPG-36). The Allies kept U- boats pinned down at sea, as May 1945 approached, while land campaigns in Europe and attacks by long-range bombers delayed production of new submarines.**

major scientific contributions to subsurface warfare came from members of Philip Morse's group, who concentrated on developing new tactics to counter new equipment and tactics heralded by the messages of the Japanese attache in Berlin. As events marched toward May 1945, the Allies kept the U-boat pinned down at sea while the land campaign in Europe and attacks by long-range bombers delayed production of Doenitz's new generation of submarines. This strategy gained the time needed for Allied land armies to cut into the heartland of Germany, to occupy her industrial centers, and to force her to surrender. In prosubmarine warfare, the SORGs continued their work to derive new tactics while Division 6 pushed to get newly developed gear into the hands of Lockwood's skippers.

National Archives

Troop transport and escort vessels in North Atlantic. Through June 1944, U-boats struggled to keep from being killed, allowing convoys to pass almost without loss. The old wolfpack tactics were proving inadequate.

I
U-Boats Struggle to Survive

In the last months of 1943 and through June 1944, the U-boats struggled merely to to keep from being killed. Smarting from the beating they took in the convoy lanes in October 1943, the Germans shifted their patrol lines to block the routes that ran from Great Britain to the Mediterranean. Here again the old wolfpack tactics proved inadequate. Constant coverage by land-based, long-range bombers, heavy contingents of escorts that now defended each convoy and stayed behind for hunts to exhaustion, and operations of support groups based on escort carriers (CVEs) allowed the passage of convoys almost without loss.

After November 1943, U-boats abandoned their old wolfpack tactics. Without refuellers, forced to remain submerged during the day to avoid radar, U-boats spread out in small groups positioned throughout likely shipping routes. But they could no longer move to concentrate on lumbering merchantmen. They lay beneath the surface in wait, hoping to place themselves in the path of a convoy and, by remaining submerged, avoid detection by escorts. Managing to keep an average of more than 30 submarines in the North Atlantic, and between 10 and 20 on the lanes to Gibraltar, BdU lost in these areas 12 U-boats a month between November 1943 and April 1944.[1]

BdU also tried to send U-boats to patrol off South America and attempted to move a flotilla into the relatively undefended Indian Ocean. Acting on warnings provided by communications intelligence, the quick responses of Allied airpower and surface ships preempted these operations. Doenitz had to give up the tonnage war to conserve his force for the attack on the armada preparing to move to the shores of France.[2]

To enable them to attack the D-Day invasion fleet, BdU began massing U-boats in the Bay of Biscay and continued to push the program to install the snorkels suggested by Dr. Walther. But the Allies understood the seriousness of the threat posed by a massive wolfpack attacking their amphibious fleet. They placed 10 escort groups on patrol across the western approaches to the Channel and backed them up with 3 support groups organized around the CVEs. Coastal command increased its patrols in the Bay and off the Channel.

In June, the timing and location of the Normandy landings took Doenitz by surprise. He ordered U-boats already equipped with snorkels to attack. By the end of the month, German submariners sank only 3 merchant vessels and 2 escorts at a cost of 12 U-boats. Of 48 German submarines that attacked into the Channel in June, July, and August, 16 survived. U-boats simply could not penetrate the Allies' curtain of antisubmarine capabilities. Once the breakout had occurred in France, Allied spearheads soon reached the submarine bases. In September, the 25 U-boats in French ports capable of making the trip to Norway began their long journey. All but four made it.[3]

Stripped of his forward bases, unable to press massed attacks, husbanding a once proud, elite force of now doubting men, Doenitz faced certain defeat. Unless he could find a way to restore to the U-boat its operational invisibility and develop counters to enemy tactics and weapons used in close attack, Germany had no hope of influencing the war at sea. BdU now pushed harder for the development of new submarines and the program to equip conventional U-boats with snorkels. The only hope to regain the operational initiative in the campaign lay in new technology and the leap over Allied capabilities that it promised.

The snorkel was an interim step to a submarine fleet equipped for continuous underwater warfare. A snorkel had approximately one-third the radar cross section of a surfaced submarine. Earlier in the war, the Germans toyed with and abandoned the idea of coating conning towers of their submarines with a compound designed to absorb the energy of incoming radar pulses. They discovered that a layer of rubber impregnated with iron attenuated the reflected energy of a radar signal. Named *Alberich*,* the coating proved difficult to apply and tended to peel from the surfaces of the submarine. Getting the compound to stay on the snorkel proved less awkward.

German scientists developed another coating based on semi-conductor paper, but could not find ways of shaping the paper to match the complex curves of the breathing apparatus. They soon settled on *Alberich*, and U-boats began deploying in 1944 with one of the early forms of what has become known in the late twentieth century as "Stealth" technology. Equipped with an *Alberich*-coated breathing apparatus, a snorkeling

---

* Named for the dwarf who, in German legend, guards the treasure of the *Nibelungen*, owners of a magic ring. In Wagner's musical drama, *Der Ring des Nibelungen* (1876), Loki and Wotan steal the ring and the treasure, and Alberich's curse follows the ring wherever it goes.

National Archives

Conning tower and snorkel of U-3008 covered with a layer of rubber impregnated with iron. Designated *Alberich*, the coating was designed to absorb the energy of incoming radar pulses, but proved difficult to apply and tended to peel from the surfaces of the submarine.

U-boat had from one-sixth to one-ninth the radar cross section of a normal submarine of equivalent class operating on the surface.

The snorkel proved a mixed blessing. While it made U-boats harder to find and attack, it tended to degrade their utility as an offensive weapon. Confined to submerged operations, a Mark VII or Mark IX U-boat could only make five to six knots continuously without having to charge its batteries frequently. Snorkeling submarines spent most of their time moving to and from their patrol areas, which cut into their search rate, that is, their probability of acquiring targets. Continuous underwater operation also proved hard on crews. Water often swept over the snorkel and forced its way into the submarine. When the snorkel closed to stop the flow of seawater, the diesels continued to suck air out of the boat; and unless the engineer quickly shut them off, the crew was forced to gasp for breath. Without the ability to surface and air out the submarine and the crew, German submariners suffered from wet, stale air that added respiratory ailments to the psychological effects of prolonged confinement. The submarine force took to the new device slowly. But in time, skippers reported kills taken in areas the British had only recently come to consider safe.[4]

However unpleasant, snorkeling operations did add to the survivability of the U-boat. By December 1944, Allied aircraft made more than half their contacts on German submarines on U-boats operating on snorkels. Radar proved less effective. Aircrews often picked up the submarine by sighting the exhaust plume at greater ranges than their radar could pick up a return. Attacking snorkeling boats proved more difficult as well. From July 1943 to May 1944, Allied aircraft damaged 40 percent and sank 25 percent of all U-boats they attacked, a tenfold improvement from the kill rates of the early days of the war. From May 1944 until the end of the war, rates of damage and sinkings per attack from the air fell to 35 and 18 percent respectively.

Though it increased chances for survival and restored to the old classes of U-boats a degree of invisibility, the snorkel did not redress the imbalance in capabilities between the U-boat arm and Allied air and surface antisubmarine warfare units. Rates of sinkings did not increase appreciably. Without the operational mobility to move and mass in response to tactical opportunities, the U-boat could only move slowly in a half-blind state to make its kill. Then, if not picked up by escorts, it slunk away. The wolves had become slow killers who attacked alone. While still deadly in close, they lacked improved capabilities for evasion and escape and proved more and more vulnerable to coordinated attacks of increasingly well-armed surface escorts. In late 1944 and throughout 1945, British and American ships armed with the newest sonar and weapons like *Hedgehog* and *Squid* * made repeated one-pattern kills on U-boats, something unheard of in the early years of the war.[5] Doenitz needed a submarine with the underwater speed and endurance to overtake the new, fast convoys without having to surface and, when attacked, could sprint away from destroyers at speeds at which the destroyers' sonars could not operate.

Starting in the summer of 1943, Doenitz began a development program to replace his entire fleet of U-boats. Small enough to be shipped on railway cars, the coastal submarine, the 200-ton Mark XXIII, was designed for operations in the Mediterranean and northern seas. With only two torpedoes, the Mark XXIII also had the range to reach coastal waters around England. Its top speed of 13 knots underwater gave it a significant capability to complicate efforts of surface escorts making depth charge attacks.

The new attack submarine, the 1,600-ton Mark XXI, would replace the Mark IX and give BdU a boat that could range 28,500 nautical miles at a cruising speed of 6 knots. With its snorkel, it could avoid dangers of operations on the surface. Its greatest strength, however, lay in its underwater speed. It had the quickness and endurance to sweep ahead of a convoy, race in for an attack, and, when escorts closed, evade at a top speed that made attacks with depth charges impossible. The XXI would pull away from smaller classes of escorts

---

* A larger more powerful version of *Hedgehog*, which threw six proximity-fused warheads ahead of the ship in two triangular patterns.

Victory in Subsurface Warfare 187

National Archives

German submarine nest. These coastal subs (200-ton Mk XXIII), which carried only two torpedoes, were designed for operation in the Mediterranean and northern seas, and could reach coastal areas of England.

and force faster destroyers to run at speeds that created water noise that made it impossible for sound operators to monitor sound returns. Heavy weather made the task even easier for the new U-boat. Even larger destroyers and Coast Guard cutters could not withstand the pounding of a high-speed chase in bad weather. In the relative quiet of the depths, a fast U-boat could glide away with comparative ease, while on the surface the hunters shook and shuddered from the hammering of trying to keep up.

Not satisfied with a new coastal submarine and the larger, longer-range U-boat, Doenitz pushed for a replacement for the 500-ton Mark VII. U-boat crews favored the Mark VII for attacks on convoys. Quick, agile, and able to take a beating, the 500-tonner had been the mainstay of the U-boat arm in the heady days of 1941 and 1942 and in the tough battles of 1943. Doenitz wanted a boat of under 1,000 tons that had the highest possible underwater speed. Using components from both the Mark VIIC and the Mark IX, Dr. Walther designed a new streamlined boat. By disposing of reserve torpedoes and designing into the pressure hull six additional rearward-facing torpedo tubes, by omitting the antiaircraft armament of the Mark XXI, and by applying his ideas about streamlining, Walther produced a design that promised even greater capabilities than those of the XXI.

The Mark XXVIW had three power plants. For normal cruising, it used the new large electric motor and MAN (*Maschinenfabrik Augsburg-Neurnberg*) diesel being produced for the Mark XXIII. On the drawing board, this powerplant looked like it would deliver capabilities similar to the Mark VIIC. While its endurance at two knots underwater looked about the same as the Mark VII, its streamlined hull gave it greater high-speed endurance. The more efficient hull helped gain a calculated surface speed of around 18 knots on diesel power. But Walther's new boat contained another powerplant he had been working on since the thirties, the closed-cycle combustion process that burned hydrogen peroxide.

Yielding 7,500 horsepower, half again as much as the combined output of the large electric motors of the XXI, the new Walther turbine promised speeds of more than 24 knots underwater. The new U-boat had a range of 11,000 to 15,000 nautical miles, depending on cruising speed; using its peroxide-fueled power plant, it had 6 hours of operations underwater at 24 knots. This range gave the new boat a capability to make exceptionally quick approaches and attacks on convoys and, when threatened, dash out of harm's way. In February 1944, Doenitz accepted Walther's design and ordered a construction program to produce the maximum number of submarines that Germany's production of hydrogen peroxide would allow. As of May 1944, the firm of Blohm & Voss began work to achieve a monthly production rate of 12 Mark XXVI submarines by November 1945.[6]

While Doenitz worked with Walther to develop the new submarine to attack convoys, German industry made herculean efforts to produce the new longer-range Mark XXI. Production specialist Otto Merkur put together a construction program designed to produce 233 of the new boats in 1944 and 114 in the first quarter of 1945. Actually, the yards only delivered 80 Mark XXIs in the last seven months of 1944 and 39 in 1945.

A number of factors cut into production. The availability of batteries slowed final assembly and eventually forced Doenitz to authorize delivery of submarines with only two-thirds of their batteries in place. Allied bombing caused delays, but not for the obvious reason. Despite a number of heavy air raids, production continued. Workers quickly repaired damage to facilities and carried on. However, the technique of assembling submarines in great sheds and then moving them like bottles through a final fitting-out process had a severe disadvantage. When bombs wrecked a newly assembled submarine, the time required to get it out of the way jammed up everything in the queue behind it, a problem exploited by Allied air force planners. Heavy bombing did not damage factories as much as it blocked the flow of finished end items. Small pinpoint raids by *Mosquitoes** proved more effective than large raids, because they took out key facilities like cranes or sank submarines in small fitting-out basins. The Soviets contributed to delays in production of new submarines by occupying Danzig in April 1945. With Danzig and the yards of Schichau went 30 percent of the production capacity for Mark XXIs and one-third of Germany's naval repair capability. Slowly, through the winter and spring of 1945, delivery of Mark XXIs ground down from 16 in January to 1 in April, but production did not stop until Allied armies actually occupied the yards.[7]

One can only wonder what might have happened if BdU had started its production program of construction a year earlier during the happier times of 1942 and had concentrated only on the Mark XXI.

The German Navy also turned out a surprising array of equipment for its submarines, new and old. Doenitz received approval for a program of construction of new DO-355

---

* The British twin-engine *Mosquito* series, said to be the masterpiece of the British aircraft designer de Havilland, was configured as a fighter, fighter-bomber, in some cases carrying 2.5 tons of bombs, a night-fighter, and as a reconnaissance and observer craft.

bombers to assist the new submarines by conducting reconnaissance over the Bay and the Atlantic approaches. Torpedo design forged ahead. By war's end, German technicians had improved the zigzagging torpedoes and the acoustically guided T-5. Not content to stop there, they developed two new versions of acoustic torpedoes, a wire-guided torpedo, and the G7es, *Lerche*, a wire-guided torpedo with an active acoustic homing system. Having captured an H2X, 3-centimeter radar from a downed bomber, the Germans developed an improved radar receiver, *Tunis*, that detected the presence of both 10- and 3-three centimeter radar. This receiver, which went into both old and new submarines, fortunately came too late.[8]

II
BdU's Moves are Watched

As Doenitz rushed to deploy new capabilities for his conventional submarines, and to augment production and delivery of his new classes of U-boats, a small group of senior decisionmakers in COMINCH and the Admiralty watched his every move. When it broadcast routine data to technicians at dockside, a new submarine testing a snorkel in the Baltic gave away the results of the trial. The Allies carefully debriefed prisoners and pieced together fragments of information about new submarines and torpedoes. No source of technological intelligence, however, matched the efficiency of the office of the Japanese Naval Attache in Berlin.

In early 1944, for instance, the Allies discovered a variety of German technological secrets. They learned that the Germans had recovered and rebuilt a 10-centimeter radar. They picked up the presence in the Atlantic of the first U-boat equipped with a snorkel, U-539. In March, the efficient Japanese attache summarized for his superiors the entire scope of the German effort to develop technical countermeasures to antisubmarine capabilities of the Allies. He described new

Victory in Subsurface Warfare 191

Survivor of the German U-boat *U-175* is rescued. The Allies gathered intelligence information from many sources to keep a watch on every move made by Doenitz in his rush to deploy conventional submarines and produce new classes of U-boats.

radar search recievers, FAT torpedoes, and *Aphrodite*, a balloon used as a radar decoy. He described BdU's emergency training and tactics for counterattacking escorts, evading attack from surface ships, and breaking through escort screens. Most important, though, the messages tipped Doenitz's hand and revealed his new classes of submarines by describing the "construction of submarines which can display high speed under the surface and have high endurance."[9]

In late spring, the sprinkle of technological tidbits accelerated into a torrent that exposed the entire German strategy for regaining the initiative in the subsurface war. In April 1944, Japanese messages revealed the capture of a 3-centimeter radar and the fact that the Germans now understood its capabilities.

Op-20-G could even report the serial number of the captured set, number 6. In May, Allied codebreakers read about the German view of the history of the development of Allied radar in the war and use of a network of fixed land-based receivers to provide early warning and locations of Allied aircraft. They also learned that Hitler had approved a new submarine campaign that relied on the two new types of submarine: The Mark XXI, a large fleet submarine, and a much smaller boat for operation in the channel and the Mediterranean, the Mark XXIII. The message cited characteristics of the new Mark XXI and Mark XXIII U-boats, to include range, speed, and armament. COMINCH now knew, for instance, that the large submarine had an underwater endurance profile that varied from 450 miles at 3 knots to 24 miles at a top speed of approximately 16 knots.[10]

From July to November 1944, as the staff of the Japanese attache learned more about German techniques for submarine warfare, they inadvertently shared them with COMINCH and the Admiralty. Their messages reported faithfully on work to counter 3-centimeter radar with the absorbent coatings for the snorkel. They revealed that the Germans did not understand the Allies' use of towed noisemakers as a means of decoying acoustic torpedoes away from their targets. They showed that BdU did not appreciate the threat from Allied acoustic torpedoes dropped from the air. Eager to explain what the Germans were doing, the attache eventually told Tokyo about problems with the T-5 torpedo, and detailed construction procedures for Mark XXI and Mark XXIII submarines, including complete dimensions of the larger U-boat and engineering specifications of its power plant.

The messages gave Allied planners tremendous insight into German tactics. For instance, they revealed that of 379 FAT torpedoes fired, BdU believed 79 had found targets. They also gave away what the Germans had found out about Allied antisubmarine tactics from prisoners of war. From the construction schedule of the Mark XXI to details on its new *Mimek* sonar, nothing important seems to have escaped investigations of the Japanese Imperial Navy's attache. Not only did Rear

Admiral Low read about new German equipment under construction, more importantly, he learned BdU's appreciation of the effectiveness of Allied equipment and its employment. He could place his priorities for development accordingly.[11] From the messages to Tokyo and the debriefings of prisoners, COMINCH obtained an almost perfect view of German plans for the future.[12]

Nor do the Germans seem to have doubted the security of their cipher systems. They certainly appreciated the potential danger of this type of compromise. On occasion, they became anxious about patterns of Allied successes. They worried especially about their losses off Capetown and in the Indian Ocean, where British aircraft and ships patrolled far less frequently. They even developed a new ciphering system based on the names of crewmen, but nothing seemed to help. BdU never seems to have grasped the possibility of compromise of the *Enigma* machine, even though it had been offered for commercial sale in its early prewar form by the company that had invented it.[13]

One must be careful about attributing too much to *Ultra*. An important factor in both the Pacific and the Atlantic, it was not, however, a panacea for the units sent out to hunt down U-boats. In a study done after the war, the Navy's operations analysts assessed data on attacks on and by the U-boats. When BdU vectored (directed, or gave a course to) a U-boat to a selected convoy, located with the help of communications intelligence, the submarine had a two-and-a-half times greater probability of a successful attack than a U-boat operating alone without direction. When in late 1943 and early 1944, the Allies read German communications in near real-time, the rate of contacts between U-boats and convoys fell to two-thirds the rate of July to December 1942. The warning provided by intercepts, improvements in Allied antisubmarine capabilities, and the decrease in U-boats on patrol cut the sinking rate in the convoy area to one-sixth the rate in the last six months of 1942. The campaign of the escort carriers against refuellers and other U-boats off the Azores resulted in 44 attacks that destroyed 15 U-boats and damaged 9 more. A U-boat

Enigma encoding machine, in use by soldiers of the German Army. The Germans apparently never doubted the security of their cipher systems, nor the possibility of compromise of the *Enigma* machine, even though it had been offered for commercial sale in its early prewar form.

compromised through intercept of its radio messages or those of BdU had a 3.7 percent chance of being attacked per day in the patrol area and a 2 percent chance of being sunk. The same submarine when not compromised by communications intelligence had a 2.1 percent chance of being attacked and a 0.6 percent chance of being destroyed. German cryptanalysis increased the search rates of the U-boats by a factor of 2½; *Ultra* more than tripled chances of destruction for a compromised submarine, from 6 chances in a thousand to 21 chances in a thousand. However, even with the advantage of *Ultra*, Allied seamen and airmen had to find and close with their prey, and once contact was established success depended on the right weapons, the right training, and the right reactions.[14]

All the technological intelligence became grist for the mills run by Morse's ASWORGs and scientists of Division 6. Low would get critical pieces of technological intelligence and feed them to Morse. Morse appreciated the accuracy and reliability of data provided by Low and had far greater confidence in conclusions drawn by his analysts. From the information given them, scientists developed conclusions about several aspects of the German technological effort. Given data on a new torpedo, for example, they could design a countermeasure. Given design parameters of a new submarine, they could predict tactical profiles and develop new tactics to allow escorts and aircraft to hunt it down and kill it.

Equally as important, with an understanding of the Germans' appreciation of American tactics and weapons, their allocation of work became more efficient. They did not waste time rushing to produce counters to possible German weapons that the Germans themselves did not think necessary. They also knew exactly where they stood in the game of technological leapfrog. For instance, they could predict with confidence that the Germans could not match with new receivers their ability to produce radar of continuingly shorter wavelength. For the most part, Morse and his counterparts not only knew they had the initiative in developing techniques for subsurface warfare, they knew in what areas and how far they were ahead and on what technologies they had to work to keep even.

III

Scientific Effort Changes Emphasis

Work on antisubmarine equipment began to fade during the latter part of 1944. As the successes of the U-boats waned, the focus of the scientific effort in subsurface warfare began to change. Many scientists felt strongly that they should only contribute their talents to military applications so long as victory lay in doubt. They did not want to work on projects that had only the potential to develop into mature weapons after the war. Winning the war was one thing; assuring American military dominance in the postwar world was quite another. In June 1944, in a paper entitled "It's Later than You Think," F. V. Hunt argued that he and his colleagues should not build up "the Navy's fat on which it must live until the next war." As a result, pressure mounted among the scientists to turn work over to the services. And as soon as an area of research seemed to have potential only for postwar applications, NDRC initiated procedures to transfer contracts over to the Navy.[15] As 1944 progressed, scientists of Division 6 began to wind up their work on antisubmarine warfare and to concentrate on the needs of the Pacific Theater, where American submariners needed scientific assistance in countering antisubmarine techniques of the Japanese Navy.

Though the emphasis on equipment waned, work on operational analysis continued apace. Morse's ASWORGs continued to publish reports and develop them into articles for the *US Fleet Antisubmarine Bulletin*. The *Bulletin* included articles on how to operate sonar gear properly. It gave the latest results of sinkings of merchantmen and U-boats and gave detailed reports of how outstanding ships had made their kills. Attributing its data on German technological developments to information gained from prisoners of war, it predicted the direction of future German tactics.[16]

Appearing over King's signature, the results of the ASWORGs' work became the Navy's fighting doctrine. Morse's analysts provided a wealth of operational information to decisionmakers in Tenth Fleet. They pointed out that human errors caused the greatest proportion of failed attacks on U-boats, rising from 47 percent of the total in 1943 to 51 percent in 1944. Again and again, operational analysis showed that training, or the lack of it, kept crews from delivering potential results possible with their new equipment. Human error remained a major factor in the lack of quality of attacks on submarines. As late as January 1944, the Navy had no standardized program and no military occupational specialty for sound operators. Operators trained on the East and West Coasts scored in radically different ways on validation tests. A young seaman could attend sound school and receive the latest program of instruction developed by scientists from Columbia or the University of California, only to find himself assigned as a clerk because he lost his occupational identity once he moved into the fleet.[17]

The Navy's reaction to the imminent appearance of the Mark XXI provides the best example of Tenth Fleet's operational advantage over BdU. As early as December 1944, using data gleaned from the intercepts of the Japanese attache in Berlin, ASDevLant had studied problems posed by the new, fast submarine. These problems and work done by Morse's analysts showed the difficulty of catching and sinking a Mark XXI U-boat with a surface ship using depth charges. A search began for better tactics and better weapons, including a new acoustic torpedo designed for use from a destroyer, and new search tactics. The navy stripped an R-class submarine so it could do 13 knots underwater, and began trials. Morse's analysts recommended the development of depth-finding sonar in conjunction with *Squid*.

Analysis showed that with *Squid*, probabilities of success in attacks on a deep-running submarine more than doubled over those with *Hedgehog*. From December 1944 to the end of the war, the *Antisubmarine Bulletin* announced to the fleet the imminent arrival of the Mark XXI U-boat, described in

National Archives

US Navy sailors prepare a *hedgehog* bomb projector for action. It threw a pattern of contact depth charges ahead of the ship, while sonar operators could still detect the target on their equipment. *Hedgehog* eliminated the blank period unavoidable in depth charge attacks astern.

increasingly more specific detail, including drawings, its capabilities, and specified tactics best suited to defeat the new submarine once it entered the battle.[18]

Scientists contributed in another more direct way by working directly on tactical problems in the field. In February 1944, magnetic anamoly detection (MAD) made its first kill on a U-boat that was attempting to slip through the Straits of Gibraltar. Throughout the war, Doenitz had been able to infiltrate submarines through this gate to the Mediterranean. Moving submerged, making only enough speed to maintain trim, U-boats rode prevailing currents into the Med silently past British forces guarding the Strait. This tactic allowed BdU to move U-boats continually into the Mediterranean to harass

Allied shipping. Once in the Med, however, U-boats did not come out.

In January 1944, PBYs of Patrol Squadron (VP) 63 began patrolling the Straits, using patterns developed by a scientist from NDRC's Division 6. Between 21 January and 15 April, nine U-boats attempted the passage. Six made the trip, often passing through at night or in foggy weather conditions that kept the PBYs on the ground. MAD successfully accounted for three of the nine U-boats, by locating the submarines and calling to the scene a combination of air and surface units that made the kills. BdU eventually decided that the toll had become too costly and, in view of declining fortunes of the Axis in the Mediterranean, stopped ordering U-boats to attempt the passage.[19]

BdU's search for its war-winning weapon continued right up to the actual surrender. Snorkeling operations cut casualties to U-boats, but, in the words of the COMINCH staff, they were "not conducive to aggressive action." [20] By the last year-and-a-half of the war, losses had shattered the will of the U-boat arm. Doenitz was never able to restore the fighting quality of his crews nor their confidence in the ability of BdU to deliver weapons that could break the Allies' superiority in subsurface warfare. U-boat crews lived to survive. This tendency not only affected the operational effectiveness of individual boats, it made German crews less willing to take the risks to exploit new weapons when they reached the fleet. As a result, the Germans' acoustic torpedo, for example, never developed its full potential. Officials at BdU admitted to their Japanese naval colleagues that crews exhibited "a desire not to encounter the enemy." [21]

Even so, when new submarines took to the water in actual combat operations, they proved that Doenitz had been right. The Allies had not deployed weapons to match them. Five Mark XXIII submarines made a total of eight patrols before the war ended. They sank six ships and damaged another. The one Mark XXI U-boat to get out on patrol had to return to base to repair engine malfunctions; as it moved again to its patrol area it received orders to cease hostilities. By developing a submarine capable of total underwater warfare, Doenitz leapfrogged the effectiveness of airborne radar and acoustic torpedoes. By deploying a submarine with an unprecedented tactical profile, based on unanticipated underwater speed and endurance, BdU countered the most advanced sonar and depth charges designed to attack conventional U-boats.[22] The US Navy had known the Mark XXIs were coming, but had not completed development of weapons and tactics to counter them.

Work done in the German yards of Schichau and Blohm & Voss pointed the way to a whole new realm of capabilities in subsurface warfare. The Mark XXI submarine had little to fear from surface escorts and, had they been ready in time, the Mark XXVIWs even less. In 1945, technological possibilities pointed the way to subsurface warfare in which submarines replaced airplanes as the best killers of their own kind.

IV
Scientists Aid Submarine Warfare

As NDRC contracts went over to the Navy, and scientists moved to other work or returned to their own pursuits, the complexion of scientific work on subsurface warfare changed dramatically. The New London Laboratory began the war as one of the original and most productive centers of work on antisubmarine equipment and techniques. In August 1943, as Low's counterattack with acoustic torpedoes and escort carriers exploited successes of the Royal Navy and Royal Air Force of May, the lab devoted only one-fifth of its energies to submarine warfare. By January 1945, three-quarters of its efforts went into helping American submarines, as opposed to the one-quarter that remained dedicated to antisubmarine warfare.[23] This statistic reflects a change in emphasis that ran through the entire program of Division 6, NDRC.

Silhouette of HMS *ARCHER*, British escort carrier, in 1943.

COMSUBPAC, Vice Admiral Charles A. Lockwood, should have been able to exploit the results of this investment of scientific talent. With authority similar to that of Rear Admiral F. S. Low, Chief of Staff, "but nominally the commander" of Tenth Fleet, Lockwood controlled the entire scope of the Pacific submarine campaign. He also had other advantages. A commander who actually participated in tests of the new gear his men were supposed to use, Lockwood understood how the gear worked and how it could best be used in combat. Like Low, who had personally evaluated the first reports of attacks by acoustic torpedoes and who took part in the classification of kills, Lockwood went out on submarines to watch the trials of new radar or FM (frequency modulation) sonar.

But Lockwood's efforts to get new capabilities into his submarines suffered in several respects. Some members of Admiral Chester Nimitz's staff had convinced Nimitz that scientists should not be roaming around the theater. This feeling led to rather severe restrictions on movements of personnel from NDRC within the operational areas. Vannevar Bush protested to the Navy's Coordinator of Research and Development, Rear Admiral Julius A. Furer, to no avail. King still shared a prejudice against civilian scientists, a bias exploited by the head of the Navy's Bureau of Ships.[24] Lockwood could arrange to get scientists out to help him when he needed, but a larger effort, on the order of that mobilized by Bush, Frank B. Jewett and John T. Tate in 1941 and 1942, was no longer possible.

Lockwood had one other advantage not available in early 1942. The value of operations research had taken hold. Lockwood had no trouble getting scientists and an IBM machine to Pearl Harbor. By March 1944, he reported to one of his important allies on the staff in Washington that the "punch card business is well in hand." To ensure the closest relation of findings of scientists to operational strategy, Lockwood tied his operations research cell directly to his strategic planner. By fall, this tie yielded significant results. As a result of their work with data on attacks on American submarines and the pattern of losses, scientists turned in findings that the number of contacts between US and Japanese submarines had doubled between January and October 1944, and that night contacts had increased 60 percent. The proportion of Japanese attacks in these contacts doubled while the proportion of attacks by Americans on Japanese submarines fell to less than half its former rate. This finding led scientists to reemphasize their earlier finding of the danger of the Japanese setting nighttime ambushes for American submarines. Accordingly, they stressed the disciplined use of random zigzagging, new radar tactics, and the need for a device to warn of the approach of an enemy torpedo.

Analysts came up with a number of other important contributions to submarine tactics. In the fall of 1944, for example, they countered the old prejudice that Japanese aircraft were homing onto submarine radar. They also analyzed plots of radar intercepts taken in the Sea of Japan to determine the locations of Japanese land-based radar that posed a threat to American submarines. In respect to equipment, they proved that the Mark 18 torpedo ran too slow and deep for universal use and had utility only against large warships. Because members of the operations research cell worked directly for Lockwood's planning shop, their ideas made an important contribution to operational planning.[25] In a way similar to the manner the operational insights of Morse's analysts found their way into Low's *Antisubmarine Bulletin*, the work of the SORGs in Pearl Harbor went from a critical point in the SUBPAC planning staff into operational plans, briefings, and the tactical bulletin now being written for the submariners in the

Victory in Subsurface Warfare 203

National Archives

U-118 under attack from planes of USS *BOGUE*, 12 June 1943.

Pacific. Linked to a key decisionmaker, the scientists' operational insights found their way quickly into the fleet.

Communications intelligence also played a major role in the American submarine campaign in the Pacific. In a short paper done after the war, Lockwood acknowledged the fact that the rates of sinkings followed the relative success of cryptologists in keeping current in breaking the Japanese Navy codes. But reading the mail and executing the order represent two very different problems. From January to October 1943, Lockwood's headquarters vectored submarines onto 810 potential targets. The submarines sighted 354 (44 percent). They attacked 120 (15 percent), sank 33 (4 percent), and damaged 58 (7 percent) of total targets made available by *Magic*. Certainly the availability of *Magic* increased the search rate of American submarines, but as for the escorts hunting U-boats, actions on contact, successful attacks, and escape depended on the right equipment, rigorous training, and the skipper's daring and guile.[26]

Lockwood and his submariners quickly recognized the value of the ideas of the scientists and the potential they held for producing the right equipment. As their understanding of the broad range of scientific work being done on antisubmarine warfare grew, they began seeing applications relevant to their way of fighting. In December 1943, the Navy requested modification of the Mark 24 acoustic torpedo to a configuration that could be employed by American submarines against Japanese escorts. This modification meant streamlining, better battery life, and greater speed. In March 1944, a variety of problems cropped up in trials, sending the new weapon back to the laboratory. Three months later, in June at Key West, Lockwood observed new trials with considerable interest, noting the Mark 27 gave "much more promise." By August 1944, COMINCH allocated 35 of the first 60 Mark 27 acoustic torpedoes to the Pacific Theater, and the Bureau of Ordnance committed to reach a level of production of 200 a month in September. Of 46 test runs to that time, 36 proved successful. With forceful support from the field, in a little over six months the hybrid team of scientists performing design and testing of prototypes and the Bureaus handling procurement and production developed a new capability for submarines to strike back at Japanese escorts that hunted them.[27]

In similar fashion, Lockwood's interest and sponsorship, combined with the growing knowledge on the part of scientists of what was technologically available and on the part of the submariners of what was operationally needed, spawned a variety of new ways for making submarines more effective. Scientists developed the new night periscope with a 3-centimeter radar that allowed a submarine to track more efficiently at night and then to make better close approaches. The new periscope went into service production at the Kollmorgen Corp., Simsbury, Conn., in September 1944.[28]

The echoscope,* the device that had not panned out as a sonar for surface ships, reemerged in time to be of help for submarines. Lockwood wanted a sonar to allow his submarines

---

* Electronic instrument for determining the distance and direction of an object, such as a submarine, by reception of a reflection of an ultrasonic pulse under water (asdic). The echoscope was an accurate short-range sonar that used frequency modulation.

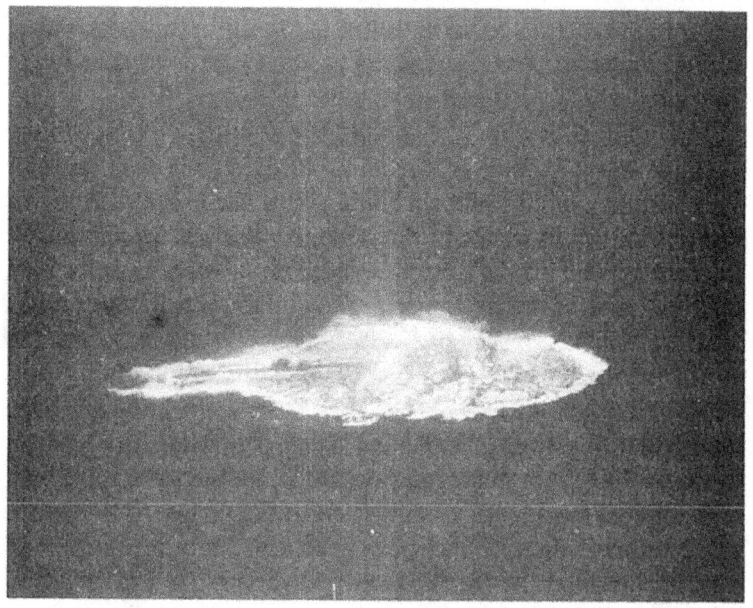

U-boat attacked and sunk by planes from USS *BOGUE*, 12 June 1943.

to infiltrate minefields that guarded the Sea of Japan. When given the operational requirement, scientists refined the echoscope to produce the QLA FM sonar. Scientists in New London and San Diego worked on a number of other devices to aid submarines. They successfully developed sensors that gave the distance and direction of exploding depth charges.

To enable a submarine to escape a surface escort that had locked on with sonar, they continued work on noisemakers or beacons that the submarine could leave in its wake and present to the enemy sound operator a signature very similar to that of its quarry. They also responded quickly with the torpedo warning indicator, TDM, which began deploying on patrol in March 1945. In addition, as scientists modified and added to pieces of equipment, new applications suggested themselves. The addition of a single switch to TDM turned it into a single-ping echo-ranging device. The hydrophone proved so sensitive it also could be used for underwater telephony and for transmission of code, as well as a variety of other uses. The work invested in a broadly based program of basic research in 1941 and 1942 and highlighted by the analysis of the SORGs now paid off in a flood of new applications.[29]

In spite of the ability to reap the benefits of investments made in basic science in the early years of the war, an efficient network of contacts throughout the staffs in Washington, and the ability to speak as the man responsible for submarine warfare in the Pacific, Lockwood did not always have his way. Bad luck and faulty design often slowed development of a new weapon. Unbeknownst to COMSUBPAC, his main contact on the staff of the Chief of Naval Operations, Captain Frank T. Watkins, had a more conservative view of technological risk than did Lockwood. Watkins pushed the scientists and the Bureaus, but from his correspondence, he seems to have been reluctant to send to the field or commit money to a weapon when failure might reflect poorly on the Navy after the war. Low had moved the Mark 24 torpedo from the laboratory to the field because he had the clout and the situation was urgent. Low fielded the weapon and reserved a decision on full employment until results from combat came in, but Lockwood had to rely on Watkins to do the pushing in Washington. Watkins was caught between the urgent need of the men in the field and pressures in Washington to make sure things were done right.

Try as Lockwood might to get new devices to the theater, Watkins and a number of officials at the Bureaus had the last word. While Lockwood's priorities were based on the realities of combat, concerns of officers supporting him seem at times to have been somewhat more institutional. At one point, a frustrated Lockwood felt obliged to remind one flag-rank officer on the staff that a real war was going on, one with real casualties. Pointing out that his command had lost 50 of its 180 fleet submarines, he wrote pointedly, "I want to leave no stone unturned which can lessen these losses".[30]

Not that officials in Washington deliberately obstructed progress, but they seem often to have been more averse to technological risk than Lockwood, who had scientific advice at least as good and perhaps better than theirs. Venting his

USS *GREENLING* (SS 213) reported the success of scientific applications suggested in 1943: New noisemakers had saved the boat while it was on patrol.

frustration over the erratic performance of the FM sonar, Lockwood wrote, "Can we get someone to get the lead out of their pants?" [31]

In spite of delays and disappointments, 1945 saw the delivery of many applications suggested in the last months of 1943. In February, USS *GREENLING* reported that the new noisemakers had saved the boat. Mark 27 acoustic torpedoes took their first kills in combat, with mixed results. Initially, the new torpedo scored well, at a rate of 88 percent. But USS *SENNET* returned from a cruise with only 1 hit for 10 firings. Lockwood continued to push for refinement of the Mark 27 and for better models of acoustic torpedoes and sound beacons, FM sonar that worked, and torpedo detectors. By March 1945, five submarines had new noise-level monitoring gear that

National Archives

Quintet of US submarines returning to Pearl Harbor after successful patrols in the Pacific in September 1945 includes, from front, *FLYING FISH*, *SPADEFISH*, *TINOSA*, *BOWFIN*, and *SKATE*.

allowed them to listen to their own sound signature, so they could isolate and correct the development of slight malfunctions in equipment that threw off telltale noises that gave the boat away. Finally, in May, after a trial of new gear mounted on USS *FLYING FISH*, Lockwood reported, "The finest FM sonar performance I've seen." [32] By June, nine of the new sets found their way into boats destined for patrol.[33]

Much of the new equipment failed to reach the fleet in time to make a significant difference. On the other hand, the speed with which laboratories designed and tested equipment like FM sonar and the speed with which contracting firms turned it out shows what is possible when operational insights, backed by analysis, scientific and engineering know-how, and authority, are combined. As T. E. Shea wrote in 1943 as he began to establish the prosubmarine effort, success depended on

> a single group to whom we can go for opinions on priority and usefulness of effort, who can conveniently get together for us the various interested parties on a problem when this seems to be in order and who can drive the program on Navy side.[34]

The work of Division 6 made a relatively modest contribution to sinking the Japanese Merchant Marine at the least cost in American lives. However, it opened the door to a whole new type of subsurface warfare, that of submarine against submarine. The head start this new type of warfare represented gave the American Navy significant advantages over potential enemies in the postwar period, an advantage that will only be understood when the remainder of the records become available to scholars.

V
An Irony: Too Late, Too Much To Do

The history of the defeat of the U-boat and the parallel successes of the American submarine arm possess an ironic twist. The Germans started too late and tried to do too much by developing three classes of submarine when they should have concentrated on one. But facing defeat as they were, they threw out the existing baggage of service tradition and invented a new class of submarine that made far more difficult the problem of attack on a submarine from the surface. Like the Germans, adversity forced American naval officers to look to science for new capabilities in submarine warfare. The Americans started to apply scientific know-how to submarine warfare only when Vice Admiral Lockwood began casting

National Archives

Japanese Destroyer *HARUSAME*, as seen through periscope of USS *WAHOO* (SS-238), after the US submarine broke her back with a torpedo near Wewak, New Guinea, on 24 January 1943. The destroyer was repaired and returned to service, despite her heavy damage. Although wartime intelligence evaluated her as an *ASASHIO*-class destroyer, her bridge clearly makes her a *SHIRATSUYU*-class DD, with her number two 5-inch gun mount removed.

about for ways to minimize losses to his command. Despite his efforts, a number of factors seemed to get in the way. The Americans started late and could not get enough done in time to make a great difference. But in both cases, with Doenitz and Lockwood, both achieved results only when they somehow got around the established bureaucracy for development of new naval weapons. They achieved fundamental breakthroughs in capability only when they dealt directly with engineers and scientists and fostered the combination of knowledge of scientific potential with an understanding of operational need and what fighting men could use in the field.

In Retrospect

LOOKING BACK, CERTAIN PATTERNS EMERGE FROM THE American experience in subsurface warfare in World War II. They suggest insights about the relationship between technological innovation and military capability and about operational art in general. The old saying, that "generals and admirals live to fight the last war," is a conclusion borne out in part by this study.

Admiral Ernest J. King never appreciated the strategic value of the submarine. In spite of a long period in 1940 and 1941, in which war seemed inevitable, American naval officers failed to understand the requirement for ships capable of conducting a protracted antisubmarine campaign. Nor did they understand the value of the airplane as a submarine killer.

Only the work of scientists who approached the problem from the point of view of scientific method, and who did not have the emotional bias of a tradition of shared experience, and who drew heavily on experiences of the Royal Navy, brought the airplane to the fore. Ironically, the US Army Air Forces, which had the most to gain by exploiting the universal utility of the airplane, went along only reluctantly. General Henry H. "Hap" Arnold proved only too happy when Secretary of War Henry L. Stimson agreed to get out of the antisubmarine business. To him, pulling back from antisubmarine operations meant that forces diverted from the really

US Navy PBY patrol bomber drops bomb during hunt for U-boat. Scientists drew on the experience of the Royal Navy to help US naval officers appreciate the value of airplanes as submarine killers.

important work of winning the war by smashing cities could return to the strategic bombing campaign.

At least for the Navy, the evidence seems to show the confining influence of the big fleet exercises of the thirties. Though King and his wartime subordinates learned a good deal about fast carrier groups and amphibious warfare, they missed the lessons that could and should have been learned about submarines. Once the war began, King held tenaciously to his ideas and only relented when political pressures became unbearable and President Franklin D. Roosevelt sent, through his Chief of Staff, Admiral William D. Leahy, a veiled though pointed message.

In the submarine arm as well, the lessons of prewar exercises had to be unlearned in the heat of combat. This unlearning took the combined efforts of innovative submarine skip-

In Retrospect 213

National Archives

President Roosevelt confers with Admiral Ernest J. King, Commander in Chief, US Fleet, second from left, and General George C. Marshall, Army Chief of Staff, on board USS *QUINCY* **(CA-71) during the Yalta Conference of allied leaders in the Crimea 2 February 1945. At left is Admiral William D. Leahy, the President's personal chief of staff during World War II.**

pers and the supporting work of scientists and operational commanders. Officers like Vice Admiral F. S. "Frog" Low, Captain Wilder D. Baker, and Vice Admiral Charles A. Lockwood saw operational problems more clearly, and willingly drew on skills of scientists to forge a winning combination of new techniques and equipment. They stood closer to operational problems, had a more intimate sense of the need, and, because of their relative youth and freedom from institutional parochialism, assessed new ideas based on their potential utility, instead of their potential threat to precedent.

Many developments in subsurface warfare in the Second World War were suggested by experiences of the First World

War. Admiral William S. Sims wrote in *The Victory at Sea* openly about techniques for tracking U-boats, the value of communications intelligence, and successes of the airplane. His opponent, Admiral Andreas V. Michelsen, corroborated the value of aircraft in antisubmarine operations. German Admiral Karl Doenitz made no secret of his ideas either. No good reason seems to present itself for the failure of imagination that kept British, American, and Japanese naval authorities alike in the dark about the deadly potential of the submarine and the many ways of countering it.

What does emerge is a corollary to the principle that military men always prepare to fight the last war. The evidence seems to suggest that the seeds of success for the next war lie in the experiences of the last, if only the generals and admirals would look for them in an unbiased way, or listen to their subordinates who immerse themselves in warfighting disciplines.

The Navy's experience with subsurface warfare also reveals a number of historical insights about technological innovation and its potential impact on winning campaigns. The most significant developments in subsurface warfare came from the deployment of asymmetric capabilities by both sides. The Germans had airplanes and acoustic sensors. But scientists unfettered by operational traditions rummaging about in laboratories came up with the idea of an air-dropped acoustic torpedo. The ability to deploy a new weapon without the enemy's knowledge offers an opportunity to attack him from a dimension he does not perceive. This phenomenon has several effects. Asymmetries in capability accelerate the killing. Unaccustomed and unexplained losses create psychological shock in the ranks of the enemy, shock that comes from an inability to understand why losses are so great and how the killing is being done. Heavy losses are hard enough to bear, but mysterious increases in attrition can check the will of the most elite organization. In addition, these losses persist not only until the enemy discovers the cause but until he reacts and actually gets his defensive counter into the fight. Thus, for a while, crews know they must go up against weapons for which they have no answer, a knowledge that unsteadies the hand of the most aggressive leader. In this phase, the most aggressive leaders are most quickly killed off as they attempt at high risk to develop new ways of fighting.

What allowed scientists of the National Defense Research Committee (NDRC) to develop capabilities that fell outside the realm of perception of combined efforts of German and Japanese military and scientific establishments? What allowed Doenitz to develop a new submarine that circumvented all the work done in England and America to strip from his U-boats their most important quality, their operational invisibility? The scientists' studies of the ocean environment and the mathematical problem of search and attack led to an understanding of operational requirements that allowed John T. Tate and his colleagues to look across the whole range of possibilities available in the work then being done in the laboratory. Faced with the realization that his U-boats could not survive on the hostile surface environment, Doenitz turned to his own scientific community to find ways of making total underwater warfare possible. A balanced scientific appraisal lay behind Tate's work; desperation forced Doenitz's hand.

The intimate relationship between knowledgeable scientists and naval officers immersed in operations made for the closest possible link between the operational problem and the potential technological solution. This intimacy depended on the removal of service bureaucracies normally charged with development and procurement. Thus Lockwood, Low, and Doenitz had the most success with technological innovation when they and the scientists together dictated requirements for materiel to the military bureaucracy. The Bureaus reacted in similar and predictable ways to ideas they found silly, like designing submarines shaped like fish or applying the technology of acoustics to the guidance of torpedoes. In both the American and German navies, commanders in charge of the campaign working hand in hand with scientists made the crucial link between technological possibility, military need, and institutional authority and sponsorship.

Captain of U-858 in May 1945.

Finally, successes of Philip M. Morse's ASWORGs, members of the Antisubmarine Warfare Operational Research Group, provide a vital insight about the relative value to World War II decisionmakers of emotion and tradition, as opposed to statistically valid data and insights. Doenitz never understood as well as Lockwood the fate of his submarines. With scientific advice close at hand, Lockwood avoided several decisions that would have had an unfavorable effect on his crews. Plus, he had an explanation for losses that was convincing to his skippers. Without adequate scientific advice, blind to the compromise of his ciphers, and for too long failing to appreciate the value of radar, Doenitz continued to press his captains to overcome their loss rates by force of will. When BdU had countermeasures to deploy, Doenitz had already lost credibility with his fighting leaders.

Lockwood, on the other hand, could immediately turn the SORGs' conclusion that Japanese submarines were ambushing his boats into a request defined in engineering terms for the laboratories in San Diego and New London. This request led to quick production of a prototype that could be tested in the operational environment by scientists and men who needed to use the new weapon in combat.

Success in technological innovation came from phrasing the operational problem in unbiased mathematical terms, and then developing equipment to take advantage of the interaction between enemy capabilities and his system for operational employment and the environment. The basic science behind many developments fielded by NDRC was known to scientists in Germany and Japan. The Japanese had magnetic anomaly detectors. The Germans had acoustic sensors for torpedoes long before American scientists began thinking about antisubmarine warfare. Scientists such as Dr. Vannevar Bush, John T. Tate, Philip M. Morse, T. E. Shea, and their colleagues simply were able to look at operational problems of subsurface warfare without regard to institutionally biased paradigms of military thinking. Once they displayed a new capability in a field trial, the availability and enthusiasm of champions like Secretary of War Henry L. Stimson and Admirals Low and Lockwood, who could circumvent the obstructionism of the nay-sayers, meant the new weapon had a chance of quickly getting to the field.

Unfortunately, scientific advice went unheeded in one area. Though scientists warned of the importance of training

Silhouette of HMS *BITER*, British "jeep" carrier, in April 1943.

in allowing ships to get the most out of new equipment, senior officers at COMINCH failed early in the war to heed the advice. Ironically, academics had to remind senior admirals of the importance of training. And because they alone developed methods for measuring operational results, scientists had to develop techniques for training individuals and teams for antisubmarine warfare. Officers like Low, Admiral Royal E. Ingersoll, and Lockwood quickly seized on the value of new ideas about training and pushed to get these new training establishments into operation.

One other insight about technological innovation in a military setting bears note. Admiral King had proved in his career to be something of an innovator. A brilliant man, an accomplished seaman, he had many qualities that should have made him more perceptive about scientific advice that promised to have a significant impact on the antisubmarine campaign. But his dogmatic, authoritarian personality and an almost bitter determination to protect the Navy from any outside meddling blinded him to realities of operational life in the Atlantic. King's personality and its role in slowing the arrival of escort carriers and antisubmarine aircraft in the Atlantic provide a telling example of the cost of a willful, dogmatic nature and institutional parochialism in a senior military leader. Though individual American naval ships and

Coast Guard cutters performed yeoman service in the Atlantic, credit for the successful defense of North Atlantic convoy routes belongs to the Royal Navy and the Royal Air Force, which killed U-boats in May 1943 at a rate that forced Doenitz to abandon the tonnage war temporarily. To Tenth Fleet goes credit for the counterattack against the refuellers that exploited communications intelligence to maximize the effectiveness of the escort "jeep" carriers. The counterattack broke the back of the U-boat arm by destroying its ability to sustain the projection of combat power into the sea-lanes.

Finally, the American experience in subsurface warfare yields insights for students of the operational art. American submarines, destroyers, and antisubmarine aircraft only began to defeat the U-boat when basic science and statistical inference yielded doctrine and equipment relevant to operational need that reached the hands of men trained in how to fight. Certainly, *Magic* and *Ultra* played a significant role in subsurface warfare and made a great contribution to decisionmaking at the operational level of command. In both the Atlantic and Pacific, communications intelligence more than doubled search rates of American surface craft and submarines as they hunted their prey. However, communications intelligence alone did not win the campaign. Finding the enemy is one thing. Killing him is another, and the effectiveness of attacks improved tenfold by war's end—a result of operational analysis, better weapons, and training.

Success in battle required the right weapons in the hands of the right men, trained and disciplined to react properly. In subsurface warfare, equipment, doctrine, and training, when matched with daring, won at sea. The plight of U-boat crews in 1944 and 1945 and of Allied merchantmen from 1940 to 1943 show what daring can achieve in the face of an enemy who has better weapons and better tactics and an equivalent will to win.

American scientists contributed to American victories in subsurface warfare in World War II in two ways. They forged better weapons of war. But most important, they measured and analyzed, in a way far more unbiased than

National Archives

USS *SENNETT* on patrol in September 1944. When *SENNETT* reported only one hit for 10 torpedo firings, Admiral Lockwood pushed for refinement of the Mark 27 and for better models of acoustic torpedoes and sound beacons, FM sonar that worked, and torpedo detectors.

their counterparts in uniform, what was happening in combat at sea and what had to be done to win. To the credit of the Navy, younger men like Captain Wilder D. Baker, Vice Admiral F. S. Low, and Vice Admiral Charles A. Lockwood saw the merit of ideas of scientists. With the support of pragmatic senior leaders like Admiral Richard S. Edwards, Admiral Chester Nimitz, and Admiral Royal Ingersoll, they were able to make these ideas an indispensable component of victory at sea.

Notes

Chapter 1

1. Vice Admiral Andreas Michelsen, *The Submarine Warfare, 1914-1918,* Office of Naval Intelligence, Monthly Information Bulletin, January 1926, Supplement Number 3, pp. 92-109.

2. Ibid., pp. 68-69.

3. Rear Admiral William S. Sims, *The Victory at Sea* (Garden City, N.Y.: Doubleday & Page, 1920) pp. 118-125, 269, 320-323.

4. Admiral Karl Doenitz, *Memoirs: Ten Years and Twenty Days,* trans. R. H. Stevens (London: Weidenfeld & Nicolson, 1959), pp. 1-8.

5. Sims, *Victory at Sea,* pp. 203-204.

6. National Archives and Research Agency (hereafter NARA), Record Group 227 (hereafter RG 227), The Records of Division 6 of the National Defense Research Committee (hereafter Div 6), John T. Tate et al., *The Summary Technical Report of Division 6* (hereafter *STR Div 6*), Volume 1, pp. 9-11.

7. Walter M. Whitehill, *History of Headquarters Commander in Chief, United States Fleet, 1941-1945,* a manuscript history at the Operational Archives of the Naval Historical Center (hereafter: NHC). See also at NHC, *The Records of the Tenth Fleet, Antisubmarine Measures Division* (hereafter: Tenth Flt, ASM Div), Box 34, folder: Tenth Fleet, F.S. Low, Memorandum, subject: "Resume of Anti-Submarine Operations Against German U-Boats in World War II" and F. S. Low "Preliminary Draft given to W. M. Whitehill, Oct '44."

8. Ibid., also Tenth Fleet, Anti-Submarine Warfare Statistical and Analysis Section (hereafter: A & S Section), Box 43, Memorandum, no author indicated, dated 2 December 1942, subject: "Anti-Submarine Warfare—December 7, 1941 to December 7, 1942."

9. Captain S. W. Roskill, *The War at Sea: 1939-1945*, ed. J. R. M. Butler (London: Her Majesty's Stationery Office, 1956), pp. 135-136, 355.

10. Thomas B. Buell, *Master of Seapower* (Boston: Little, Brown and Company, 1980), pp. 54-122; Fleet Admiral Ernest J. King and Walter Muir Whitehill, *Fleet Admiral King, A Naval Record* (London: Eyre & Spottiswoode, 1953), pp. 40-87.

11. Library of Congress, *The Papers of Ernest Joseph King* (hereafter: LC, King Papers), Box 23, folders for Operations Problems I, II, & III and Tactical Problems I & II.

12. Ibid., Box 30, see draft article entitled "U.S. Naval Aviation" in the folder: US Naval Aviation—1935.

13. Ibid., Box 30, paper entitled "Naval Strategy and Tactics."

14. Ibid.

15. Doenitz, *Memoirs*, pp. 1-13.

16. Ibid., pp. 18-28.

17. Ibid., pp. 19-21, 29-36.

18. Ibid., p. 23.

19. Whitehill, *Fleet Admiral King*, pp. 92-93; see also LC, King Papers, Box 31, Ernest J. King to Commander W. M. Whitehill, USNR, 20 September 1950.

20. William T. Y'Blood, *Hunter-Killer* (Annapolis, Md.: Naval Institute Press, 1983), pp. 3-9; and Whitehill & King, *Fleet Admiral King*, pp. 237-239.

21. Ibid. I will use the terms sonar and asdic to refer to underwater echo-ranging gear improved between the wars by the development establishments in both the United States and the United Kingdom. The navies of both countries profited from the parallel development of this technology.

22. Doenitz, *Memoirs*, pp. 150-151, 115-117.

23. Ibid., pp. 75-99; and *Conduct of the War at Sea*, pp. 1-9.

24. Charles M. Sternhell and Alan M. Thorndike, *Anti-Submarine Warfare in World War II* (OEG Report No. 51) (Washington, DC: Office of the Chief of Naval Operations, 1946), pp. 7-15. This

report also was published as Volume Three of NDRC, Division 6's Summary Technical Report. Tate et al., *STR Div 6*, Vol. 1, p. 25.

25. Ibid., p. 13.

26. Ibid., pp. 84-88.

27. Ibid., p. 15; *STR Div 6*, Vol. 3, pp. 14, 22-24; and Roskill, *The War at Sea*, Vol. I, pp. 10-11, 46, 134-135, 350-351, 359.

28. Tate, *STR Div 6*, pp. 8-20, 84-89; and Roskill, *The War at Sea*, Vol. I, pp. 356-357.

29. NARA, RG 227, Div 6, Box 72, Minutes of Section Meetings Book I, *Report of Committee on the Submarine Problem*; and Box 42, *Draft History*, p. 5-2.

30. Ibid., RG 227, Div 6, Box 39, folder: Section C-4, *Steps in the Formation of Section C-4*, dated 6 September 1941.

31. Tate, et al., *STR Div 6*, Vol. I, pp. 21-22; see also NARA, Div 6, Box 42, *Draft History*.

32. NARA, NDRC Directors' Files, The Files of Frank B. Jewett (hereafter: Jewett Files), Box 1513, Folder: 49. C-4 Submarine Detection A and folder: 49. C-4.01.

33. NARA, RG 227, OSRD, Office of Field Services (hereafter OFS), Anti-Submarine Warfare Operations Research Group— ASWORG, "Review of Activity, 1 April 1942 to 31 August 1944," p. 5.

34. NARA, RG 227, Div 6, Box 59, "Material Brought Back from London by Dr. Tate—Rough Notes."

35. Ibid., NARA, RG 227, Div 6, Box 39, Bureau of Ships, "Memorandum of Conference Between Representatives of the Bureau of Ships and Section C-4 of the National Defense Committee," 5 September 1941.

36. NARA, RG 227, Div 6, Box 38, NDRC, Section C-4, Minutes of Meeting, 22 September 1941.

37. NARA, RG 227, Div 6, ASWORG, Review of Activity, p. 5; Tate, *STR Div 6*, Vol. 1, p. 81; and Div 6, Box 39, E.H. Colpitts, Memorandum for Dr. John T. Tate, 4 August 1941.

38. NARA, RG 227, Div 6, Folder: Memorandum to Rear Admiral Van Keuran, Navy Conference 9/5/41, Significant Steps in the Organization of the NDRC Submarine Detection Program.

39. NARA, RG 227, Div 6, Box 39, Research and Development Program, no author given.

40. NARA, RG 227, Div 6, Box 59, Memorandum of Meeting of NDRC on Sub-Surface Warfare, New London, Conn., 10 December 1941; Box 39, Memorandum: Conference at the US Navy Underwater Sound Laboratory at Fort Trumbull, New London, between representatives of the Bureau of Ships and Section C-4 of NDRC, 6 October 1941.

41. NARA, RG 227, Div 6, Box 59, John T. Tate. Memorandum to Dr. F.B. Jewett, 26 November 1941.

42. NARA, RG 227, Div 6, Box 42, "Draft History," pp. 4-2 to 4-22; and Div 6, Box 39, Summary of Projects Discussed, 10 December 1941; and *STR Div 6,* Vol. 3, p. 21.

43. NARA, RG 80, Secretary of the Navy—Chief of Naval Operations Files (hereafter: SecNav CNO Files), RADM R. K. Turner to Chief of Naval Operations, 8 November 1941, subject: Anti-Submarine Devices, Capt. H. W. Hill, Memo to Admiral Turner, 4 November 1941, Subject: Anti-Submarine Devices. These files are under file number A16-3(17) and are filed by year by file number.

Chapter 2

1. John T. Tate et al., *STR Div 6,* Volume III, p. 84, Figure 1.

2. Karl Doenitz, *Memoirs,* pp. 181-82.

3. Naval Historical Center (NHC), Doenitz, Karl, Admiral, *The Conduct of the War at Sea,* Division of Naval Intelligence, 1946, p. 18.

4. NARA, RG 457, Special Research History 009, "Allied Communications Intelligence and The Battle of the Atlantic," pp. 29, 85-88; and Thomas Parrish, *The Ultra Americans* (New York: Stein and Day, 1986), pp. 157-61.

5. See NARA, RG 457, SNRA 0204 and 0220.

6. NARA, RG 457, Special Research History 002, "War Secrets in The Ether," p. 152.

7. Captain S. W. Roskill, *The War at Sea,* Volume II, pp. 93-104; Doenitz, *Conduct of the War at Sea,* pp. 17-18; *Memoirs, Ten Years and Twenty Days* (London: Weidenfeld and Nicolson, 1958), p. 206; and Vice Admiral Friedrich Ruge, *Der Seekrieg,* Cdr. M. G. Saunders, trans. (Annapolis, Md.: US Naval Institute, 1957), pp. 252-53.

8. Roskill, *The War at Sea,* Volume II, p. 104; John T. Tate et al., *STR Div 6,* Volume III, p. 25; NARA, RG 227, The Records of the National Defense Research Committee (NDRC) Division 6, Box 58, Memorandum: Antisubmarine Warfare, Facts and Possibilities.

9. Montgomery C. Meigs, "This Must Mean the Philippines," *Proceedings,* August 1985, pp. 72-78.

10. A number of references give oblique and polite allusions to the extremes of character of Admiral King. See Buell, *Master of Seapower,* pp. 74, 88-89, 106, 111, 114, 131 for an excellent discussion of King's personality, based on extensive interviews and correspondence with officers who worked closely with King.

11. Buell, *Master of Seapower,* pp. 197, 235-37; Whitehill, *Fleet Admiral King,* pp. 114, 115, 146-47. Library of Congress (LC), King Papers, Box 31, Ernest J. King to Commander Walter M. Whitehill, 20 September 1951, and King to Whitehill, 12 December 1950.

12. Buell, *Master of Seapower,* pp. 155-57, 237-39; King and Whitehill, *Fleet Admiral King,* pp. 140-47.

13. This statement is a strong claim. The skeptical scholar should peruse the excellently kept records available at the Operational Archives of the Naval Historical Center. In the Double Zero Files of Commander in Chief, US Fleet (COMINCH), no comprehensive documents can be found concerning antisubmarine warfare that predate the conferences of mid-1943. These files were King's personal files. Nor are these types of materials to be found in the records of Tenth Fleet, the division created by Admiral King in May 1943 that took over antisubmarine warfare. Antisubmarine folders of the Secretary of the Navy, Chief of Naval Operations files available at the National Archives in RG 80 under file number A16-(3)17 offer no clues; nor do the COMINCH Double Zero Files at NARA. However, an informal study was prepared by Rear Admiral F. S. Low in October 1945. Low began his association with antisubmarine warfare in the fall of 1942 and commanded Tenth Fleet. See F. S. Low, "Resume of Anti-Submarine Operations Against the German U-Boats in World War II" in Box 34 of the Records of Tenth Fleet, Antisubmarine Measures Division. This paper by the officer most intimately involved with antisubmarine warfare states that the first all-encompassing statement of strategy came on 27 April 1943.

14. NARA, RG 313, CINCLANT Files, Box TS 554, folder: A14-1/Convoy, for the order signed by King to direct submarines to patrol stations in the Atlantic in November 1941; Box 596, folder: A4-2 January-May 1942. Baker's Memo is in NHC, Tenth Fleet, ASM Div, Box 27, Folder: Antisubmarine Measures Appreciation, and carries a date of 24 June 1942.

15. NARS, RG 227, Div 6, vol. 3, p. 28; NHC Rear Admiral J. M. Worthington, "Admiral Royal E. Ingersoll History," pp. 88, 279, 314-15, 338; NARA, RG 313, Box 324, folder: A16-3(20) Antisubmarine Warfare, E. J. King, letter, dated 24 January 1942, subject: Antisubmarine Tactics; folder: A16-3(21) Sub Warfare Unit Lant Flt, Record of Telephone Conversation, 7 February 1942, between RADM Lee, COMINCH, and Cmdr Moses, CINCLANT.

16. King & Whitehill, *Fleet Admiral King,* pp. 164-65, 239; NHC, Tenth Fleet, ASM Div, Box 34, W. M. Whitehill, Memorandum of conversation with Rear Admiral F. S. Low (FX-01), 19 September 1944.

17. For King on convoy vicinity, see Tenth Fleet, ASM Div, Box 34, Memorandum to the Secretary of the Navy, Subject: Antisubmarine Warfare; Organization of Special Air Task Forces; Tate et al., STR Div 6, Volume III, p. 28.

18. NARA, RG 313, CINCLANT Flag Files, Box 324: A16-3(20), E. J. King, COMINCH, letter, 24 January 1942, subject: Antisubmarine Tactics; W. D. Baker, to Commander in Chief Atlantic Fleet, subject: Anti-submarine Warfare, 7 March 1942; Record of Telephone Conversation between RADM Lee, COMINCH and Cdr Moses, CINCLANT, 7 March 1942; STR Div 6, Volume I, p. 80.

19. NHC, Tenth Fleet, Analysis & Statistics Section, Box 43, Serial 740, subject: Antisubmarine Warfare Unit—Establishment of.

20. NHC, Columbia University, Oral History Research Office, Admiral Royal E. Ingersoll, Memoir, p. 86-92; Rear Admiral J. M. Worthington, "Admiral R. E. Ingersoll," unpublished manuscript at NHC, pp. 279, 605; and "CINCLANT Administrative History" at the Department of the Navy Library at the Naval Historical Center, pp. 300-12.

21. Roskill, *War at Sea,* Volume II, pp. 97, 101.

22. NHC, Tenth Fleet, ASM Div, Box 34, F. S. Low, Memorandum, subject: Resume of Operations Against the German U-boats in World War II; and Philip M. Morse, *In at the Beginnings: A Physicist's Life* (Cambridge, Mass.: MIT Press, 1977), pp. 172-77.

23. Ibid., p. 29.

24. Ibid., pp. 31, 32.

25. Ibid.

26. NHC, COMINCH Double Zero Files, Box 42, R. S. Edwards, Memorandum for Admiral King, subject: Submarine Situation, dated 27 July 1942.

27. Ibid.

28. LC, The Papers of Julius A. Furer (hereafter: LC, Furer Papers), Diary, entries for 1 and 2 January 1942; and NARA, RG 227, Div 6, Box 38, Minutes of Section Meeting, 3 March 1942.

29. NHC, Tenth Fleet, ASM Div, Box 24, "Conference of Representatives of the Navy and Section C-4, NDRC, 12 March 1942"; NARA, RG 227, Div 6, Box 39, Folder: Navy Conference—3/12/42; Box 71, Minutes of Section Meetings—Book I, Minutes of Meeting on 1 June 1942; and Box 59, Folder: Subsurface Warfare Committee. For an example of conversion see RG 227, OSRD Special Subject File, Box 15, Karl T. Compton to V. Bush, 29 January 1942; and V. Bush to Dr. Karl T. Compton, 9 February 1942.

30. NARA, RG 227, Div 6, Box 39, Folder: Navy Conference—3/12/42.

31. NARA, RG 227, Div 6, Box 39. See folders on Navy Conferences and Miscellaneous Navy Conferences; Box 67, Folder: Project "61" SECRET, December 1941 to December 1943.

32. NARA, RG 227, Div 6, Box 71, Minutes of Section Meetings—Book I, Minutes of Meeting on 1 June 1942.

33. Tate et al, STR Div 6, Volume I, pp. 231-41.

34. Morse, *In at the Beginnings,* pp. 58, 172-74, 181-83; NARA, RG 313, CINCLANT Flag Files, Box 323, Folder: A16-3(20) Antisubmarine #2, Major C. F. Reynolds and J. R. Pelham, "Aircraft Attacks on U-boats"; CNH, Tenth Fleet, ASM Div, Box 24, Folder: ASW General Organization, Tactics, Doctrine, Training.

35. NARA, RG 227, Div 6, Box 58, Folder: General—Naval Liaison, Memorandum, "Antisubmarine Warfare, Facts, and Possibilities."

36. NARA, RG 227, Office of Field Services (hereafter: OFS), "Review of Activities," p. 38; Div 6, Box 70, Philip Morse, Memorandum: Proposals for Systematic Tests of Antisubmarine Attack Procedures; see also Morse, *In at the Beginnings,* pp. 171-82.

37. NARA, RG 227, Div 6, Box 58, Folder: General—Naval Liaison, Memorandum: Antisubmarine Warfare, Facts and Possibilities. See also NHC, Command File, ASWORG, Preliminary Report on the Submarine Search Problem, 1 May 1942; and the Papers of Rear Admiral Paul R. Heineman, Box 6, US COMINCH, "Searching for Submarines."

38. NHC, Tenth Fleet, ASM Div, Box 24.

39. NARA, RG 227, Div 6, Box 60, Folder: G-OSRD Mission, V. O. Knudsen, V. O. Knudsen to John T. Tate, 15 July 1942.

40. NARA, RG 227, Div 6, Box 58, Folder: General—Naval Liaison, John T. Tate to Dr. Vannevar Bush, 14 July 1942, with enclosure: "Antisubmarine Warfare, The Job of Planning and Improving its Conduct."

41. The Diary of Henry L. Stimson, Sterling Library, Yale University, microfilm edition (hereafter Stimson Diary), entry for 16 February 1942. I am indebted to the discussions of this issue that appear in Henry L. Stimson and McGeorge Bundy, *On Active Service in Peace and War* (New York: Harper Brothers, 1948), p. 506; and Elting Morison, *Turmoil and Tradition* (Boston: Houghton Mifflin, 1960), pp. 566-68.

42. Stimson Diary, entry for 14 April 1942.

43. Ibid., 7 June 1942.

44. Ibid., 7 July 1942.

45. Edward L. Bowles interview on 11 May 1982, notes in author's possession; Stimson and Bundy, *On Active Service,* pp. 464-69; Morison, *Turmoil and Tradition,* pp. 561-64; and Stimson Diary, entries for 11 March 1942 and 1 April 1942.

46. Arthur B. Ferguson, "The AAF in the Battle of the Atlantic" in Wesley Frank Craven and James Lea Cate, eds., *The Army Air Forces in World War II, Volume I* (Chicago: University of Chicago Press, 1948), pp. 526-41; and Stimson Diary, entries for 16 February 1942 and 5 and 20 May 1942.

47. NARA, RG 80, Secretary of the Navy—Chief of Naval Operations File (hereafter: SecNav/CNO File), Box 322, Note: FK to Admiral King, undated.

48. Stimson Diary, entry for 7 July 1942; and NARA, RG 107, Files of Assistant Secretary of War for Air, Memorandum for the Secretary of the Navy, 29 June 1942, subject: Control of Submarine Warfare; NARA, RG 80, Box 322, Frank Knox, Memo-

randum for the Secretary of War, 14 August 1942, Subject: Control of Submarine Warfare; and Henry L. Stimson to Dear Frank, 8 September 1942, with attached memo from Knox and Vice Admiral R. S. Edwards.

49. Ibid.

50. See note 25.

51. Ferguson, "The AAF in The Battle of the Atlantic, pp. 534-35.

52. NARA, RG 218, Records of the Joint Chiefs of Staff, CCS 476.1 (6-25-42) Antisubmarine Weapons, Report on Antisubmarine Devices, Part III, 22 July 1942.

53. Stimson Diary, entry for 23 July 1942.

Chapter 3

1. NHC, BdU War Logs, "Estimate of U-boat Situation," 18 November 1942; and Situation Report for 19 December 1942.

2. NARA, RG 457, SRH 009, "The Battle of the Atlantic, Vol. 1," pp. 34-49; SRH 008, "The Battle of the Atlantic, Vol. II," p. 113; John T. Tate et al, *STR Div 6,* Vol. III, p. 39; and Samuel E. Morison, *The Battle of the Atlantic* (Boston: Little, Brown & Company, 1947), p. 314.

3. NHC, BdU War Logs, 2 October 1942.

4. Ibid., pp. 42, 44.

5. NARA, RG 457, SRH 009, p. 25.

6. The British cryptanalytic agency, called the Government Code and Cypher School, moved about the start of World War II to a Victorian house on an estate called Bletchley Park in the town of Bletchley, about 45 miles northwest of London. Its codebreakers included members of famous families and others who later became famous in their own right: chess champions, novelists, publishers, and mathematicians such as Alan Turning, who first expressed the fundamental concept of the electronic computer, and Gordon Welchman, who devised what he called the "diagonal board" that enabled the reading of more German messages faster. "The place glowed white-hot with talent," says David Kahn in *Kahn on Codes: Secrets of the New Cryptology* (New York: Macmillan Publishing Company, 1983), p. 110.

7. NARA, RG 457, SRH 009, pp. 29, 85-86; SRH 025; F. H. Hinsley, *British Intelligence in the Second World War* (New York:

Cambridge University Press, 1981), volume II, pp. 163-179, 551, 561.

8. NARA, RG 457, SRH 008, *The Battle of the Atlantic,* Vol. II, pp. 7-11, 18, 19.

9. NARA, Div 6 Records, Box 42, "Draft History," p. 6-16; Tate et al., *STR Div 6,* Vol. III, pp. 13 & 30; CNH, BdU War Logs, 11 June, 1 & 15 July, and 3 September 1942.

10. Ibid., 21 August 1942; see also Karl Doenitz, *Memoirs* (London: Weidenfeld and Nicolson, 1958) p. 253. One must read Doenitz's *Memoirs* with some care, for he often claims in retrospect to have had a steadier hand and better strategic insight than the entries in his War Diaries will support. It is not really clear how well Doenitz understood the threat posed to the operational invisibility of his U-boats by radar-equipped aircraft.

11. Doenitz, *Memoirs,* p. 354.

12. Tate et al., *STR Div 6,* Vol. 3, pp. 30, 31; Doenitz, *Memoirs,* pp. 95, 233, 253, 270, 353; CNH, Admiral Karl Doenitz, *Conduct of the War at Sea,* p. 33.

13. Doenitz, *Memoirs,* pp. 233-238, 243.

14. NHC, WWII Command File, ASWORG, Memorandum 43, 1 November 1943, p. 12; NARA, RG 313, CINCLANT Files, Box 597, RADM Martin K. Metcalf, "History of Convoy and Routing."

15. John M. Waters, *Bloody Winter* (Annapolis, Md.: Naval Institute Press, 1984), pp. 76-78; Marc Milner, *North Atlantic Run* (Annapolis, Md.: Naval Institute Press), pp. 177-180.

16. Donald Macintyre, *The Battle of the Atlantic* (New York: The Macmillan Company, 1961), pp. 148-166; Captain S. W. Roskill, *The War at Sea, Vol. II* (London: Her Majesty's Stationery Office, 1956), pp. 199-215; NARA, RG 227, OFS, ASWORG, *Review of Activity,* p. 16.

17. *Operation Torch* was a British proposal to invade French North Africa, approved by President Roosevelt to "help Russia" by opening a Second Front as soon in the war as possible. The *Torch* invasion started on 8 November 1942 and continued until 14 February 1943. After a rocky start, and absorption of some tough lessons by the Americans, the Tunisian campaign showed that American and British forces could fight efficiently as one team under one commander against a common enemy. See F.D.R., Memorandum for the: no subject, dated 6 May 1942, President's Safe File, Franklin D. Roosevelt Library, Hyde Park, N.Y.

18. Doenitz, *Memoirs,* pp. 276-277; Roskill, *The War at Sea,* pp. 212, 213, 314-328; The Naval Historical Collection, The Naval War College, Thomas B. Buell & Walter M. Whitehill Historical Collection, Cornelius Bull's Notes, 30 November 1942.

19. For the quotation see: NHC, Tenth Fleet, ASM Div, Box 3, Folder A16 (3). Commander Destroyers, US Atlantic Fleet to Commander in Chief US Atlantic Fleet, Subject: Anti-Submarine Warfare-Recommended Changes in Policy, 12 February 1943; NARA, RG 313, CINCLANT Flag Files, Box 379, Folder A16-3(2), Anti-Submarine Warfare Information, T. L. Lewis to Commander in Chief United States Fleet, 15 March 1943, "Condensed Step by Step Conning Procedure."

20. Tate et al., *STR Div 6,* Vol. III, pp. 34-36, Samuel E. Morison, *The Battle of the Atlantic,* pp. 303-326, 403-409.

21. Morison, Samuel E., *The Atlantic Battle Won* (Boston: Little Brown & Company, 1975), pp. 16-20; Naval Historical Collection, Buell Whitehill Collection, Box 4, R.E.Libby, Memorandum to Fleet Admiral King, 12 February 1946, Subject: Notes Covering Period 7 December 1941 to Casablanca; see also Cornelius Bull's Notes for 30 November 1942 and 19 February 1943.

22. NARA, RG 107, Files of Edward L. Bowles, Expert Consultant to the Secretary of War: General, Vannevar Bush to Edward L. Bowles, 7 November 1943.

23. NARA, RG 313, CINCLANT Flag Files, Box 379, folder: A16-3(2) Anti-Sub Warfare Information, T.L. Lewis to Dear Bill, 3 January 1943. Ingersoll presents an enigma for naval historians. S.E. Morison dedicated his second volume about the Battle of the Atlantic to him, yet Thomas Buell reports in *Master of Seapower* that King believed Ingersoll contributed little to the antisubmarine campaign. Ingersoll added to the dilemma. He left no papers, and his family reports that after retirement he put aside his military interests and rarely spoke of the war. In the vagaries of the preservation of CINCLANT records, Ingersoll's private and secret working flag correspondence has either disappeared or has been inadvertently concealed in the masses of paper that still exist. There are, however, some faint footprints in the sand. Ingersoll was a loyal, highly principled man. On occasion he came to Washington and met with King. There also is in the index cards to the COMINCH Secret Files in RG 38 at NARA at least one reference to an Ingersoll letter hand-carried to Admiral Edwards for King's and

Edwards' eyes only. The yeoman making the entry only found out about the letter indirectly. It is not in the files. There also are throughout these files, particularly under numbers A14-1 and A16-3(9), see Boxes 255 & 259, letters from Ingersoll that are specific and blunt and deferentially suggest how COMINCH might better support CINCLANT's operations. I suspect that Ingersoll knew King well and understood that in order to be able to disagree privately with King, something he probably did often, he had to maintain the lowest of public profiles. Admiral Royall E. Ingersoll was most likely one of those rare men who followed the rule that the greatest results come from men who do not care who gets the credit.

24. NHC, Tenth Fleet, ASM Division, Box 35, Folder: Tenth Fleet Organization, Memorandum for Admiral Edwards, 25 January 1943, no author cited.

25. NARA, RG 38, Records of COMINCH-1943, folder: A16-3(9) Submarine & Anti-Submarine Warfare; J.P.W. Vest, Memorandum to Assistant Chief of Staff (Operations), 5 January 1943.

26. Ibid., J.M. Haines, Memorandum to Assistant Chief of Staff (Operations), 8 January 1943, Subject: Anti-Submarine Warfare—Strategical Analysis; RG 227, Files of the Office of Field Services (OFS), Boxes 284-282.

27. NHC, Tenth Fleet, ASW A & S Section, Box 43, folder: Anti-Submarine Warfare 41-42.

28. NHC, Naval Department Library, Commander in Chief Atlantic Fleet, *United States Naval Administration in World War II,* Vol. I, pp. 467-469, 495; and Vol. II, p. 159.

29. NHC, Tenth Fleet, ASM Division, A & S Section, Box 263, Folder A16-3, US Lant Flt, Anti-Submarine Warfare Unit, Serial 0520, 12 June 1943.

30. NARA, RG 457, SRH 009, p. 50.

31. Hinsley, *British Intelligence in the Second World War,* Vol. II, p. 608; CINCLANT Administrative History, pp. 464, 465.

32. Ibid.

33. NHC, Records of the Strategic Plans Division, Box 37, Admiral Ernest J. King, Address to the Atlantic Convoy Conference, 1 March 1943.

34. Ibid.

35. NHC, COMINCH Double Zero Files, Combined Staff Planners, *Measures for Combating the Submarine Menace,* 1 March 1943. For Bowles' argument see his paper delivered to the conference. Dated 8 March 1943, it is in Box 37 of the Files of the Strategic Plans Division.

36. NHC, COMINCH Double Zero Files, Combines Staff Planners, *Measures for Combating the Submarine Menace,* 1 March 1943. 37. NHC, Tenth Fleet, ASM Division, Boxes 34 and 35, see especially the folders marked "Tenth Fleet" and "Tenth Fleet – Organization." A number of memoranda indicate a movement in January and February to get a change to the command structure. See also: NARA, RG 218, Records of the United States Joint Chiefs of Staff, Lt. Abbot Smith, "History of the Joint Chiefs of Staff," pp. 106-121.

38. These files appear in several places. See NARA, RG 165, Records of the War Department General and Special Staffs, W.D.C.S.A. Anti-Submarine Operations, Edward L. Bowles, Memorandum for General Marshall, 1 March 1943, subject: "The Acute Problem of Ocean-Borne Transport and Supply." Bowles' Report, supporting memoranda, and ensuing correspondence of the next three months are found here. See also: NHC, COMINCH Double Zero Files, Box 42. King's subordinates had copies of all of the correspondence between Marshall and Stimson and their subordinates.

39. NARA, RG 165, D.C.S.A. 560, H.L.S., Memorandum for General Marshall, 14 March 1943. Stimson's Diaries for March and April 1943, see especially the entries for 25, 26, and 29 March and 1 April. Other sets of correspondence concerning these issues are in RG 38, COMINCH Secret Files for 1942 and 1943, Boxes 255, 260, & 672.

40. Bowles quotes Marshall on page 1 of his memorandum cited above.

41. This memorandum is in the correspondence cited above; however, its significance is highlighted by its presence in CNH, Tenth Fleet, ASM Div, Box 35, Tenth Fleet – Organization. For a history of the Army Air Force Anti-Submarine Command during this period, see Arthur B. Ferguson, "The Anti-Submarine Command" in *The Army Air Forces in World War II,* Frank Wesley Craven & James Lea Cate eds. (Chicago: University of Chicago Press, 1949).

42. Forrest Pogue, Marshall's biographer, told me in an interview that in interviewing General Marshall, when the discussions

touched on matters critical of individuals, a hard stare signaled that the interviewer should move on. For Marshall to make an "on the record" criticism of the Navy's performance of its duty was rare indeed.

43. NHC, Tenth Fleet, ASM Div, Box 36, W.D. Sample, Memorandum for Admiral Low, 19 June 1943; and Double Zero File, COMINCH, Box 38, Folder: Gen. Marshall/ADM King—A/S Air.

44. NARA, RG 38, HQ COMINCH, Folder: A16-3(9), Admiral E. J. King, Memorandum for the Secretary of the Navy . . . delivered by hand by Admiral King to the Secretary of the Navy, 4 April 1943.

45. The relevant documents are at NHC, Tenth Fleet, ASM Div, Box 34, Folder: Tenth Fleet; see especially Low's Resume on Anti-Submarine Operations Against German U-Boats in World War II. See Low's *Memoir* in the Buell, Whitehill Collection. Interview by the author with Eugene L. Bowles, 11 May 1982, in author's possession. In a letter to King in May 1942, Ingersoll proposed alternatives very similar to those adopted by Low in 1943. See NARA, RG 38, Box 259, Admiral R. E. Ingersoll to Commander in Chief United States Fleet, 26 May 1943.

46. For King's thinking at this point see Cornelius Bull's Notes for 5 April 1943, in the Thomas Buell/W. M. Whitehill Research Collection in the Naval Historical Collection at the Naval War College Library. A number of papers cover the period of the formation of Tenth Fleet. Both Samuel E. Morison's *The Atlantic Battle Won* and Whitehill's *Fleet Admiral King* treat this topic deferentially. The Navy's program was in a shambles, and they knew it. See the materials in NHC, Tenth Fleet, Div. Box 27, Folder: Anti-Submarine Measures (Appreciation and Summary); Box 34; and Box 35, Folder: Tenth Fleet Organization. For Roosevelt's displeasure see NHC, Double Zero File, Box 1, Fleet Admiral Leahy; in the two memos of Leahy to King dated 18 March 1943 and 3 April 1943, note the wording.

47. Ibid.; also Box 34, Folder: Tenth Fleet, Box 35, Folder Tenth Fleet—Organization, and Box 36. See also, Box 40, Folder: Research Council Correspondence, V. Bush to Admiral Ernest J. King, 20 April 1943. ASWORG, "Review of Activities," p. 17; and *STR Div 6,* Vol. 1, p. 93.

48. In addition to the references cited above see: JEJ, "Anti-Submarine Conference held by Mr. Jewett in New York, April 20, 1943"; no author cited but probably John T. Tate, "Aspects of

Antisubmarine Warfare," both in NARA, RG 227, Div 6, General Technical Records, 1941-46, Box 63. See also Digest of Minutes, Conference on Anti-Submarine Warfare #10, 9 March 1943 in Div 6, General Admin Records, 1941-46, Navy Conferences, Box 39.

49. Ibid. *Aspects of Antisubmarine Warfare,* Edward L. Bowles, Memorandum to General Marshall, 3 March 1943, subject: Recommendations—Army Air Antisubmarine Effort, in NARA, RG 165, Army Chief of Staff Decimal Files, 560, Box 98, Entry 13.

50. NHC, World War II Command Files, ASWORG Memorandum 34, 24 June 1943, a document that obviously builds on Morse's comments in the Antisubmarine Conference Report of 20 April 1943 cited above. For SC 121, Tenth Fleet, ASM Div, Box 5, Folder A16(12) Analysis of Attacks (SM). NARA, RG 227 OSRB Director's Special Subject Correspondence Files, Folder: Submarines—Anti-submarine Research Program, Memorandum Report on the Anti-submarine Research Program of NDRC as of 15 April 1943.

51. Ibid., NARA, RG 227, John T. Tate, Memorandum to Dr. Vannevar Bush, 1 March 1943, subject: Present Status of the More Important Anti-Submarine Weapons Under Development by Divisions 3 and 6; JEJ, *Antisubmarine Conference; STR Div 6,* pp. 41-41.

52. Ibid.

Chapter 4

1. One can find the entire correspondence on this contentious issue in several locations: NARA, RG 165, Decimal Files, WDCSA 560; NHC, Commander in Chief US Fleet Double Zero Files, or in the Samuel Eliot Morison Papers. See also Stimson Diary entries for 29 March; 1, 4, and 14 April; 26 May; and 14 and 15 June 1943.

2. Ibid., Box 35, Folder: Tenth Fleet Operation Plan and Folder: Tenth Fleet Organization, see R. S. Edwards, Memorandum for Staff Study, 30 April 1943, subject: Establishment of Tenth Fleet; Box 45, folder: FX 43, Analysis of Attacks.

3. Ibid., Box 27, Folder: Antisubmarine Measures (Appreciation and Summary) contains Low's "Appreciation" and feedback from members of the staff asked for comment. For a comment on Low's personality, see NHC, Morison Papers, Box 71, folder: Morison, S. E., Rear Admiral, Notes on Interviews, Interview with Captain Vest at Bridgeport, Conn., 18 December.

4. NARA, RG 107, Secretary of War Decimal Files, 400.01, Submarine-Sadu, Dr. Bowles' Sadu Papers, Atlantic Fleet Confidential Letter 8CL-43, 1 April 1943; RG 227, OSRD Director's Special Subject Files, Box 15, COMINCH Serial 0355, 3 February 1943, subject: Aircraft Antisubmarine Warfare Detachment—Establishment of and in The Records of Division 6 of NDRC, Box 687, Progress Report of Group M, Division 6, 9 September 1943, Volume III. NHC, Tenth Fleet, Box 34, folder: Tenth Fleet, F. S. Low, Memorandum for File with W. M. Whitehill's note, "Preliminary Draft given to me by Rear Admiral Low October 1944."

5. For the Antisubmarine Warfare Unit, see: NARA, RG 38, COMINCH confidential files for 1942, '43 and '44 under file numbers: A16-3(41) & A16-(42). Morison states that with the formation of Tenth Fleet, "For the first time naval pilots and crewmen, technicians, and men of science worked side by side in the same detail with one purpose." See *Atlantic Battle Won,* p. 50. Morison is wrong on two counts. Airmen, sailors, and scientists had been working together for a year in Ingersoll's Antisubmarine Warfare Unit. The critical distinction involves institutional authority. ASDevLant's (Antisubmarine Development, Atlantic) relation to Commander Tenth Fleet gave the results the sponsorship of the Commander in Chief US Fleet. This relationship fundamentally changed the rules of the game. Institutional guerrilla warfare was no longer required to get things done. When Low approved a recommendation from ASDevLant and had it published over King's signature, it became Navy policy. Furthermore, for over a year, the Army Air Force had a combined team of airmen and scientists working for the First Bomber Command at Langley Field. They did a good deal of early work to develop search and attack techniques for long-range bombers, first on B-18s and later on B-24s. With Marshall's agreement to take the Air Force out of antisubmarine warfare, the group at Langley broke up, and many of the scientists and operational analysts went to work for the Navy. See also: NHC, Tenth Fleet, ASM Div, Box 34, folder: Tenth Fleet, E. J. King, Serial 01550, subject: Antisubmarine Measures, 19 May 1943. Low in his *Resume* calls this the "standard directive for A/S warfare from its issue until the end of the war."

6. Philip M. Morse, *In At The Beginnings,* p. 184; and NARA, RG 227, Office of Field Services, *ASWORG: Review of Activity,* p. 17.

7. NHC, Navy Department Library, Commander in Chief Atlantic Fleet, "United States Naval Administration in World War II," first draft narrative, Volume I, pp. 485-87.

Notes to pages 118-127   237

8. NARA, RG 457, SRH 008, *The Battle of the Atlantic,* Volume II, p. 123.

9. NHC, Tenth Fleet, ASM Div, Box 34, folder: Tenth Fleet, COMINCH Serial 01550, 19 May 1943.

10. Ibid., F. S. Low, "Preliminary Draft," October 1944.

11. Thomas Parrish, *The Ultra Americans* (New York: Stein and Day, 1986), pp. 160-61. For King's message to the Admiralty, COMINCH to Admiralty, 251628 April 1943, the original copy is in the Ernest J. King Papers, NHC, Box 13, Folder: Antisubmarine OPS Against German U-Boat WWII.

12. For the best description of how Ultra was derived see: NARA, RG 457, SRH-368, "Evaluation of the Role of Decryption Intelligence in the Operational Phase of the Battle of the Atlantic," pp. 10, 11,

13. NARA, RG 218, Records of the Joint Chiefs of Staff, CCS 476.1, Joint Staff Planners, Note: Devices for Antisubmarine Warfare, 8 March 1943 with enclosure and RG 227, Div 6, Box 689, Completion Report, Contract #OEMsr-20 Vol. III. NHC, Tenth Fleet, ASM Div., Box 4, Folder: S68(2) Instructions—Magnetic Anomaly Detector (2) and A & S Section, Box 47, Folder: ASM Conferences (1), Digest of Minutes, Conference #17, 15 June 1943.

14. NARA, RG 227, Div 6, Box 689, Memorandum for File, Expendible Radio Sono-Buoy and MAD Submarine Search Test, April 1943. NHC, Post-World War II Command File, University of Pittsburgh Staff, "The History of the United States Naval Research and Development in World War II," draft manuscript, pp. 1194, 1194fl.

15. NARA, RG 227, *STR Div 6,* p. 40; RG 298, Records of the Office of Naval Research, Coordinator of Research and Development, Box 38, John T. Burwell, Report of Conference, 3 July 1943; and NHC, University of Pittsburgh History, pp. 1114, 1114a.

16. NARA, RG 227, Div 6, Box 42, "Draft History," pp. 6-23, 6-24; NHC, Post-World War II Command File, ASWORG Memoranda 34, 38, 39, & 41; Tenth Fleet, A & S Section, Box 47, Digest of Minutes, Antisubmarine Conference #21, 10 August 1943. RG 298, Coordinator of Research and Development, J. T. Burwell to Admiral J. A. Furer, 9 March 1943, subject: Attendance at Meeting in New York of Division 6, NDRC, on 8 March 1943.

17. Eberhard Rossler, *The U-boat, The Evolution and Technical History of German Submarines,* Harold Erenberg, trans. (London: Arms and Armour Press, 1981), pp. 154-68.

18. RG 457, SRH 008, 69-77; SRMN-037, COMINCH File: U-Boat Intelligence Summaries, January 1943-May 1945, pp. 37-39. Captain S. W. Roskill, *The War at Sea 1939-1945,* Volume II (London: Her Majesty's Stationery Office, 1956), pp. 362-82; and Morison, *Atlantic Battle Won,* pp. 65-84.

19. Ibid., RG 457, SRMN-037, pp. 54, 55 & 67, 68.

20. NHC, COMINCH Double Zero File, Box 50, CTU 24.3.10 to CINCLANT, messages 141656, 201814, & 211128 May 1943; COMINCH to CINCLANT, 291853 May 1943.

21. Ibid., Roskill, *War at Sea,* pp. 373-82; and NARA, RG 457, SRMN 037, pp. 49-51.

22. SRH-008, p. 77.

23. RG 457, SRH-008, p. 74.

24. NHC, BdU War Logs, To All Boats Message #1769, 24 May 1943.

25. Roskill, *War at Sea,* Vol. III, pp. 380-81; and RG 457, SRMN-037, pp. 53-68.

26. A number of different sources make different claims about reasons for Allied success in convoy battles of May and April. Roskill, *War at Sea,* Vol. II, pp. 376-79 rightly notes the contribution of air and surface escort groups. Doenitz in *Conduct of the War at Sea* gives credit to Allied strength in the air and to radar; see p. 23 and *Memoirs,* p. 332. Samuel E. Morison highlights the combination of weapons and the emergence of escort carriers as well as efforts of surface and air escorts; see *Atlantic Battle Won,* pp. 81-84. But in terms of casualties inflicted on the Germans, escort carriers played only a supporting role; their significant contribution came later, after the critical spring battles. While noting the contribution of jeep carriers, the Administrative History done by the CINCLANT staff after the war emphasized the turn in the weather, the Royal Navy's campaign in the North Atlantic, and the Biscay campaign. The numbers seem to support this view and that of Roskill. The most readily available tally of U-boats killed is in US Naval History Division, US Submarine Losses—World War II (Washington, DC: US Government Printing Office, 1963), pp. 159-74.

27. NARA, RG 227, OSRD Director's Special Subject Correspondence Files, Box 15, V. Bush to Dr. Frank Jewett, 9 April 1943.

28. Ibid., Notes on British Mission of Dr. Vannevar Bush, 7 July-29 July 1943.

29. Ibid., NHC, COMINCH Double Zero File, Box 50, see messages from ComASDevLant to ComTenthFlt; Tenth Fleet, ASM Div, Box 27, folder: Antisubmarine Measures (Appreciation & Summary), Draft Memorandum, subject: Study of Counter Measures to Antisubmarine Action, 17 July 1943; Box 28, folder: A/S Miscellaneous, F. S. Low, Memorandum to the Admiral, 9 September. NARA, RG 227, OFS, ASWORG, "Review of Activities," p. 37.

30. See NARA, RG 457, SRMN-037, look through the Intelligence Summaries for June and July 1943. NARA, Div 6, "Draft History," 5-52, 5-53 explains how in one instance scientists responded to a hypothetical threat with work directly applicable to a real problem.

31. NHC, Post-World War II Command file, ASWORG Memorandum 42, "Countermeasures to the Acoustic Torpedo," 20 November 1945; US Fleet Antisubmarine Bulletin, November 1942; COMINCH Double Zero File, Box 51, ASDevLant to Com-Tenth Flt, 1222103 and 122152 October 1943. Compare the information contained in all three of these documents. For antiradar tactics see the University of Pittsburgh History, pp. 1436-1439 in the same files.

32. NARA, RG 38, COMINCH Top Secret Files, Box 672, F.S. Low for COMINCH to Commander in Chief US Atlantic Fleet, 21 October 1943, subject: Aircraft with Special Equipment for U-boat Radar Investigation.

33. There is a tendency to attribute too much of the Allies' success in this area to Ultra. The scientists knew that the source of a good deal of their information came from other than "DF" or POW reports. Often Group M received operational data they knew to be more accurate than design capabilities of the Allies' direction finding equipment. Morse confronted Low with this information and was let in on the secret. This insight had two results. Because Morse had great confidence in his operational data, he and his subordinates had more confidence in their findings. Plus he knew the significance of a hypothetical question from Low concerning the possibility of the Germans acquiring a new type of weapon. See Morse, *In at the Beginnings,* pp. 184-86.

34. Rossler, *The U-boat,* p. 196; NARA, RG 457, pp. 180-184; SRH-008, *The Battle of the Atlantic,* Vol. II, pp. 144-147, SRH-024, *The Battle of the Atlantic,* Vol. IV, pp. 6-12.

35. Ibid., pp. 198-204.

36. Ibid., pp. 205-12; Doenitz, *Memoirs,* pp. 341-57; NARA, RG 457, SRH-009, *The Battle of the Atlantic,* Vol. I, pp. 63, 74.

37. Rossler, *The U-boat,* pp. 208-212.

38. Ibid., pp. 214-234.

39. Rossler, *The U-boat,* p. 224.

40. Ibid., pp. 145, 146, 196.

41. NARA, RG 227, *STR Div 6,* Vol. III, pp. 54-56; RG 457, SRMN-037, pp. 22-30, Rossler, *The U-boat,* pp. 188-194.

42. Morison, *Atlantic Battle Won,* pp. 110-111.

43. NHC, Tenth Fleet, A & S Section, Box 45, Folder: Escort Groups and Supports Groups, Message: COMINCH to CINCLANT, 14 June 1943; Box 48, folder: Tenth Fleet Organization: Message: COMTENTHFLT to CINCLANT, 3 July 1943; Morison Papers, Box 71, folder: Morison, S. E., RADM, Notes on Interviews, Admiral Morison's Interview with Captain Vest at Bridgeport, Conn. 18 December 1954.

44. NARA, RG 457, SRH-008, *The Battle of the Atlantic,* Vol. II, pp. 105-06, 125, 132-44, 149-51; SRMN-037, pp. 100-103.

45. Morison, *Atlantic Battle Won,* pp. 117-19; NHC, COMINCH Double Zero File, Box 50, USS *SANTEE* to COMINCH, 031545, July 1943, CINCLANT to COMINCH, 231634 June 1943, COMINCH to CINCLANT, 101517 July 1943, COMTENTHFLT to CINCLANT, 171923 July 1943. See also NARA, RG 457, SRMN-037, pp. 107-11. WNRC, The Files of OP-312, Accession Number 10613, 2/82:31-2-1, see the envelope for incident #4900.

46. NARA, RG 457, SRMN-037, pp. 134-40; Worthington, Ingersoll History, pp. 427, 563. NHC, COMINCH Double Zero File, Box 39, Folder: Memoranda to Admiral, January 1943-September 1944, F. S. Low, Memorandum for the Admiral, 11 August 1943.

47. NARA, RG 457, SRH-024, *The Battle of the Atlantic,* Vol. IV, pp. 23, 30.

48. NARA, RG 457, SRMN-037, pp. 172-87.

49. Ibid., p. 190.

50. Ibid., pp. 196-248; SRH-025, pp. 40-42; RG 227, *STR Div 6*, Vol. III, pp. 54-56; Doenitz, *Memoirs*, pp. 418-20. Roskill, *The War at Sea*, Vol. III, Part I, pp. 37-57; Morison, *Atlantic Battle Won*, pp. 153-77.

Chapter 5

1. NHC, Commander, Submarine Force, Atlantic Fleet, *History of United States Naval Administration in World War II—Submarine Commands*, p. 320, World War II Command File, Commander Submarine Force, US Pacific Fleet, *Submarine Operational History, World War II*, pp. ii, 552.

2. NHC, Operational Archives, World War II, pp. 507-11, 531-33, 588, 640-41; Norman Polmar, *The American Submarine* (Annapolis, Md.: The Nautical and Aviation Publishing Company of America, 1983), p. 59.

3. NARA, RG 80, SecNav-CNO Files, Box 322, A16-3(23), FF6-4, War Activities, US Submarines, Asiatic Fleet, 1 December 1941 to 1 April 1942; NHC, Submarine Operational History, pp. 2-5, 108.

4. Ibid., pp. 103-08, 124-26.

5. Clay Blair, *Silent Victory* (Philadelphia: J. P. Lippincott, 1975), p. 359-61.

6. NHC, Nimitz Command Summary, Estimate of Situation for 24 December 1941 with changes to 28 December 1941.

7. Ibid., entries for 19 February 1942, 15 April 1942, 16 June 1942, and the Estimate of Situation for 26 May 1942 and An Estimate of Enemy Intentions, August 1942; also *Submarine Operational History*, pp. 25-28, to substantiate that senior submariners in theater understood the problem.

8. Ibid., Estimate of Capabilities, 1 October 1942; see also the entry for 22 November 1942 and Serial 222125, CINCPAC to COMINCH; *US Strategic Bombing Survey (Pacific)*, Naval Analysis Division, *The Campaigns of the Pacific War* (Washington, DC: US Government Printing Office, 1946), pp. 60, 105-25; NHC, *Submarine Operational History*, pp. 18-25.

9. Strategic Bombing Survey, *Campaign of the Pacific War*, pp. 378-81; NHC, "Submarine Operational History," p. 262.

10. Ibid., p. 49.

11. Blair, *Silent Victory*, pp. 359-61; Samuel E. Morison, *Breaking the Bismarks Barrier, 22 July 1942 – 1 May 1944* (Boston: Little Brown and Co., 1954), p. 5; and John Costello, *The Pacific War* (New York: Rawson, Wade Publishers Inc. 1981), pp. 453-55.

12. NHC, *Submarine Operational History*, p. 29; and King Papers, Box 1, Folder: Conference Notes, see entries for 29 February 1943.

13. NHC, *Submarine Operational History*, pp. 41-46, ii 654-ii 663; King Papers, Box 10, folder: Conference Notes, entries for 30 May 1943; LC, The Papers of VADM Charles A. Lockwood, Box 13, folder: Official Correspondence, April 1943, Capt J. B. Griggs to Dear Jimmy, 22 March 1943.

14. LC, Lockwood Papers, Box 13; and NHC, *Submarine Operational History*, pp. 39-40.

15. LC, Lockwood Papers, Box 13, see Lockwood's correspondence with Griggs, Comstock, and ADM Edward L. Cochrane for the months of April, June, and July 1943.

16. Ibid.; also see Lockwood's letter to "Dear Frog" of 22 August 1943 in the folder entitled Official Correspondence, August 1943.

17. NCH, *Submarine Operational History*, pp. 403, 404; COMINCH Double Zero File, F. S. Low, Memorandum for the Admiral, 27 August 1942, "PRIVATE"; and Tenth Fleet, ASM Div, Box 28, Folder: A/S Miscellaneous, F. S. Low, Memorandum for Admiral Edwards, 29 August 1943.

18. NARA, RG 38, COMINCH Files, Box 672, E. J. King to Chief of the Bureau of Ordnance and Chief of the Bureau of Ships, 2 August 1943.

19. NARA, RG 227, Div 6, Box 62, Folder: Pro-Submarine Program, G. P. Harnwell to E. H. Colpitts, Memorandum, subject: Pro-Submarine Aspect, Training Group, Section 6.1, NDRC Program, 15 December 1943; Box 689, Final Report on Contract OEM sr-20. RG 298, Records of the Coordinator of Research and Development, Report of Conference on Proposed Development Program for New and Improved Submarine Equipment, 14 September 1943. NHC, *Submarine Operational History*, pp. ii 405-ii 420.

20. NARA, RG 227, Div 6, Box 62, Folder: Secret, Pro-Submarine Program, Elmer Hutchinson to Dr. G. P. Harnwell, 17 December 1943.

21. NCH, *Submarine Operational History*, pp. ii 404, ii 405; Tenth Fleet, ASM Div, Box 40, Folder: Research Council—Correspondence.

22. Blair, *Silent Victory*, pp. 777-81; NHC, Submarine Commands, Administrative History, pp. ii 390-ii 398 and Appendix II to Volume III; *Submarine Operational History*, p. 412; and NARA, RG 227, Div 6, Box 62, Folder: Secret—Pro-Submarine Program, T. E. Shea, Memorandum for: Capt. Allan R. McCann, 6 December 1943.

23. NHC, World War II Command File, *University of Pittsburgh History*, pp. 1114a, 1114b, 1452-55; and *Submarine Operational History*, p. ii 553.

24. NHC, Tenth Fleet, ASM Div, Box 5, Folder: A16(12), Submarine Analysis of Attacks; and *Submarine Operational History*, pp. 568-72.

25. NHC, Commander Submarines, US Pacific Fleet, Tactical Information Bulletin No. 6, 22 November 1943.

26. *Strategic Bombing Survey, Pacific Campaigns*, p. 379; and NHC, *Submarine Operational History*, pp. 50-111, 112; and COMSUBPAC, Tactical Information Bulletin #6, 22 November 1943; Nimitz Command Summary, 23 October 1943.

Chapter 6

1. *STR Div 6*, Vol. III, p. 53; SRH 008, pp. 177-82, Roskill, *The War at Sea*, pp. 369-71. I have included only U-boats sunk in the Atlantic, the Bay of Biscay, and the approaches to the Mediterranean. The total is higher if losses from the Arctic, South Atlantic, and Mediterranean are included.

2. CNH, Tenth Fleet, A & S Section, B: 49, Folder: COMINCH Bi-Weekly U-boat Trends, #34, January 1944.

3. Ibid., #49, 2 September 1944; SRH 008, pp. 189-213; SRH 025, pp. 31, 32; *STR Div 6*, Vol. III, pp. 64, 65.

4. SRH 025, pp. 15, 16, 29-31; *STR Div 6*, pp. 74, 159. Rossler, *The U-boat*, pp. 198-204.

5. Ibid.

6. Rossler, *The U-boat*, pp. 246-60; NARA, RG 457, SNRA 3064 and 3069.

7. Ibid., pp. 240-65.

8. Ibid., pp. 344, 345. NARA, RG 457, SNRA 2611, and RG 165, Digests of Information from Prisoner of War Sources: No. 49, 26 January 1945; No. 51, 7 February 1945; No. 55, 18 April 1945. CNH, Post-World War II Command File, *US Fleet Antisubmarine Bulletin,* January 1945, Vol. II, No. 8, p. 9. *STR Div 6,* Vol. I, pp. 153-60; Vol. III, pp. 76, 77.

9. NARA, RG 457, SNRA 914 to 918, message: 03/060930/1944, translated on 011035 April 1944. See also SNRAs: 775, 827, 829, 858, 932; RG 165, Digest of Information from Prisoner of War Sources, Nos. 6 and 7, 8 and 15, January 1944; SRH 009, p. 65.

10. NARA, RG 457, SNRAs: 1154, 1155, 1450 to 1454, and SRH 025, pp. 50-55.

11. The translations of intercepted messages from the Japanese attache to Tokyo are voluminous and contain a wealth of data about the German program for submarine warfare. See especially SNRA: 1899 to 1901, 2347 and 2348, 2414 to 2418, 2825, 2826, 2854 to 2856, 2922 to 2924, 2952 to 2953, 2969 to 2974, 3075 to 3087, 3290 to 3291, 3303 to 3304. For information obtained from Allied prisoners of war, see: SNRA 2362 to 2366; for German countermeasures to Allied tactics, see: 1112 to 1114.

12. NARA, RG 165, "Digest of Information from Prisoner of War Sources," Numbers 37 through 46, dated 12 August to 20 November 1944. These reports tended to complete outlines provided by messages to Tokyo. From these outlines came the names of the first skippers for the first Mark XXIs and more details on their design, location of testing of the *Mimek* sonars, and more information on German tactics.

13. NARA, SRH 024, pp. 134-143.

14. NARA, RG 457, SRH 368, "Evaluation of the Role of Decryption Intelligence in the Operational Phase of the Battle of the Atlantic."

15. NARA, RG 227, Div 6, Box 57, Folder: G-Laboratories SECRET, F. V. Hunt, "It's Later Than You Think"; Box: 71, Minutes of Section Meetings, Book II, Minutes of Meeting on 21 September 1987; see also NDRC Minutes of Meetings in Box 1501A of F. B. Jewett's Files. Note especially the minutes for 3 November 1944.

16. CNH, a complete set of the Bulletins is in the World War II Command File.

17. Ibid., Tenth Fleet, A & S Section, Box: 47, Folder: ASM Conferences (2), Digest of Minutes, Conference #26, 25 January 1944.

18. NARA, RG 298, Records of the Coordinator of Research and Development, John T. Burwell, Memorandum to the Coordinator, 12 December 1944, Subject: Trip to Surface Division ASDevLant and Naval Ordnance Unit, Fort Lauderdale, Fla. NHC, Tenth Fleet, ASM, Box: 28, Folder: A/S Miscellaneous; World War II Command File, ASWORG Memorandum 46, *Probability of Success of Ship-Borne Anti-Submarine Ordnance;* US Fleet Anti-Submarine Bulletins for November 1944 through May 1945.

19. NARA, RG 227, Div 6, Box 42, Draft History, pp. 9-7; *STR Div 6,* Vol. III, p. 50. NHC, Morison Papers, Box 72, Folder: Study of MAD Barrier in the Straits of Gibraltar.

20. Ibid., A & S Section, Box: 49, Folder: COMINCH Bi-Weekly Submarine Trends, #56, 15 December 1944. See also Doenitz, *Memoirs,* pp. 423-524.

21. NARA, RG 457, SNRA 1837-1842.

22. NARA, RG 457, SRH 008, pp. 222, 223. NHC, Morison Papers, Box: 72, Folder: Rohwer, Dr. Jurgen, Merchant Ship Losses; Records of the Underwater Warfare Division, Box: 9, Surrendered German Submarine Report, Type XXI.

23. NHC, Submarine Command, "Draft Administrative History," Vol. II, p. 404a.

24. NHC, Tenth Fleet, ASM Div, Box 36, Folder: Admiral King—Memorandums, W. S. DeLany, Memo to Admiral King, 30 August 1943; Box 40, C. W. Nimitz, Serial 01987, To COMINCH, Subject: Assignment and Visits of Scientists to The Pacific Ocean Area, 18 May 1944. LC, Furer Diary, 22 May 1944 and 2 October 1944 as well as other entries for the intervening period.

25. NHC, Tenth Fleet; Undersea Warfare Div, Box 15, Folder: Captain Watkins' Correspondence. 1943-45, C. A. Lockwood, to Dear Allan, 1 March 1944; ASM Div, Box 41, folder: Submarines: Miscellaneous Memos, SORG Memorandum SS35, 23 December 1944; WWII Command File, *University of Pittsburgh History,* pp. 1452-55.

26. NARA, RG 457, SRH 011.

27. NARA, RG 227, Div 6, Box 67, Folder: Project 61 SECRET, *STR Div 6,* Vol. I, pp. 212-213. LC, Lockwood Papers, Box 14, Official Correspondence, January-June 1944, C. A. Lockwood to

Dear Admiral Furer, 16 June 1944; also other materials on the same subject. NHC, Undersea Warfare Division, Box 6, Folder: Submarine Officers Conference, August 1944.

28. Ibid.

29. *STR Div 6,* Vol. I, pp. 201-07.

30. Lockwood's correspondence in his papers at the Library of Congress gives a telling picture of his frustrations and his constant restatement of his priorities for new gear to Capt. Frank T. Watkins. See in Box 14 the folders for correspondence between Watkins and Lockwood in May through October 1944. For Lockwood's reminder, see Lockwood to RADM L. E. Denfield, USN, in the folder marked Official Correspondence, September-October 1944. Officers of flag rank seldom in their official correspondence raise emotional issues in pointed terms. It is remarkable for Lockwood in wartime to have felt the requirement to remind a fellow admiral of the fact that men's lives were at stake. Much of this correspondence appears as well in NHC, Undersea Warfare Division, Box 15, Folder: Capt. Watkins Correspondence 1943-45.

31. Ibid., C. A. Lockwood to Dear Frank, 26 January 1945.

32. NHC, Undersea Warfare Division, Box 15, Folder: Capt. Watkins Correspondence, 1943-45, E. E. Yeomans to Dear Frank, 9 February 1945; Frank T. Watkins to Dear Admiral (RADM Ralph W. Christie); 5 March 1945, C. A. Lockwood to Dear Frank, 24 March 1945. For the quotation cited see C. A. Lockwood to Dear Frank, 21 May 1945. LC, Lockwood Papers, Box 14, Folder: Official Correspondence February 1945.

33. Ibid., C. A. Lockwood to Dear Frank, 23 June 1945; Submarine Force Pacific Fleet, Submarine Bulletin, Volume II, Number 1, March 1945.

34. NARA, RG 227, Div 6, General Administrative Records 1944-46, Box 42, Folder: Secret—Pro-Submarine Program, T. E. Shea to John T. Tate, 30 September 1943.

Selected Bibliography

Primary Sources

National Archives and Records Administration

Record Group 38
Secretary of the Navy, Chief of Naval Operations Files for 1942, 1943, 1944, and 1945.
Commander in Chief, US Fleet, Files for 1942, 1943, 1944, and 1945.
OP 412, War Operations Files, 1942-1945.

Record Group 80
Secretary of the Navy, Chief of Naval Operations Files for 1941, 1942, 1943, 1944, and 1945.

Record Group 107
Records of the Secretary of War and the Assistant Secretary of War.
Files of the Expert Consultant to the Secretary of War.
Decimal Files of the Office of the Assistant Secretary of War for Air.
Secretary of War's Safe File.

Record Group 165
Army Chief of Staff Decimal Files.
Digests of Information from Prisoner of War Sources.

Record Group 218
Records of the US Joint Chiefs of Staff.
"History of the Joint Chiefs of Staff," draft manuscript.
Combined Chiefs of Staff, Decimal Files.

Record Group 227
Records of the Office of Scientific Research and Development (OSRD).
Files of Frank B. Jewett.
Files of the Office of Field Services.
Files of Divisions 6, 14, and 15, NDRC.
OSRD Director's Special Subject Correspondence Files.

Record Group 298
Records of Naval Research, Coordinator of Naval Research and Development.

Record Group 313
Records of Naval Operating Forces.
Files of Commander in Chief US Atlantic Fleet.
Files of Commander in Chief Submarines Pacific Fleet.

Record Group 457
Admiralty COMINCH ULTRA Message Exchange, 25 June 1942-17 October 1944 (SRMN-035).
COMINCH File: Assessment of U-boat Fleet at the End of WWII, June-October 1945 (SRMN-040).
COMINCH File: U-Boat Intelligence Summaries, January 1943-May 1945 (SRMN-037).
COMINCH File of U-Boat Situation Estimates, 15 June 1942-21 May 1945 (SRMN-036).
Functions of the "Secret Room" (F211) of COMINCH Combat Intelligence, Atlantic Section, Antisubmarine Warfare, WWII (undated) (SRMN-038).
Historical Review of OP-20-G (SRMN-152).

Special Research Histories (SRH):
002 — War Secrets in the Ether.
008 — The Battle of the Atlantic, Vol. II.
009 — The Battle of the Atlantic, Vol. I.
011 — Communications Intelligence, The Role of Submarine Warfare in the Pacific.
024 — The Battle of the Atlantic, Volume III.
025 — The Battle of the Atlantic, Volume IV.
142 — U-Boat Campaigns and Ultra.
149 — Brief History of Communications Intelligence in the US Navy.
152 — OP-20-G, US Navy, Historical Review.
197 — Communications Intelligence Organization, Liaison & Collaboration, 1941-1945.
201 — Collection of German U-Boat Admonition Experience Messages, 1943-1945.
235 — COMINT Contributions to Submarine Warfare in WWII.
279 — OP-20-G, Communications Intelligence Activities, 1942-1946.
305 — The Undeclared War, History of Radio Intelligence.
368 — Evaluation of the Role of Decryption Intelligence in the Operational Phase of the Battle of the Atlantic.

Translations of Japanese Naval Attache Messages (SRNA 0001-5324)

Library of Congress

Julius A. Furer Papers
Ernest J. King Papers.
Charles A. Lockwood Papers.

Massachusetts Institute of Technology, Special Collections

Philip M. Morse Papers.

Naval Historical Center, Naval Department Library

Commander in Chief, Atlantic Fleet, US Administration in World War II, First Draft Narrative, Volumes I-IV.

Naval Historical Center, Operational Archives

Commander in Chief, US Fleet, Files.
Eastern Sea Frontier, War Diary.
Oral Interview Collection.
World War II Command File.
Post-World War II Command File.
Records of the Tenth Fleet.
    Antisubmarine Measures Division Files.
    Analysis and Statistics Section Files.
    Convoy and Routing Division Files.
Samuel E. Morison Papers.
Strategic Plans Division Files.
Translations of the BdU War Logs.
Undersea Warfare Division Files.

Naval Historical Collection, Naval War College

Thomas B. Buell-Walter M. Whitehill Research Collection.
The Sterling Library, Yale University.
Diary of Henry L. Stimson, Microfilm Edition.

Interview by author: Edward L. Bowles, 11 May 1982.

Secondary Sources

Alger, John. *Thoughts Toward a Definition of the Operational Art*. National War College Monograph. Washington, DC: National War College, 1986.
Blackett, P. M. S. *Studies of War*. New York: Hill & Wang, 1962.
Blair, Clay. *Silent Victory*. Philadelphia: J. P. Lippincott, 1975.

Boyd, William B., and Buford Rowland. *U.S. Navy Bureau of Ordnance in World War II.* Washington, DC: US Government Printing Office.

Bridgman, Leonard, ed. *Jane's All the World's Aircraft 1945-46.* New York: MacMillan & Co., 1946.

Collins, John M. *Grand Strategy: Principles and Practices.* Annapolis, Md.: US Naval Institute Press, 1973.

Costello, John. *The Pacific War.* New York: Dawson, Wade Publishers, Inc., 1981.

Cushman, John H. *Command and Control of Theater Forces-Adequacy, Options, and Implications.* Cambridge: Center for Information Policy Research, 1982.

Doenitz, Karl, Admiral. *Die U-Bootswaffe.* Berlin: Verlag E. S. Mittler & Sohn, 1939.

——————. *The Conduct of the War at Sea.* Division of Naval Intelligence, 1946.

——————. *Memoirs: Ten Years and Twenty Days.* Translated by R. A. Stevens. London: Weidenfeld & Nicolson, 1959.

Ferguson, Arthur B. "The AAF in the Battle of the Atlantic," in *The Army Air Forces in World War II,* Volume I, Frank Wesley Craven and James Lea Cate eds. Chicago: University of Chicago Press, 1948.

——————. "The Antisubmarine Command," in *The Army Air Forces in World War II,* Volume II, Frank Wesley Craven and James Lea Cate, eds. Chicago: University of Chicago Press, 1949.

Friedman, Norman. *Submarine Design and Development.* Annapolis, Md.: U.S. Naval Institute Press, 1984.

Fuller, J. F. C. *Armament and History,* London: Eyre & Spottiswoode, 1946.

——————. *The Conduct of War.* New Brunswick, N.J.: Rutgers University Press, 1961.

Furer, Julius A. *The Administration of the Navy Department in World War II,* Washington, DC: Naval History Division, 1959.

Gordon, Don E. *Electronic Warfare: Element of Strategy and Multiplier of Combat Power,* New York: Pergamon Press, 1981.

Harnwell, Gaylord P. "Assistance to the Navy in Technical Training," in John T. Tate, *A Survey of Subsurface Warfare in World War II,* Washington, DC: Office of Scientific Research and Development, 1946.

Hinsley, F. H. et al., *British Intelligence in the Second World War,* four volumes. New York: Cambridge University Press.

Holley, I. B., *Ideas and Weapons,* New Haven, Conn.: Yale University Press, 1953, reprint ed., Washington, DC: Office of Air Force History, 1983.

Holmes, W.J. *Undersea Victory.* Garden City, N.J.: Doubleday and Co., 1966.

_____. The U-Boat Wars. New York: Arbor House, 1984.

Hoyt, Edwin P. *Submarines at War.* New York: Stein and Day, 1983.

Kozaczuk, Wladyslaw. *Enigma,* trans. Christopher Kasparek, University Publications of America, 1984.

Michelsen, Andreas V. "The Submarine Warfare, 1914-18," *Monthly Information Bulletin of the Office of Naval Intelligence,* January 1926, Supplement Number 3.

Metcalf, Martin K., "History of Convoy and Routing, Headquarters of the Commander in Chief United States Fleet, 1939-1945," Record Group 313, National Archives and Research Agency, Washington, DC.

McNeil, William H., *The Pursuit of Power,* Chicago: University of Chicago Press, 1982.

Milner, Marc, *North Atlantic Run,* Annapolis, Md. Institute.

Morison, Elting E., *Turmoil and Tradition,* Boston: Houghton Mifflin, 1960.

Morison, Samuel E., *The History of the United States Navy in World War II,* 11 Vols. Boston: Little Brown, 1957.

_____. *Strategy and Compromise.* Boston: Little Brown and Co., 1959.

Morse, Philip M., *In at the Beginnings: A Physicist's Life,* Cambridge, Mass.: MIT Press, 1977.

_____. "Of Men and Machines," *Technology Review, 49.* November 1946: 30-33.

Mulligan, Timothy, *Records Relating to U-Boat Warfare, 1939-45,* Washington, DC: National Archives and Records Administration, 1985.

Naval History Division, *United States Submarine Losses in World War II,* Washington, DC: Office of the Chief of Naval Operations, 1963.

Parrish, Thomas. *The Ultra Americans,* New York: Stein and Day, 1986.

Pokrovsky, G. I. *Science and Technology in Contemporary War,* trans. Raymond L. Garthoff. New York: Praeger, 1959.

Polmar, Norman. *The American Submarine.* Annapolis, Md.: The Nautical and Aviation Publishing Company of America, 1983.

Selected Bibliography 253

Rohwer, Jurgen. *The Critical Battles of March 1943,* Annapolis, Md.: US Naval Institute Press, 1977.

Roscoe, Theodore. *United States Submarine Operations in World War II.* Annapolis, Md.: US Naval Institute Press, 1949.

Roskill, Stephen Wentworth. *The War at Sea, 1939-1945,* 3 volumes in 4. London: Her Majesty's Stationery Office, 1954-61.

Rossler, Eberhard. *The U-Boat, the Evolution and Technical History of German Submarines,* trans. Harold Erenberg. London: Arms and Armour Press, 1981.

Ruge, Friedrich. *Der Seekrieg,* trans. M.G. Saunders. Annapolis, Md.: US Naval Institute Press, 1957.

Sims, William S. *The Victory at Sea.* Garden City, N.J.: Doubleday, Page & Co. 1920.

Spector, Ronald H. *Eagle Against the Sun.* New York: Vintage Books, 1985.

Stimson, Henry L. and McGeorge Bundy. *On Active Service in Peace and War.* New York: Harper Brothers, 1948.

Spindler, Arno. *History of German Submarine Warfare,* trans. Howard Pyle III, Naval Department Library, Naval Historical Center.

Vander Vat, Dan. *The Atlantic Campaign.* New York: Harper & Row, 1988.

Waters, John M. *Bloody Winter.* Annapolis, Md.: US Naval Institute Press, 1984.

Whitehill, Walter M. and Ernest J. King. *Fleet Admiral King, A Naval Record.* London: Lyre & Spottiswoode, 1953.

Whitehill, Walter M., *History of Headquarters Commander in Chief, United States Fleet, 1941-45,* unpublished history at the Naval Historical Center, Operational Archives.

Worthington, J. M., *Admiral R. E. Ingersoll,* unpublished history at the Naval Historical Center, Operational Archives.

Abbreviations

AAF	Army Air Forces
ACV	Auxiliary Aircraft Carrier; US Navy symbol
ASDevLant	Antisubmarine Development Detachment Atlantic
ASDIC	Antisubmarine Detection Investigation Committee (A group in WWI that helped devise the device that bore its name in WWII.)
ASV	Airborne Surface Vessel Detection
ASW	antisubmarine warfare
ASWORG	Antisubmarine Warfare Operational Research Group
B-dienst	*Beobachtungdienst,* German cryptological unit
BdU	*Befehlshaber der Unterseebooten* (Commander in Chief of Submarines)
CCS	Combined Chiefs of Staff
CINCLANT	Commander in Chief, US Atlantic Fleet
CINCPAC	Commander in Chief, US Pacific Fleet
CNH	Center for Naval History
CNO	Chief of Naval Operations
COMINCH	Commander in Chief, US Fleet
COMSUBLANT	Commander, Submarine Force, US Atlantic Fleet
COMSUBPAC	Commander, Submarine Force, US Pacific Fleet
CVE	Letters designating Escort Aircraft Carrier in US Navy terminology; also called "jeep" carrier

Div 6	Division 6 of the National Defense Research Committee (NDRC)
DUKW	amphibious 2½-ton cargo-carrying truck
FAT torpedo	*Federapparat,* German torpedo
FM	Frequency modulation (sonar)
LC	Library of Congress
MAD	Magnetic Anomaly Detection (device)
MAN	*Maschinenfabrik Augsburg-Neurnberg*
MIT	Massachusetts Institute of Technology
NARA	National Archives and Research Agency
NDRC	National Defense Research Committee
NDRL	National Defense Research Laboratory
NHC	Naval Historical Center
OFS	Office of Field Services
OSRD	Office of Scientific Research and Development
PBM	Patrol Search Plane; US Navy designation for Mariner aircraft
PBY	Patrol Bomber; US Navy designation for Catalina aircraft
PPI	Plan Position Indicator
radar	*ra*dio *d*etecting *a*nd *r*anging; instrument for determining, by radio echoes, the presence of objects and their range, bearing, and elevation
RAF	Royal Air Force
RG	Record Group
SADU	Sea-Search Attack Development Unit
SECNAV	Secretary of the Navy
SESE	Secure Echo-Sounding Equipment (sonar)
sonar	*s*ound *n*avigation *a*nd *r*anging; underwater sound equipment for submarine detection and navigation.
SORG	Submarine Operations Research Group
STR	Summary Technical Report

TDM	Torpedo Detection Modification
U-Boat	German naval submarine, with a designation of "U-" (for *Unterseeboot*)
USCGC	US Coast Guard Cutter
VLR	very long range
VP	Letters designating Patrol Squadron in US Navy terminology
WPG	Letters designating US Coast Guard (W) Patrol Gunboat (PG); USCGC *SPENCER* (WPG 1), for example

Index

Aircraft, as ASW weapons, 6, 9, 10. *See also* Escort Aircraft Carrier (CVE) groups; First Bomber Command; Royal Air Force
  British use of, 19, 23, 75, 77-78, 87, 91
  Japanese, 162
  long-range, 81-82, 86, 87, 88, 94, 128
  scientists promote, 55, 59-60, 61, 62, 69, 100-101
  success against U-boats of, 67, 75, 77-78, 89, 124, 146
  weapons and equipment for, 100-101, 106
Alberich, 183-185
Allied Antisubmarine Survey Board, 117-118
Anglo-German Naval Treaty (1935), 9, 13, 14
Antisubmarine Development Detachment Atlantic (ASDevLant), 106, 115, 138, 197
Antisubmarine Warfare Unit, 51, 52, 85, 101, 115, 126
Antisubmarine Warfare Operational Research Group (ASWORG), 58-62, 195, 216-217
  contributions to doctrine and tactics of, 61-62, 85, 98, 101-103, 125-126, 138, 139, 180, 196-197
  relations with naval officers of, 58-59, 60-61, 116

Antisubmarine warfare (ASW). *See also* Antisubmarine Warfare Operational Research Group (ASWORG); Army Air Forces (AAF); National Defense Research Committee (NDRC); Navy, US; Royal Air Force; Royal Navy; Tenth Fleet
  Allied prewar neglect of, 8-13, 16-17
  British efforts in, 1939-1941, 20, 21-23
  doctrine and tactics for, 21, 58-63, 85, 99-103, 125-126, 138, 139, 180, 196-199
  German countermeasures to, 78, 80-81, 140-146, 150, 183-185
  Japanese efforts in, 158, 161-162, 175-176
  pressure for US offense in, 62, 67, 69, 71, 87-96
  systemic approach of scientists to, 24, 29-36
  US countermeasures to, 125-126, 134-140, 171-173
  US defensive strategy in, 47-49, 53, 87, 91, 99-100
  US offensive strategy in, 97-98, 112-122, 127-134, 146-151
  weapons and equipment for, 54-58, 67-69, 103-107, 111-112, 122-125
  in World War I, 5-8
Aphrodite, 138, 145
Army Air Forces (AAF), 65-66, 112, 211-212

259

Arnold, Henry H. (Hap), 65, 112, 211-212
Atlantic Convoy Conference, 90-92, 118

Baker, Wilder D., 51-52, 58, 213, 220
Battle of the Atlantic (phases of), 19-24, 70, 85-86, 109, 111. *See also* Antisubmarine warfare; U-boats
Befehlshaber der Unterseebooten (BdU) (Commander in Chief of Submarines). *See* Doenitz, Karl
Beobachtunsdienst (B-dienst), 77, 81
Biscay, Bay of, 75, 78, 87, 91, 124-125
Bowles, Edward, 65, 92-93
Britain. *See also* Royal Air Force; Royal Navy
and antisubmarine warfare in World War I, 5, 6-7
countermeasures developed by, 19, 21-22, 23
cryptology in, 76-77, 89, 193
operational analysis in, 51, 60, 87
and safeguarding of intelligence sources, 119-120
unprepared at start of war, 8-9, 10, 19
views on ASW issues of, 83, 87, 91, 92
Bush, Vannevar, 24-26, 52-53, 97-98, 134, 136, 137
as adviser to Stimson, 65, 67, 69, 93

California, University of, 32, 168, 169

Casablanca Conference, 86, 87
Colpitts, Edwin H., 26
Colpitts Report, 26
Columbia University, 31-32, 168, 169, 171
Commander in Chief, US Fleet (COMINCH) (as organizational unit). *See also* Antisubmarine Warfare Operational Research Group (ASWORG); King, Ernest J.; Tenth Fleet
organization of ASW efforts in, 46-53, 89, 92, 94-98, 118, 126, 218
views of junior officers in, 87-88, 92
Communications intelligence
assessment of, 193-195, 219
German use of, 40, 77, 193, 195
on German weapons development, 115, 120, 138-139, 179, 180, 190-193
in Pacific theater, 203
used against U-boats, 97, 114, 119-122, 147, 193-195
Comstock, Merrill, 168
"Convoy vicinity," concept, 49, 91
Convoys. *See also* Shipping losses
as means of defense, 21, 37, 49, 81-83, 127-128
in World War I, 5, 6
Cryptology. *See also* Communications intelligence; Signals intelligence
British, 76-77, 89, 193
German, 40-41, 77
Pacific campaign and, 203
US, 96, 114, 120

Dealey, Samuel D., 124
Depth charges, 10, 34, 57, 105-106, 125
Direction-finding gear, 6-7, 22, 86, 103
Division 6 (National Defense Research Committee), 106, 168, 170, 180, 195, 196, 200, 209
Doenitz, Karl, 7
  appointed Commander in Chief of Submarines (BdU), 13
  closely controls U-boats, 23, 75-76
  deploys U-boats, 39, 41-42, 53, 67, 70, 73, 75, 85, 147, 149-150
  develops new U-boats, 78-80, 179, 186-188, 199-200
  fails to anticipate countermeasures, 17, 23-24, 39, 43
  links scientific research to operational problems, 183-190, 209-210, 215
  problems of, 20, 42-43, 78, 217
  response to sudden losses of, 127, 129, 131-134
  seeks countermeasures, 78, 80-81, 140, 142, 143, 145, 146
  strategy and tactics of, 13-15, 17-19, 23, 37, 73, 74-76, 179, 182
Dyer, George C., 47

Echoscope, 33, 172-173, 204-205
Edwards, R. S., 46, 53, 67, 99, 167

Enigma machine, 77, 193. See also *Ultra*
Escort Aircraft Carriers (CVE) groups, 86, 126-127, 146, 147-149, 150, 151
Escort vessels, British, 21-22, 23

Fido, 57, 173
First Bomber Command, 65-66, 112
Furer, Julius A., 138, 201

GATO-class submarine, 154-155
German High Command, 20, 41, 42
German submarines. See U-boats
Germany. See also Doenitz, Karl; U-boats
  advantages held by, 39-43, 81-83
  communications intelligence in, 40, 77, 193, 195
  cryptological unit in, 40-41, 77
  prewar developments in, 13-15
  strategic objective of, 177-179
  technological innovation in, 78-81, 126-127, 179, 183-190, 199-200
  in World War I, 5, 7
Griggs, Capt. John B., 167-168
Group M. See Antisubmarine Warfare Operational Research Group (ASWORG)
Guadalcanal, battle of, 161, 163

Hart, Thomas C., 158
Harvard University, 32, 57
Hedgehog, 125, 186
High-Frequency Direction Finding Gear (HFDF), 6-7, 103
Hitler, Adolf, 20, 41, 143
Hopkins, Harry L., 93
Horne, Frederick J., 44
Hunt, F. V., 196

Ingersoll, Royal E.
 relations with King of, 48, 49-50, 51
 role in ASW campaign of, 51, 52, 83, 85, 115, 116, 146, 148-149, 218
Integral tonnage concept, 17-19

Japan. *See also* Pacific Theater
 antisubmarine efforts of, 158, 161-162, 175-176
 Naval Attache of, in Berlin, 190-193
 shipping losses of, 163, 175
Jewett, Frank B., 26, 28, 31
Jodl, Alfred, 41
Joint Committee on New Weapons and Equipment, 67-69

Kettler (Col.), 41
King, Ernest J.
 antisubmarine warfare views of, 48-49, 52, 86, 87, 91, 99
 appointed Commander in Chief, US Fleet (COMINCH), 43-44
 background and strategic orientation of, 10-13, 16, 211
communications intelligence and, 120
 organization of ASW efforts under, 46-53, 92, 94-98, 118
 personality and working relations of, 44-46, 49, 66, 67, 201
 personality of, affects ASW efforts, 13, 48, 49-51, 63-64, 66, 67, 201, 212, 218
Knox, Frank, 64, 67
Knudsen, Verne O., 60, 62

Leahy, William D. 96
Lockwood, Charles A., 201-202, 204, 206-207, 209-210, 212, 220
 development of ASW countermeasures and, 164-165, 166-168, 169, 171
 links scientific work with operational problems, 202, 209-210, 213, 215, 217
Long-Range Electronic Navigation (LORAN), 101, 105, 125
Low, F. S. ("Frog")
 attitude toward scientists of, 97-98, 116, 220
 concern for training, 95, 115, 218
 conducts offensive campaign, 118-120, 146-147, 148
 helps in Pacific theater, 166, 168, 169, 171
 links scientific developments with operational problems, 138-140, 213, 215

as Tenth Fleet commander, 95, 96, 97-98, 113-116, 193
MacArthur, Douglas, 158, 159
Magic, 203
Magnetic Anomaly Detection (MAD) devices
  Allied, 26, 33, 34, 54-55, 101, 106, 123-124, 198-199
  Japanese, 162
Marshall, George C., 44, 55, 71, 93, 94, 112
McNarney, Joseph T., 65
Memoirs (Doenitz), 15
Merkur, Otto, 143, 188
Michelsen, Andreas V., 214
Midway, battle of, 161, 163
Morse, Philip M., 34, 52, 58, 89, 92, 134, 138. See also Antisubmarine Warfare Operational Research Group (ASWORG)
Morton, Dudley W. (Mush), 165
Mousetrap, 34, 56-57

National Defense Research Committee (NDRC), 26-28, 101, 105-107, 122-123, 134, 137-138, 196
  Division 6 of, 105-106, 168, 170, 180, 195, 196, 200, 209
  Section C-4 of, 28-36, 54-58, 62
  work in Pacific Theater of, 112, 168, 170, 171, 179, 196, 200
Naval Research Laboratory, 9, 28

Navy, US. *See also* Antisubmarine warfare; Antisubmarine Warfare Operational Research Group (ASWORG); Commander in Chief, US Fleet (COMINCH); King, Ernest J.; Pacific Theater; Tenth Fleet
  Antisubmarine Development Detachment Atlantic (ASDevLant), 106, 115, 138, 197
  Antisubmarine Warfare Unit, 51, 52, 85, 101, 115
  barriers to innovation in, 15-16, 26, 33-34, 36, 206, 211, 212-213, 215, 218
  before World War II, 9-13, 16-17, 211, 212-213
  Bureau of Aeronautics (BUAER), 33, 106
  Bureau of Ordnance (BUORD), 33, 168
  Bureau of Ships (BUSHIPS), 26-28, 29-30, 33, 201
  command arrangements in, 33, 34, 43-44, 46-48, 49-51
  relations between scientists and, 33-34, 35-36, 54, 58-59, 60-61, 116, 196
Night periscope, 171-172, 204
Nimitz, Chester, 1, 44, 161, 164, 201
Noble, Sir Percy, 91
Noisemakers. *See* Sonic decoys
Normandy invasion, 182-183

Office of Scientific Research and Development (OSRD), 93
Operation Torch, 83, 85

263

Operational analysis
  in Atlantic theater. *See* Antisubmarine Warfare Operational Research Group (ASWORG)
  in Britain, 51, 60, 87
  Germans lack adequate, 217
  in Pacific theater, 168, 169, 173-174, 177, 202-203

Pacific Theater
  communications intelligence in, 203
  Japanese ASW efforts in, 158, 161-162, 175-176
  Japanese shipping losses in, 163, 175
  new US submarine tactics in, 164, 165-166, 168, 169, 173-175, 202-203
  scientists' role in, 153-154, 168-174, 177, 201-203
  US defensive efforts in, 153, 158-161
  US offensive in, 163-166, 174-176
  US problems and mistakes in, 153, 155-156, 159, 162-163
  US submarines in, 154-155, 157-158, 175
  weapons development for, 171-173, 204-209
Pillenwefer, 80, 138, 145
Prize Ordinance, 5

Radar
  Allied use of, 65, 78, 100, 103, 125
  developments for ASW, 22, 54, 103, 105, 125
  for US submarines, 155, 165, 171-172
  German countermeasures to, 78, 140-142, 150, 183-185

Roosevelt, Franklin D., 16-17, 26, 43-44, 93, 94-95, 212
Royal Air Force (RAF), 19, 23, 78, 87, 111, 127-128, 134, 219
Royal Canadian Navy, 86
Royal Navy, 29
  defense of merchant ships by, 20, 23, 52, 86, 87, 111, 127-128, 133-134, 219
  unprepared for ASW, 8-9, 10, 19
  weapons and tactics developed by, 21-22
Rudeltaktik (wolfpack tactics), 15, 21, 74-76, 127, 129, 131

Scientists. *See also* Antisubmarine Warfare Operational Research Group (ASWORG); Bowles, Edward; Bush, Vannevar; Jewett, Frank B.; Morse, Philip M.; National Defense Research Committee (NDRC); Submarine Operations Research Group (SORG); Tate, John T.
  comprehensive approach of, 24-36, 211, 215, 217, 219-220
  contributions of, summarized, 208-209, 211, 215-218, 219
  cooperation between British and American, 29, 87, 92
  Pacific Theater developments and, 168-174, 177, 196, 200-203
  and postwar weapon development, 196, 209

264

push for offensive operations, 39, 87, 89, 92, 93, 95, 99, 100-101
training issues and, 26, 29, 54, 57-58, 62, 83, 89, 107, 126, 197, 217-218
work in field by, 60-61, 83, 107, 198-199, 201
Sea-Search Attack Development Unit (SADU), 65
Section C-4 (National Defense Research Committee (NDRC)), 28-36, 54-58, 62
Shea, T. E., 209
Shipping losses
Allied, in 1942, 70, 83
Allied, in 1943, 71, 89-91, 129, 130, 131, 133
in American waters, 41, 53
British, in 1939-1941, 20, 22, 23, 37
Japanese, 163, 175
Shockley, William, 34
Signals intelligence, 76-77, 121-122
Sims, William S., 6, 214
Snorkel, 141-142, 182, 183-185, 199
Sonar
developments, 28, 29, 32-33, 54, 55, 100, 105, 155, 205, 207, 208
Japanese, 162
operators, training of, 54, 57-58, 62, 197
World War I, 7
Sonic decoys, 138, 139, 172, 205, 207
Sonobuoys, 33, 55, 106, 123-124
Speer, Albert, 143
Squid, 186, 197

Stark, Harold R., 16, 44, 46
Stimson, Henry L.,
consults with scientists, 64-65, 67, 69, 92
critical of Navy leadership, 63, 64, 69, 71, 93-94, 112
supports use of air power, 65, 66, 67, 93-94
Submarine Operations Research Group (SORG), 169, 173-174, 180, 201-203
Submarine Warfare Bulletin, 175
Submarines, German. *See* U-boats
Submarines, US. *See* Pacific Theater

Tate, John T., 52, 89
heads Section C-4, 28, 29-30, 31, 34, 62-63, 134, 137, 138
Pacific Theater and, 168-169
Technological innovation
American. *See* Antisubmarine Warfare Operational Research Group (ASWORG); National Defense Research Committee (NDRC); Scientists; Submarine Operations Research Group (SORG)
British, 21, 22
conditions affecting military use of, 15-16, 209-210, 211, 214-218
Doenitz fails to anticipate Allied, 17, 23-24, 39, 43
German, 78-81, 126-127, 179, 183-190, 199-200
Tenth Fleet, 96, 97-98, 112-114, 116

265

Torpedo Detection Modification (TDM), 173, 205
Torpedoes
 acoustic, development of US, 26, 33, 34, 57, 106, 123, 173, 204
 acoustic, German, 80-81, 145, 149, 150, 190
 acoustic, use of, 130-131, 148, 149, 207
 German, 17, 20
 problems of US submarine, 155-156, 163, 165
Training, 83, 85, 95, 107, 115, 116, 197, 217-218
 British, 21-22
 of sonar operators, 54, 57-58, 62, 126, 197
Triton, 76, 77, 89

U-boats. *See also* Doenitz, Karl; Shipping losses
 attacked in Bay of Biscay, 75, 78, 87, 91, 124-125
 BdU control over, 23, 75-76
 deployment of, 19, 39, 41-42, 53, 67, 70, 73, 75, 85, 127, 129, 133-134, 147, 149-151, 181-182
 development of new, 78-80, 126-127, 179, 186-188, 199-200
 losses, of before 1943, 20, 23
 losses of, 1943 and after, 89, 127, 129, 130, 131-134, 149, 150, 182-183, 185
 Mark XXI, 142-143, 186-189, 199-200
 Mark XXIII, 186, 199
 Mark XXVI, 188

morale on, 127, 199
 and Normandy invasion, 182-183
 number of, 17, 20, 21, 37, 53, 69, 118
 production of, 40, 73-74, 81, 188-189
 reasons for early successes of, 39, 40, 41, 77
 reprovisioning at sea of, 40, 74, 118-119, 147
 snorkel equipped, 141-142, 182, 183-185, 199
 tactics of, 19, 21, 74-76, 127, 129, 131, 146, 150, 179
 tactics of, prewar development of, 7, 14, 15
 Walther, 78-80, 140, 142, 188
 weaknesses of, 24, 118-119
U-bootswaffe, Die (Doenitz), 15
Ultra, 114, 190-195
Underwater sound-ranging gear. *See* Sonar
United States. *See also* Antisubmarine warfare; Army Air Forces (AAF); Navy, US; Pacific theater
 attacks along East Coast of, 39, 41, 52-53
 unprepared for antisubmarine warfare, 8-13, 15-17
 in World War I, 6, 7
US Fleet Antisubmarine Bulletin, 196, 197
US Pacific Fleet. *See* Pacific theater
USS *HARDER*, 124
USS *SANTEE*, 147-148

Van Keuran, A. H. 29-30
Versailles Treaty, 9, 13
Victory at Sea, The (Sims), 6, 214

Walther, Hellmuth, 78, 142, 188
Walther submarine, 78-80, 140, 142, 188

War Department. *See* Stimson, Henry L.
Washington Naval Treaty, 9
Watkins, Capt. Frank T., 206
Wolfpack tactics. *See* *Rudeltaktik*
Woods Hole, Oceanographic Institute at, 31
World War I, 3, 5-8, 213-214

The Author

Colonel Montgomery C. Meigs is a serving Army officer currently assigned to the Joint Staff as a strategic planner in J-5. He commanded 1st Squadron, 1st Cavalry along the "Iron Curtain" between West and East Germany, and Troop A, 3rd Squadron, 5th Cavalry in combat in Vietnam. He earned a PhD in history from the University of Wisconsin-Madison, and has held postdoctoral Fellowships at the Council on Foreign Relations and the National Defense University.

www.ingramcontent.com/pod-product-compliance
Lightning Source LLC
Chambersburg PA
CBHW071659160426
43195CB00012B/1516